To LAWRENCE → NANCY
FROM BULB CHANGER
TO BUILDER
TO AUDIER

LOVE

13/4

HARD ACT
TO FOLLOW

HARD ACT
TO FOLLOW

MICHAEL SELLERS

AND

GARY MORECAMBE

BLAKE

Published by Blake Publishing Ltd,
3 Bramber Court, 2 Bramber Road, London W14 9PB, England

First published in Great Britain in 1997

ISBN 1 85782-1505

British Library Cataloguing-in-Publication Data:
A catalogue record for this book is available from the British Library.

Typeset by BCP

Printed in Great Britain by
Creative Print and Design (Wales), Ebbw Vale, Gwent.

1 3 5 7 9 10 8 6 4 2

This book is dedicated to Hannah, William, Jack, Henry, Arthur and Dereka — *our* children.

Except for Felix Francis and Gail Morecambe, who wrote their own pieces, all contributions were written by the authors from taped interviews.

ACKNOWLEDGEMENTS

The authors would like to extend a huge personal thank you to all those who have helped us in the preparation of this book.

We are particularly indebted to Jennifer Edwards, Felix Francis, Kate Gayson, Martina Jones, Ian McCorquodale, Hayley Mills, Christian Moore, Gail Morecambe, Sheridan Morley, Richard Olivier, Scott Stringfellow and Nick Wisdom.

For their support and practical help, we would also like to thank Phil Day, Anthony Haas, Jennifer Luithlen, Joan Morecambe, Tracey Morecambe, Gareth Owen, Alison Sellers and Doris Spriggs.

Thanks go to Martin Sterling for giving up time to do our background research, and a big thank you to all at Blake Publishing for their willingness to put up with unexpected delays and their general co-operation and kindness.

A final thank you to Paul Simpson, who came up with the title for the book.

CONTENTS

INTRODUCTION

While promoting a book some ten years ago, I was invited to do a radio phone-in in Liverpool to tackle questions on Morecambe and Wise. One caller, profuse in his admiration and love for the double-act, finally finished his monologue by saying how lucky I was to be Eric Morecambe's son, and that I should always remember how lucky I am. I quickly explained to the gentleman that I had always considered myself very lucky and fully intended to continue to do so.

Some hours later, possibly when back at my hotel enjoying a cigar and a whisky, I found myself reflecting further on that caller's remarks. To his mind, and he was perhaps representative of many, there was only one story: I was the son of a hugely loved comic icon, so life must have been perfect, and therefore I was enviably fortunate. However, it struck me squarely that this image was not wholly true, and that one day I would give a full and balanced account of what life with a 'star' parent was all about.

When I met Michael Sellers for the first time, we both found we had been thinking along the same lines and we had much to say to each other on the subject. We decided it would not only be interesting to record our own feelings in book form, but to discover how other siblings of the famous had lived their lives under the shadow of fame.

This book is the culmination of that idea and it is up to you, the reader, to make of it what you will. Even as the child of a famous parent, I have been profoundly surprised by some of the anecdotes within these pages and now feel that, on reflection, maybe that phone-in gentleman was right — I should feel lucky.

Gary Morecambe, 1997

BLAKE EDWARDS

PRODUCER/DIRECTOR, (1922–)

lake Edwards, an actor turned producer/director, has enjoyed a hugely successful career. He began directing movies in the mid-1950s.

His earliest acclaimed films were *Breakfast at Tiffany's* and *Days of Wine and Roses*. However, it was through the 'Panther' movies — *The Pink Panther* and *A Shot in the Dark* — that he was to find true international recognition.

After a break of some years, he reunited with Peter Sellers to make what has become a cult film, *The Party* (1968), and later worked with Sellers to make more 'Panther' films, which brought him further box-office success. In 1979, he directed *10*, a film that starred Dudley Moore and won Edwards the greatest critical acclaim of his career. He is married to the actress Julie Andrews.

The following contribution comes from Jennifer Edwards, 38, who is the daughter of Blake Edwards from his marriage to actress Patricia Walker. She has one brother, Geoff, and lives in Los Angeles with Mark, and youngest daughter, Hannah, who is three. Jennifer is an actress who first made her name as Heidi in the film of the same name.

JENNIFER EDWARDS:

My mother virtually gave up acting to become Mrs Blake Edwards. The story goes that my father was driving past her when he noticed her long legs. He rushed up to her and introduced himself, and that was the beginning of their relationship.

This was at a time when he was starting to get seriously into the writing and directing side of the film business, having been a 'B'-movie actor for years. I believe *Operation Petticoat* was the first major feature he directed.

My parents had been together for six years by the time I was conceived in 1956. My brother, Geoff, was born in 1959. When he and I talk about our past lives, we don't remember really being a family. Rather, I remember incidents; things I did with my father, mother and brother, but all as separate events. I don't remember my parents as a couple, which I find slightly strange.

The one specific thing I remember of that time is being in Rome while the 'Panther' movie, *A Shot in the Dark*, was being made. We had Thanksgiving there, and everyone — my mum, dad and grandparents — was sitting around the table. But that is the only time that I can recall us behaving like a family. There were Christmases and other family get-togethers, but for some reason I've blocked them out. I don't quite know why and, again, Geoff is the same.

My parents split up in the mid-1960s. My dad and stepmother, Julie Andrews, have talked about when they met, but my mum always felt they started the affair before the split.

When Dad left Mum he would come and take Geoff and me out once a week. One week, he wanted to know what movie we'd like to see and it was *Mary Poppins* starring, as irony would have it, Julie Andrews. For weeks after we insisted that he keep taking us to that movie, so we must have seen it ten or more times. Then, one day, he told us that we were going to meet a friend of his and see another movie. We drove to the MGM studios and went into a screening-room and there was Julie Andrews — or Mary Poppins, as far as we were concerned. We watched a screening of *The Sound of Music* which hadn't yet been released. There were a few people there, I guess, but in my memory it was just us, her and my dad.

In those days, the screening-rooms had really long floors that rolled away from the front row of seats. Julie had brought a picnic along and we laid blankets out on this floor and watched the film. In retrospect I think, 'What a wonderful way to introduce your kids to your stepmother — through a film that has her happily cavorting around with little children.' But at the time I thought, 'What is Mary Poppins doing with my dad?'

Dad had a few 'in-betweens' before Julie. I remember running around the house and bumping into Jill St John in the hallway and thinking, 'Why are you here?' But it was quite apparent, just from that evening at the screening of *The Sound of Music* that this lady was a serious contender.

It's funny, but I never wanted my parents to get back together. I'm sure one day in therapy I'll figure it all out, but I sensed immediately that it was right that they not be together. It wasn't that they argued, I just had an innate feeling as a child that there was unhappiness between them. So I was one of those kids who just knew they were better people without each other. Whereas I always felt that Dad and Julie *are* supposed to be together.

I went through a lot. As soon as Dad left my mother, she tried to kill herself for the first time. She'd taken a load of pills and I found her. I was only seven, but had the sense to push the burglar alarm in the house to get attention, then phone my maternal grandmother. Sadly, that was just the beginning of a long line of such attempts. In fact, they didn't stop until I was about seventeen.

I remember walking into a room and seeing her crying. She said, 'Dad and I are not going to be together any more. Please don't tell your brother this, but we're going to get a divorce.' I said, 'Oh dear,' and went straight into my brother's room and woke him and said, 'Guess what? Mum and Dad are getting divorced!'

I'm not so sure about the moment of realising that I had a famous father, but the first time that I was aware of being somewhat privileged is waking up on my birthday when Mum and Dad were still together and looking out my bedroom window and seeing an entire carnival in our front driveway in Beverly Hills. It was like waking up to find Disneyland had moved into your yard. Granted, my best friends were Jamie and Kelly Curtis and Carrie Fisher and the like, but that was normal, as was going downstairs and finding Tony Curtis or Robert Wagner sitting on the couch — they were my dad's closest friends.

I never really knew what my dad did for a long time. He used to say he was going to shoot and I used to have visions of him on the Bel Air golf course firing guns at targets. My brother and I weren't taken on 'sets' until *The Great Race* in 1963. That was the first time I fully understood what he did.

It was slightly different because he was behind the camera. Kelly and Jamie Curtis were able to know at once what was going on because they could see their dad on the screen.

Once I was pulled into the acting environment I became hooked. The first film I did was *Heidi* when I was ten. What happened was I was visiting Elkie Sommers who was filming in LA, and someone asked Elkie who I was — this 'someone' turned out to be a talent scout who knew *Heidi* was being cast. When my dad got a call about it, he was told they'd seen something like 1,100 girls for the part, but they wanted to 'test' me. I think he thought, 'well, she hasn't ever done anything like this — she doesn't have a hope in hell.' Ironically, Dad actually directed the screen-test. Within a few days of the 'test' we were in the swimming-pool and my dad and brother were giggling and laughing and talking behind my back. 'What is it?' I kept asking. 'Shall I tell her?' asked Dad. 'Yeah, yeah, go on,' said Geoff. 'Well,' Dad said, 'it looks like they want you to play Heidi.'

It was really exciting, although I don't suppose anyone thought I was likely to get it because they were testing legitimate actresses. I hadn't even performed in a school production up until then. But that role clinched it for me. I knew then that all I wanted to do was act.

The US critic Walter Winchell said of my performance in *Heidi*, that I was the most exciting young actress since Hayley Mills was a child.

I was offered other stuff after *Heidi*, but Dad turned them down. I think he wanted me to be a 'normal' kid who went to school and so forth. It wasn't until I was fourteen and wandering around the house — always acting — that my parents realised that it was the only thing I wanted to do. So I was fourteen when I did my next film.

I was living with Mum in London at this time. I went to about four schools, including a convent school. I never really wanted to leave London. It was my home and I was very happy there. But I also had to consider that, when I was on breaks, I would go out to the States to visit my dad and that I would work there. Knowing I wanted to be an actress, I felt I had to be in LA. My Mum agreed, because Geoff had remained in London only a year before moving back to LA to live with Dad.

My mother said, 'We're leaving!' and I said, 'We're not!' But we did. I really believed I would only do a year in LA and then return to England, but now I probably wouldn't go back if you paid me. When I've visited England in recent years I've found it not to be the place it was. Not that living in LA is easy in such an unpredictable profession. The last film I did was *Son of the Pink Panther*, followed by a play about a year later, and it's been really slow since.

From a very early age I remember knowing that, if people knew who my parents were, I would be treated differently. Therefore, for a long time, I wouldn't say anything. I didn't even mention that I acted because I wanted to be just one of the gang. To this day it still haunts me. I can have very close friends for years, then, if they don't get a job on one of my dad's films, they don't talk to me any more. I find that very frightening. If confronted with it, I'm sure they'd say that has nothing to do with it, but if you examine the chain of events, it does happen. Or, conversely, a really intimate friend becomes very successful in their own right and then drops me. I find myself thinking, 'why were they friends with me in the first place?' In that respect, it was difficult growing up with the parents I have.

I am extremely proud of who my parents are and of their accomplishments — they are two people who have really survived some pretty shitty stuff in this town and they don't compromise. They always seem to keep their heads above water. Even when Dad has gotten angry, he's always seemed to channel it into creative expression to get it out of his system. Their fame has been a double-edged sword for me — I'm both wary and proud.

As unstable as my mum was for a long time, she is now one of the best parents you could wish for. She worked really hard to get through that period and remarried about twelve years ago. She and her husband have a motor-home and travel the country periodically. She was a costume designer for a long time, but had a stroke about five years ago that affected her right hand and leg, but she has more or less recovered from it. We speak almost daily on the phone and try to see each other once every couple of months.

As far as my father and stepmother go, they are two of the best people I have ever known. They are constantly trying to learn about themselves, trying to make themselves better people and, therefore, better parents. I've made mistakes like everyone else and my dad is the first person I turn to — I feel really sorry for people who don't have that connection with their parents. Dad and Julie worked hard to make a 'home' to the point that, when Julie was doing her TV special, my Dad pretty much dropped out of the business for a year so that he could be at home with us while she was tied up with work. Julie would work till eleven at night, but Dad would be there when we got home from school. Family always came first with them.

Having a second home in Switzerland was useful because we could really get away as a family. At one time they did say, 'That's it! Let's go and live in Switzerland and raise the kids there,' and it did happen for a couple of years in the mid-1970s, but I wasn't with them. However, we did spend most of our Christmases in Switzerland.

Dad and I see things so similarly that we react before anyone else does. We think the same way — and I must add that my brother is the same. If the three of us are at a funeral together then forget it, you'd better separate us. In fact, many times Julie has had to sit between my father and me at special occasions to prevent us from giggling together.

I still have problems coming to terms with the past and what happened with my parents because I find that I'm angry about not having a mother throughout my early years. What I mean is that I was *her* mother — I had to take care of her. There were many times when I had to stick my fingers down her throat to bring up an overdose and that was a really bad experience for a young kid.

As a child, I used to say to her, 'How can you do this to me and to my brother?' She would say that, at that moment, it did not occur to her that she was doing anything to anyone other than herself in an attempt to stop her pain. We've both come very far since then, and I've forgiven her all of the suicide attempts because now, as an adult, I can understand how she felt. She was so self-involved that depression took over to a certain degree. When you feel like that you don't think about the consequences for those around you.

What it did for me was make me very co-dependent and constantly want to take care of everybody to the point of not taking care of myself.

Kids tend to think that when their parents split up, they did something to cause the split. I recall feeling like this and it made me fearful of men leaving me. In my two marriages, I was the one to leave. Both parties knew it wasn't working out, but it was me who said enough is enough. Maybe a part of it is a fear that they would have stuck with it and wouldn't have left, but both marriages were miserable and I couldn't have tolerated those situations continuing indefinitely.

When friends have left, it has therefore been more traumatic. Most people would say, 'Fuck 'em! It's their loss,' or whatever. But it goes to the core of my being and I feel abandoned.

I do realise that I choose men who are very similar to my dad in many ways and they tend to be similar in negative rather than positive ways. Moody, angry — that kind of thing. Maybe I'm still trying to work it all out, because I remember as a child being concerned about my dad's moods. That has certainly been prevalent in my relationships with men.

When I lived with the man who was to become my first husband and father of my first child, my father cut me off completely. He wouldn't talk to me for three years. He was correct in what he said — he felt that it was not a healthy relationship and told me things about my first husband that I didn't believe — or chose not to believe — but which turned out to be true. To be honest, I figured everything out in the first eight months of living with him and knew it wasn't right. Then I became pregnant and thought, well I'm only eighteen and all of that and tried to stick it out. It lasted three years in all. Although Dad was correct, his way of handling it was to abandon me again — or that's how it felt.

We got back on good terms for a while, but then I started living with Peter, who was to become my second husband, and the same thing happened — he didn't approve from the beginning. That was 1981, I was 24 years of age and had a three-year-old kid.

I visited Dad right after Peter and I married and I said, 'Look, I want a relationship with you. I don't care on what terms, but I need to have a relationship with my father. Life is too short.' Whatever I said certainly made a difference. We started out on a relationship that has grown closer than we could have dared hope.

More recently, there have been times when I have to confess to using the fact that I am Blake Edwards' daughter. It doesn't always help, though — I've actually lost jobs because of who my dad is. I've been up for jobs and almost hired by producers for network television when the director has found out who my dad is and, because my dad hadn't hired him on some prior occasion way back, I've been dropped. I thought about changing my name at one point, but when you start out at ten you've already established who you are to a great degree.

There are people who my Dad knows and who knew me when I was growing up, and I have called them and said I needed some help getting a script off the ground, and they're helpful in so much as I probably wouldn't have been able to get a script to them if I hadn't been Blake Edwards' daughter.

I wrote to Mel Brooks recently, who happens to be my dad's neighbour. I'd heard he was making a film, *Dracula, Dead and Loving It*. I said in the letter that I hoped it wasn't an intrusion, but I am a huge fan of his — which I am — and a huge vampire freak. 'If you want,' I said, 'I'll read for you, scream for you, bite someone's neck for you — anything.' I kept it light by saying, 'As you have seen, my parents are busy at the moment with builders doing construction work at their house, so they might be over to borrow a cup of sugar — or some money.' He phoned me personally and said, 'My God, we're already shooting. When did you hear about it?' Basically, I was too late, but the promise of future work is there, which is genuinely kind of him.

I've put in a good word for others so I start to feel, why not? Why should I feel I'm any different in terms of getting ahead?

Working with my dad was an incredible experience. He's very objective and is quite simply a wonderful director. He doesn't overshoot, and is really good at not tiring out his actors. He knows what he wants and he gets what he wants. Of course, being his daughter he might have greater expectations. I know that when I work with him, I feel that I want to be that much better. I see it a lot with him and Julie when they work together. He's maybe a little harder on her and she's a little harder on herself. However, first and foremost, he truly loves actors. Therefore, he doesn't cast actors in a role that he doesn't feel they're going to do well. He's very respectful of actors. And he's very brave. He'll try things out. If he's comfortable with people, no matter what side of the camera they are on, he likes to use them over and over again — he has great loyalty. I've seen him coax performances out of actors that I've never seen them achieve in any other movies. Whether he does it by taking someone by the hand for an hour and half and walking them around and talking to them about what's going on, I'm not sure. I have certainly seen him do that.

When you mention films like *The Days of Wine and Roses*, *Breakfast at Tiffany's* and *Experiment in Terror*, and tell people that they were my dad's, people go,'Wow! Really? They were great movies.' But if you just mention the name Blake Edwards, they say, 'Oh yeah — the guy who directed the "Panther" movies.'

Personally, I think his best films were *The Days of Wine and Roses*, *The Party*, which for me is still an amazing study in comedy, *Victor Victoria* and *The Great Race*. *Breakfast at Tiffany's* can still make me cry.

10 was a remarkable film and it still holds up well. Strange to think that George Segal was up for it before Dudley Moore finally took the lead. It wouldn't have had the same feel if George had done it. Dudley was perfect for that particular role.

In *The Party* the entire dining-room sequence, which runs to about eight minutes with virtually no dialogue, is remarkable in the way it can hold your attention. The kitchen doors swing open so you see what's going on in the kitchen, swinging back to knock Peter Sellers from his chair every time. It's quite brilliant.

One of my favourite shots my dad ever did was in *Victor Victoria* with the cockroach in the café. All of a sudden, he pulls back, creating the proscenium of this café with everyone running around screaming and crazy, although you don't hear it, you just see it. He's been very inventive.

He enjoys shooting a lot in master shots, not even coming in for close-ups much of the time. This is very rare. Most directors come in for the close-up, then an over-the-shoulder, reverse angle and so on. Sometimes it plays much better to see the entire proscenium.

I think it's why Dad's done well on Broadway. One critic — a film critic, in fact — once said that on the stage his production looked like one big proscenium. Well, that's what the stage is, so what a stupid thing to say! But Dad did shoot his films in that way, almost like it was set on a stage.

The other night, Dad and I were watching part of *Bye Bye Birdy* television musical. Both of us were sitting there saying, 'What are you doing talking to the camera?' It was directed like a television show, not like a musical. They were coming in for close-ups while people were dancing. We were thinking, 'Wait a minute! I'd like to see these people's feet, thank you very much. I'd like to see what they're doing.' People were singing to camera but being shot from the left. Who the hell are they singing to? Because it wasn't shot correctly, it just didn't work.

Continuity is a big thing with me — as an actor, I'm very aware of it. I recall seeing something a while back involving a very famous actor of whom I was a huge fan. I couldn't believe though that, as an actor, he could miss what I could see. He had a ring on his left hand for about three-quarters of the movie, then for one scene it was on his right hand. Even though he should have noticed himself, at the very least the continuity person should have spotted it.

It happens all the time. There's a continuity story about the famous actress who is naked in bed except for a blanket that covers her from the waist down. In part of the shot the sheet is up and in the next part the sheet is down. Now, how can you miss that one? You don't see a tit, then you see a tit! With my father, that would have been re-shot — no matter what the cost, or even if they had to rig up the bed in his trailer to do it. Woody Allen would have done the same thing, no question. Total, consummate professionals.

Hannah, my three-year-old, pulled out a video of Dad's recently. It happened to be *Victor Victoria*. She looked at the cover and said, 'There's Grandma. I wanna watch this.'

I put it on and as it started she asked, 'Where's Grandpa?' I explained he was not in it but that he wrote it and basically made the movie. You could see that the concept went right over her head.

She'll also watch *Heidi* because she likes to see me when I was a little girl. It's nice that there's a record of work for her.

I think Hannah, rather than Katie, my first child, will be the one who will end up in the business — though not if I can help it — because she's very animated. Katie talked about it at one point, saying she wanted to get into commercials, but she's never really serious about it. My attitude has always been that if you want to do it, then go to school and study. She does some modelling, but at nearly twenty she's almost too old for that, unbelievable as it seems.

If Hannah really wanted to act, I can't say if I would or wouldn't help her. It's so hard to be a parent in this business and have a young child in the business, too. For instance, I wouldn't want her to be on a 'set' without me or her dad there. Equally, I don't want to be on somebody else's 'set', looking like the typical stage mother.

We've talked about letting her do some print work or commercials now, because she's so photogenic and natural in front of the camera. That way, we can put some money away for her for college. At her age she probably won't know what she's done. At the same time, it's taking her to auditions with mothers who can be rather pushy. I'm not sure I want her to be in that environment. The weird thing is that, if she were in the business, she'd be the fifth generation of our family. Very few families can make such a claim. My great-grandfather started it all by directing silent movies.

Geoff has also worked with Dad on a few things, as both writer and co-editor. He co-wrote a couple of the 'Panther' movies, and *The Man Who Loved Women*. He has also done some second-unit directing, and now seems to want to concentrate mostly on directing.

It's amazing how much the film industry has changed. There are people casting and producing stuff who I've never even heard of and they have all this power. They don't necessarily know who I am. Then again, there are those who do know me because I've been around a long time, and they'll automatically say, 'No, no, she's not right for this.' That's frustrating because they haven't seen me for eight years or so and hopefully you're constantly evolving as an actor. Their judgement is based on an old movie.

I was trying to get into something recently and the casting director said, 'No, she's too off-beat for this.' And my manager said, 'She's not off-beat.' But I said, 'No, that's OK. I like being off-beat. I take that as a compliment.' I do feel I cannot be pigeon-holed. I don't want to be a leading lady. I've done romantic comedies, but they've been off-beat characters. I'm not going to be Michelle Pfeiffer — I'm more Joan Cusack.

Big stars are now doing television and taking roles from the likes of me, who would normally have done that type of role. And of course you have people from TV shows starring in movies. So it goes — it's a different business. A lot of people in sitcoms switch over to other sitcoms to be a guest star. Where do we fit in now?

I've had the opportunity to meet many people over the years. The first time I met William Holden sticks in my mind. At first it didn't really sink in, then I thought about the films I'd seen him in and I remembered watching him work as an actor and show such a knowledge of the mechanics. He'd ask what lens was on the camera and they'd tell him and then he'd know how far he could move before he was out of frame. 'Wow!' I thought. 'Now that's a consummate professional.' We knew each other over the years, then *S.O.B.* came along and I had a small role in that. We became really close during that time. He was very much like a father figure to me.

Several years earlier, Holden had taught me to play a card game that he liked, called 'Spite and Malice'. Very few people know how to play it. It uses two decks of cards and is quite intricate. We'd play between 'takes' and he would get really upset because I was a good player and I used to beat him. I'd tell him, 'OK, we'll play three out of five and if I win, you stop smoking.' But he never did. He'd just say, 'Re-match! Re-match!'

It's very sad to think he's gone. He was probably one of the last 'greats', not just as an actor but also as a person.

Peter Sellers obviously featured in our lives. Dad directed all those 'Panther' movies in which Peter starred. One of the last times I saw Peter was with my father. We were all in Switzerland during a holiday season. Peter phoned me a couple of times at the chalet while I was out there, suggesting we get together for a drink. I met him at the Palace hotel and we sat at the bar. While he nursed his third drink, he told me in his loosened state that he reckoned he'd made a few mistakes with his children and that he wished he could change things and so on. It was an enlightening moment and very poignant, too.

During this visit to Switzerland, we all ended up at the same restaurant. During this particular period, it was rare to be together like this, as Dad and Peter had had their fall-outs and weren't too sure if they liked each other.

I was running up the stairs of this restaurant and rounded the corner and literally went bowling into Peter. I was wearing a purple trouser suit that was made of brushed cotton. Peter had an obsession with the colour purple for some reason, and my reaction was to cover myself like he'd seen me naked. I found myself apologizing, worried in case he was going to suddenly vomit or something. But he, to my surprise, was very calm about it and just laughed saying, 'Don't worry, it's OK.'

We were sitting near Peter, but at separate tables. Dad remembers Peter getting up and going outside. After about five or ten minutes Dad said to me and Julie, 'I'm going out to check on him.' This was a very natural thing to do, as it had just started snowing very heavily.

Dad opened the restaurant door on to an empty street that was rapidly disappearing in heavy piles of snow. Across the street, Peter was standing underneath a street lamp.

Dad watched him turning into a snowman for a few minutes and realised that the man was in some kind of a trance. Dad walked across the street and placed a hand on his shoulder. He said, 'Peter!' But Peter didn't respond. So he said it again and eventually Peter looked up and said, 'Oh, Blake!' Dad asked him if he was OK. He said he was fine and Dad suggested he came inside. Peter said he'd be in in a minute, so Dad left him standing there looking pathetic and lonely. It was to be the last time Dad would see him. He's told me since what a strange and macabre last memory it is to have of him. Peter was just right out of it by then.

The games that went on when making those 'Panther' movies was incredible. I doubt anyone in movie history had so many out-takes. Dad and Peter would so often just end up on the floor rolling around laughing. Everyone who worked with Peter on those films broke up at one time or other during filming.

As a child, I remember visiting the Sellers' house, Elstead, right after having my appendix out, and getting straight on to a trampoline. There was the great pleasure of showing Sarah (Sellers) my scar. Sarah and I were close friends. She'd come out to LA for consecutive summers — maybe three — and stay the whole time here.

I went with Sarah to a twenty-first birthday — we were no more than fifteen years of age. We both had a crush on the same guy there. His name was Jim Korsen and eventually we did date for some months, and we've stayed really good friends. The first time he called me at the house, Sarah got really upset and I felt so badly about it. But I liked him, so too bad! All's fair in love and war.

We saw a lot of the Sellers family from time to time. Peter rented a house at Del Resto and the images are clear in my head, but there's no sequence to events. Sarah and I smoked a lot of 'joints' there and she'd become really goofy. She'd make me laugh so much and I would laugh so hard at her laughing. She had a big mop of hair that she'd pull across her face when she felt shy, and I remember Julie saying to her, 'Come out from behind your hair, Sarah.'

One of the most memorable moments for me was when Dad and Julie were filming *Darling Lilly*. They were shooting in a house in France — I didn't really know where it was — when all of a sudden the Duke and Duchess of Windsor were standing there. I could barely talk once it dawned on me this was their house and there they were.

The shoot lasted about a week. The Windsors had six pug dogs and they let me walk them. I must have been twelve and there I was walking these snivelling dogs and thinking, I'm walking the ex-King of

England's dogs. Very bizarre. But they were just the nicest people. Mrs Simpson was quite a lady.

Dad's known for his practical jokes. He had a guy work for him several times as a barber-cum-masseur-cum-whatever. This guy had terrible constipation while on location and asked the prop man if he had anything he could take. He was told that he only had horse laxatives. The guy was that desperate he took them. The prop guy warned my Dad that this had happened, so Dad told everyone to watch for this guy to see when he ran off into the forest. Sure enough, a couple of hours later he started clenching and running. Dad sent the prop man after him, having already told him what to do. When this guy was going through his motions the prop man quietly slid a huge shovel underneath where he was going. When he'd finished, he just pulled the shovel back. The guy gets up, pulls his trousers back on, looks around to see what he's done and is horrified to see nothing there.

My dad did a movie recently called *Skin Deep*, which has this incredible condom scene. At the Broadway opening of *Victor Victoria*, John Ritter, who starred in the movie, sent Dad a packet of condoms as an opening-night gift . I was there when he opened it. 'I know what I'm going to do,' Dad said to me. 'I'm going to make them look like they've been used, then send 'em right back.' Much appreciated, thanks for the loan, sort of thing.

I tend to refer to Dad and Julie as my parents. She's been in my life for over thirty years. But it's been a rocky road at times for them. Dad and Julie came from similar places — both came out of bad marriages. They were both very involved with analysis, trying to find themselves and work on themselves.

I think if I'd known then what I know now about being an actor I might have gone to medical school or something — it would have been a bit more stable. I said to Mark the other day that I never thought I would feel this way but I really would like a lot of money. I don't care what that implies, I'd just like to have a lot of money and be really comfortable and not worry every month about how we're going to get by. To be able to prioritise, and send Hannah to the school I want her to go to without having to worry about it would be great.

I'm not the type of person who has anxiety attacks, but a month or so ago I woke up about in the middle of the night with this horrible sense of sadness. It was terrible; I felt like someone close had died. I was almost in tears. The thing that was running constantly through my head was that I would never act again. I thought about this for a while and realised just how important it is to me. The idea of not being an actor just makes me so sad that I think that's why I keep persevering. I write as well and do other things, but it just isn't the same; it just doesn't fulfil that need in me.

Perhaps if I'd gone into medicine, because that does genuinely fascinate me, it's possible I would have developed the same sort of passion as I have for acting. Being so young, that was all that I saw for my future. It never even occurred to me to go to college and I regret that terribly. The sad thing is, I never really learned another trade. I don't have the skills to be otherwise employed. And I'm too creative. I couldn't sit in an office taking dictation.

I love the law as well — at least until the O.J. (Simpson) trial. It has always fascinated me, but I'm not so sure that I could sit in a building, stuck within the same four walls, reading law books all day.

I wish I could do something that I really, really loved and at the same time make a good living from it. Well, isn't that what everybody is ultimately looking for?

DICK FRANCIS
WRITER, (1920–)

Dick Francis was a famous jockey long before he became famous as one of the best-selling authors in the world. He entered racing as an amateur jockey in 1946, becoming a professional steeplechase jockey in 1948. He rode regularly for HM Queen Elizabeth the Queen Mother and was champion rider for the 1953–54 season.

On his retirement from the saddle in 1957, he became racing correspondent for the *Sunday Express*. His first book was his racing autobiography, *The Sport of Queens*, published in December of that year. His first novel, *Dead Cert*, appeared in 1962 and there has been one every year since. Thirty-four international bestsellers later, he is widely acclaimed as one of the masters of thriller writing.

His awards include the Crime Writers' Association's Cartier Diamond Dagger for his outstanding contribution to the crime genre, two Edgar Allan Poe Mystery Writers of America awards, an honorary Doctorate of Humane Letters from Tufts University of Boston and an OBE from The Queen.

He lives in the West Indies with his wife, Mary.

The following contribution is by Felix Francis, younger son of Dick and Mary Francis. Felix was born in 1953, is married to Anne and they have two sons, Matthew (17) and William (10). Felix was a teacher of

A-Level physics, but he has been his father's full-time manager since 1991. He is also a director of World Challenge Expeditions Ltd, a London-based company that teaches leadership to young people by sending them on trekking expeditions to the Third World. Felix has led expeditions to the jungles of Borneo and South America and to the Himalaya mountains of northern India. Felix's elder brother, Merrick, left school to be an amateur jockey but soon moved on to training racehorses. In recent years, he has swopped four legs for four (or more) wheels and now owns and manages Lambourn Racehorse Transport Ltd (LRT), the largest horse transport company in England. He lives in Lambourn with his wife, Alex.

FELIX FRANCIS:

I was just three when Devon Loch decided to deposit my father on to the Aintree turf just 30 yards short of winning the 1956 Grand National for HM Queen Elizabeth the Queen Mother. As a former champion jockey, Dick Francis had been well known in the horse-racing world for many years, but this spectacular sporting failure catapulted his name on to the front pages. The incident obviously made quite an impression on Francis Junior as apparently (I have no memory of this) I was observed to scamper along on all fours and then fall flat on my stomach shouting loudly that I was playing at being Devon Loch, 'Down I go, BUMP!' My father's reaction to this less than tactful action is, fortunately, unrecorded, but it seems to me now that it was something of a miracle that I survived to see my fourth birthday.

One of my greatest sadnesses is that I have no memory of my father as a jockey. It was just before my aforementioned fourth birthday in February 1957 that he decided to retire from race riding. It was also before the days of regular televised horse racing and certainly before video recording. The only film I have is a flickering black-and-white Pathé newsreel of that infamous 1956 Grand National and every time I see it I hope that this time, just once, Devon Loch might actually win!

Dick Francis was 36 when he finally hung up his racing boots. The life of a steeplechase jockey is full of ups and downs. The ups seem to be fleeting and the downs hurt. Their most important attribute is a total disregard for personal safety, hurtling over stiff birch fences at speeds of up to 30 miles per hour astride half a ton of horse flesh. On average a steeplechase jockey will hit the turf (still at 30 mph) once every ten rides. Top jockeys can ride up to twenty or thirty races a week, which means an average week will have two or three falls. Jockeys have to learn to bounce and then curl up to avoid being kicked by the other horses. The body can only take so much. Ten years is about the limit and, at 36, my father was rather old to still be riding over the sticks. But he had started late.

The Second World War proved to be a major inconvenience in the race-riding plans of Dick Francis. Instead of joining a racing stable as he had hoped, at the age of nineteen he joined the Royal Air Force. Five-and-a-half years' service followed, in North Africa and at home in England, initially as a member of the ground crew and then as a pilot, first of fighters then of heavy bombers. Whatever the risks of riding over fences, they must be less than those of spending the hours of darkness at the controls of a Lancaster at ten thousand feet over Germany in early 1945. So it was at the age of 26 that my father became a professional sportsman.

My parents married in 1947 and six years later I arrived, younger son of an ex-fighter pilot and champion jockey. Who needs heroes with a father like that? But, of course, to me he is just my dad.

'What's it like to be the son a famous father?' An often asked question.

'What's it like not to be?' I reply. Both are impossible to answer.

As I have grown older and moved out of the nest to create a family and home of my own, I am able to look back at my childhood from a more detached perspective, to try to view my father in the way others might have seen him.

My earliest memory is from when I was four. Merrick, my elder brother, went by bus to school and I remember my father and I driving him to the bus stop in the mornings. It was not actually going to the bus that I remember, it is coming home again. We used to stop at the bakery in Didcot to pick up trays of freshly baked bread for the village shop. I remember the smell and being allowed to eat a miniature cottage loaf piping hot from the oven.

Having retired from the fray, my father was employed as a racing corresponding for the *Sunday Express*. I realise now what a change the step from saddle to notebook must have been. Risking one's life and being literally in the thick of the action replaced by being one of *them* instead of one of *us*. Nowadays many successful sportsmen move from the track, court or pitch, into the media to act as knowledgeable specialists, but in the 1950s participants were participants and the Press were the Press and the two did not mix. Mutual trust was scarce.

No longer a jockey, he was barred from the world he knew and loved — the jockeys' changing-rooms. His new abode was the Press room where he would be viewed with caution by ex-colleagues and new colleagues alike. It is a measure of the man that he soon broke down people's fears and suspicions.

The change in employment brought with it a change in circumstances. Successful jockeys are well paid. Self-employed and paid per ride, so they should be. A fall, an injury, can wipe out their earning potential for a day, for a week or for ever. Seven years at the top proved to be lucrative and my parents were able to design and build a new house at the foot of the Berkshire Downs in the year I was born. This remained their home until they moved to warmer climes in 1986. One article a week for a Sunday newspaper did not pay as well and times were harder. My father has never been an extravagant man and even today, when worldwide book royalties have raised his annual earnings into six figures, he still collects unfranked stamps for further use. He is not mean — far from it. He is just careful, and this characteristic stood him well in the lean years of my childhood. Make no mistake, we were not poor. However, Dick Francis was higher on the scale of fame that he was on the scale of affluence, a situation far from uncommon for retired sportsmen both then and now.

I cannot remember a time when horses were not an integral part of the Francis household. Strangely, for a 'racing family' we never had cats or dogs. I think my father would have had them but my mother was against. Merrick subsequently had a dog as soon as he left home and nowadays there are always at least two curled up in front of the Aga in his kitchen, acting as living speed bumps to trip up the unwary. I tended to follow my mother's philosophy and, fortunately, my wife is not a doggy person either. I am allergic to cats (no joke with a name like Felix), so we now make do with a pond full of goldfish and Wally, my son's hamster. But I digress. Childhood memories involve lots of horses and ponies.

I never had a pony of my own, unlike my brother who was given one by a family friend. This fact has never made me feel that I was deprived. Indeed, I always had ponies to ride as we used to look after a succession of ponies that belonged to other people who, I suppose, had a pony but no field while I had a field but no pony. Neat. I was never that close to the ponies I rode. I love those Thelwell images of ponies in bed sleeping with their owners — such love and affection. Somehow I was not able to love an animal whose sole intention seemed to be to dump me on the ground and decamp at the earliest opportunity. My brother's pony, Joanna, had a wicked habit of slowly lifting a front hoof and then stamping down on my toes as I tried to apply a saddle to her back. Couple this with my father's belief that all horse-riding should be done early (dark) on a winter's morning (freezing) to gain maximum benefit and you can being to understand why I belong to the 'both ends are dangerous and the middle is uncomfortable' school of equine instruction. Not that I would have dared to say so at the grand age of seven in 1960.

On most days during the school holidays and on Saturdays during term time, it was almost expected that I would rise early to 'ride out'. Every day, except Sundays, racehorses are exercised on the Berkshire Downs and my father used to ride horses at exercise for a local trainer for many years after he retired from riding them in races. The horses have to work early as the trainer will be at the races later in the day. 'First lot', as it was known, left the stables at 7.30am sharp. As the stables in question were a mile across the hill from our house, I had to rise from my warm, comfortable bed at 6.30, catch the pony in the dark with a torch (their eyes glow like cats-eyes), apply saddle and bridle and ride over the hill in order to follow the racehorses up on to the Downs. I suppose it must have sometimes been light and warm in the summer, but in my memory it was always pitch black and frosty. As a child, my father spent much of his school time playing truant to go riding. I never actually wished that the school holidays were shorter, but school days certainly held some attraction for me.

On reflection, I have to admit that not all riding was done at such an early hour and Merrick and I did have many happy hours in the saddle or riding bareback. Together with two friends, Francis and Susan Cundell, son and daughter of the trainer over the hill (literally, not metaphorically), we formed our own 'falling-off club'. Sixpence (bareback) or a shilling (saddled) was handed over to the kitty for each fall. At Christmas, we used the kitty for a party. On one occasion when we were looking after a particularly lively pony, the kitty actually paid out a shilling if we managed to ride around a course of jumps *without* falling off. Needless to say, the kitty still made a good profit that day.

My father was very keen that both his sons should learn to ride and to ride well. As a youngster he was an exceptional rider and won many awards. He is very proud of the fact that he helped to train the ponies on which The Queen and Princess Margaret first rode.

He used to lean out of his office window and shout instructions. 'Get your heels down!' he would bellow; 'Sit up straight.' 'Get your elbows in.' He wanted us to be horsemen; we, of course, wanted to be jockeys. In the fashion of the 1960s we would shorten our stirrup leathers so that we could crouch in the saddle. It looked good, even if we did have to subscribe more often to the 'falling-off' kitty. Dad was always against us riding so short, but we wanted to be Lester Piggott not Dick Francis!

Looking back, Merrick and I were, generally, fairly well-behaved children. On those occasions when we were in trouble, Dad would try to get angry to tell us off. He had a habit of sending us to our rooms and giving us a sharp kick on the bottom as we went past him. It didn't take us long to work out that our mistake was to turn our backs. Consequently, we would retire backwards like courtiers from the monarch. He would be unable to keep a straight face as we would circle round him and we would be forgiven. Only once did we find ourselves in real trouble. Merrick and I had contrived to behave so badly towards our nanny that she packed her bags and left. We had been sent to our room and, to our horror, our father appeared in the doorway with his riding whip in his hand. Our mother came to our rescue telling him not to do anything he would later regret. A close call. Nothing we did ever actually resulted in the use of the implement. Not yet anyway.

'Tidy up quickly, your father's home!' My mother's traditional Saturday afternoon call. My father wrote an article about the coming week's racing, so he was not a reporter as such, except for once a year on Grand National day. Every Friday we went up to the *Express* newspaper's offices in Fleet Street, London, with his copy for the Sunday paper, but he needed to be at the races on the Saturday in case a major story broke so that he could write a report for the following day. Often, we would all go with him and I still know my way around England by the racecourses. However, on wet, cold and miserable Saturdays, Merrick and I would stay at home and watch 'Grandstand' and 'World of Sport' on the television. We liked the racing, but wrestling was our passion. The sitting-room would be turned into the ring and one of us would be Mick MacManus and the other Jackie Pallo. It didn't matter which, the result was always the same. I would lose. There are many advantages of being an older brother, and winning at wrestling on the sitting-room floor is one of them. A three-year age gap is a major handicap when you are eight. I used to 'tag' my mother, but she never came to my rescue. 'If you choose to fight you must expect to get hurt' she would say; 'Life isn't fair.' How right she was. Saved by the 'Tidy up quickly, your father's home' was all I could hope for.

Dad was and remains a very tidy person. Not quite obsessive, but he does do the washing up between courses. 'Boy!' he would shout, 'go and make your bed!' Making beds has always been something I have hated. It seems such a waste of time when all that is going to happen is that you are going to unmake them again later. Think of the time saved for other, more important, activity if beds could be left unmade. Perhaps I will invent the self-making bed. In the meantime, duvets are a great idea!

On Christmas morning, while Merrick and I would tear our way into our presents, Dad would carefully unwrap his, saving each piece of paper. Sticky tape would be carefully removed and the paper folded for re-use. Now there is nothing more infuriating than someone who takes so long to open presents that they still have some left when all of yours are finished. Especially when you started with three times as many as they did. How I longed for him to let rip, just once. I even used to stick lots of tape on his present in the hope that I would force him to tear the paper in frustration but, of course, this tactic usually backfired as he just took twice as long to remove it.

Christmas morning always followed a ritual in the Francis household. My mother has always been a keen present-giver and we had Christmas stockings well into adulthood. She became tired of wrapping before she did of giving and occasionally our 'stockings' would be Harrods Food Hall carrier bags with unwrapped goodies and nicknacks within. Stockings would not be opened immediately on waking but would be brought to the sitting-room where the family would gather in dressing-gowns. Usually, my maternal grandmother would be staying and she would make tea. My father would wash up. How he ever found anything to wash up at 7.30 am on Christmas morning defeats me, but he did. How is it that grown-ups can be so frustratingly slow in getting ready to open presents? It must be an art that develops with age, for I am now accused of the same failing by my two sons.

My mother decided that I should know the big secret about the fat man in red with the white beard before I went to school aged six. She was worried that I might be distressed to learn from other boys that 'he' didn't really come down the chimney on Christmas Eve. I can't remember being particularly surprised at the revelation, but I do remember distressing others at school by shattering their illusions. When my own son seemed to me to be rather too old at eleven to still put sherry and mince pies next to the fireplace, I tried to break the bad news to him gently. He replied that of course he knew but didn't want to let on in case the presents stopped coming. Smart kid.

After stockings and breakfast, my father would insist on Merrick and me joining him at church. We were not a regular church-going family, but Christmas was special. Blewbury village church was blessed for many years by an eccentric, lovable vicar called Hugh Pickles. Reverend Pickles was cricket crazy. He used to take his holidays when the England cricket team was touring in the West Indies and he would follow them from island to island, becoming close friends with the players. His Christmas sermons would always include some reference to cricket and they would regularly be a critique of the touring MCC team selection. The Wise men would be equated with the team selectors and I think that he expected the Second Coming to be in the form of an English fast bowler or opening batsman. Sadly, Hugh died in 1989 but not before he saw his beloved Oxford Diocese cricket team win the Church Times Cup for the first time.

My father wrote his autobiography in 1957, shortly after the Devon Loch incident when the name Dick Francis was high in the nation's psyche. Having ridden for the Queen Mother for more than four years, he called the book *The Sport of Queens*. He has said many times that he wouldn't call it that these days! The book was suggested by an authors' agent, John Johnson, brother of Celia Johnson. John's mother was a friend of my grandmother. The family connection was made and John was sure that, as a result of Devon Loch, an autobiography would sell. At first the task seemed daunting, but my father had always been a great letter writer and, applying the adage that everyone can write their life story, he set to work with encouragement from my mother. To his great delight and surprise, the book sold very well indeed, as it still does to this day.

By 1961 he had been toying with the idea of another book for some time. Several hundred articles for the *Sunday Express* had taught him much about writing, in particular how to hook a reader and hang on. I don't remember any great decision being made to write a novel, but I was probably too young to realise anyway. *Dead Cert* was published in January 1962 and, suddenly, I was the son of an author not a journalist. This stunning change of circumstances did little for my standing in the playground hierarchy where I was teased mercilessly for having 'Felix' for a name. 'Felix the cat' the Michaels, the Christophers, the Roberts *et al* would chant. For a while I hated my name. But not for long. I soon realised that it was good to be different. Nowadays, the only disadvantage I can think of is that other people remember my name while I immediately forget theirs.

Dead Cert was an instant success, selling well at home and being accepted for publication in the USA, France, Germany, Spain and Japan. There was talk of film options. Such was the encouragement that, in January 1963, my father set to work on a second novel. So started an annual routine that has continued for more than thirty years. The bitterly cold weather of the early months of 1963 put a stop to all horse racing due to the frozen and snow-covered ground. For Dick Francis, this was a mixed blessing. It gave him more time to get on with the novel, but he still had to write a piece each week for the *Sunday Express* on non-existent racing.

Understandably, I remember the winter of 1962–63 for other reasons. The snow came on the day after Christmas and the big freeze set in for months. There was still snow lying in the garden at the beginning of May. The snow fell, melted slightly, then froze hard leaving an icy crust. My father took a cine film of my mother ice-skating across the garden on the frozen surface of the snow. Merrick and I built an igloo out of ice blocks and we spent hours sliding down a long hill on metal trays. My mother spent most of the winter sitting on an electric heater wrapped up with coat, gloves, hat and fur-lined boots, and that was *inside* the house. When she did venture out to join in the tobogganing she managed to hit a spot where the ice crust had been broken. The result was a pair of black eyes and cut nose. She retired to bed for the duration.

The 1960s proved to be the decade of greatest change in the Francis family. My father started it as a retired jockey who wrote a bit. Ten years later, he was a best-selling author who once rode as a jockey. My mother learnt to fly. She had a couple of lessons to assist my father in some research for one of the novels and simply carried on until she became one of the top qualified women pilots in the country, even writing a book for student pilots. Merrick left school in 1968 and moved into the world of horse racing, becoming assistant to Ryan Price, a top racehorse trainer. I started and finished the decade as a schoolboy, albeit at opposite ends of the educational process, but the 1960s left their mark on me, too.

I went away to school in Mill Hill, north London, in September 1966. It was a relief to escape from my prep school where the headmaster, Mr Robertson, ruled with fear. I am sure he modelled his technique on Mr Squeers from *Nicholas Nickleby*. He used to carry a thin wooden chair leg about 12 inches long in his deep trouser pocket. If he found any of his young charges misbehaving (a common occurrence) he would apply a few smart blows to the offender's backside with the said chair leg. More serious offences would occasion a trip to his study to be dealt with more painfully with a longer cane. I have since lived in fear of the smell of stale pipe tobacco. His wife was like Mrs Bumble from *Oliver Twist* — except that no one would be as foolish as to ask her for more. Our problem was how to dispose of the first serving, not how to obtain a second. Mrs Robertson had the windows of the dining-room nailed shut after finding lumpy mashed potato all over her flower beds beneath them. Tapioca pudding was my least favourite of her culinary delights and I would have to sit there until it was finished. Torment. Somehow I have never been able to make my own children clear their plates if they don't want to.

Mill Hill School was like paradise in comparison. Here the younger boys were only bullied by the older ones and not by the teachers as well. All boarding-schools went through a dramatic period of change in the late 1960s, moving away from the tyrannical establishments as depicted in *Tom Brown's Schooldays* to more caring and more comfortable centres of learning. Parents demanded that their children be happy at school and that corporal punishment be a thing of the past. I witnessed this change at first hand and cold showers, freezing dormitories and regular beatings now seem as alien as trench warfare.

My father used to write to my brother and me every week. He would send us a letter each; one week I would get the top copy and Merrick would have the carbon, the following week the reverse. He would tell us what he had been doing and often his letters would start with fact and quickly become fiction. I wish I had kept them. Great stories of his days out hunting and the adventures of his imagination. All signed 'lots of love, Pop'. My letters home tended to be shorter: 'Please send more cash, love Felix'. Only once did I write on more than one side of paper. He had written to ask whether I could help with some research for a book. Could I design a bomb that would be made to explode by remote control? Hence the radio-controlled bomb in *Rat Race* was designed by a sixth-form physics student.

In 1968, my schooling was interrupted by a spell in hospital. My left hip had been giving me trouble for some time and, in January, it collapsed completely. Rapidly I found myself flat on my back in the

Nuffield Orthopaedic Centre in Oxford and there I stayed until May. I had a slipped left femoral epiphysis, a rare condition that occurs when the bones grow but do not harden. Hence my left hip had bent and finally dislocated under my own body weight.

It was a difficult time for my parents. They felt guilty about not having done something sooner and frustrated that they could do little now. I had been suffering some leg pains for almost a year and all investigations had shown nothing. 'Growing pains' we were told. Not so.

An orthopaedic hospital is a strange environment. Very few of the inmates are ill. Most are just waiting for bones to fix or ligaments to mend. Hours and hours, days and days, weeks and weeks of lying still just waiting for the body to right itself. In my case it meant months of traction and two operations, once when my left hip was remodelled and pinned.

We did have a school of sorts in the hospital and, nowadays, I sympathise with the poor women who struggled hard to teach a dozen or so delinquents of assorted ages and abilities whose only common feature was that they were a captive audience. I recall that we were not the best behaved class in educational history. What could she do? She could hardly keep us in after school, as we were not going anywhere anyway.

The boy in the next bed to me had a neat trick. He was in hospital to have a curve in his spine corrected and this involved taking some bone from his leg and placing it up against his spine to straighten it. He was encased in a plaster cast from the top of his head to his knees and, without being lifted, he could move only his left arm. While lying almost face down on his right side, he could pick up his water jug with his left hand, and without being able to see behind him, he would throw the contents neatly over our hapless teacher as she walked by. Consequently, he was not a popular student. In fact he was not a popular patient either, as he had a habit of often repeating the feat and soaking anyone foolish enough to get too close, especially the nurses. They would move his jug out of reach, but the cleaners would always refill and replace it. He was tolerated as his brain was as twisted as his back, poor lad.

Long-term hospitalisation is something I would not wish on anybody. However, having been there myself, I would not have missed it for anything. The experience taught me so much about myself and about others. I also discovered girls.

Up to that time all I knew about 'IT' was what I had been taught by the daughter of a family friend in the back of a Landrover on the way home from school. Let me explain quickly that this was theoretical instruction rather than a practical demonstration. Her father was a farmer and she learnt about such things from watching the animals. My father asked me when I was about thirteen if I knew where babies came from. 'Of course I do,' I replied, to his huge sigh of relief, I actually knew where calves and piglets came from. Hospital taught me more.

Not from the other patients, who were all boys, but from the nurses, who were all girls, most of them seventeen- and eighteen-year-old trainees. Glorious young nymphs and so sexy in their uniforms. I rapidly fell in love with all of them, but Christine Baker, the night nurse, will always be my favourite. I used to dream that we were running together naked along a beach. When I woke, I found myself still tied to a bed with ropes and pulleys and weights. Frustration.

My mother would visit me every day and my father would come as often as he could. Living in an institution, one too easily becomes totally immersed in its trivia to the exclusion of life outside. By this stage my father was enjoying increasing success as an author and he was busy with novel number seven. My mother had continued to fly. Now, in 1968, she was an experienced pilot who was studying for an Instrument Rating, a sort of degree in flying. She was also busy writing her flying textbook. When I finally returned to the real world in the summer, it came as something of a surprise to find out how much they had done, as well as visiting me.

*   *   *

The start of the 1970s found my father busier than ever. The books continued to make great strides and *Forfeit* won the Edgar Allen Poe Award for the best mystery novel of the year in the USA. My father went to New York for the presentation as a very proud man. Few, if any, foreign writers had won this prestigious American award. I wasn't there, but all accounts report that his speech was a great success. At least he didn't repeat his rendition of his favourite verse. At the champion jockey's dinner in 1954, he is well remembered for standing on the table and reciting to the (all-male) audience all nine verses of 'The Great Farting Contest of Stilton-on-Tees'.

The regular annual routine had by now become an accepted way of life for the Francis family. My father starts writing in January, as soon as the Christmas and New Year holidays are over. He writes in longhand in a wire-bound notebook before transferring it to typescript, originally on a trusted portable typewriter but nowadays on a word processor. The book is due at the publisher by the end of May, in order to be ready for autumn publication. It is a task that requires considerable self-discipline and determination and one that seems to get harder each year as people's expectations grow. Every year there is always a difficult week or so after the book is finished and before he has received word from the publishers as to whether they like it. Confidence is not high during this period and it was always a wise time to keep out of trouble when we were young.

After the book is 'in' and after proofs have been read and corrected in June, it is time for a well-earned rest. June has always been the traditional holiday time for my parents. It is the off-season for National Hunt racing. Both as a jockey and a journalist, Dad had to take his vacations during this time even though school holidays were later. When Merrick and I were small we used to go and stay with our maternal grandmother who lived near our school in Abingdon. If asked, my parents would say that they went to Staines for their holidays. For those of you who do not know Staines, suffice it to say that it is not a usual holiday destination. However, my father and mother would slowly make their way down the river Thames to Staines before turning round and making their steady way back towards Oxfordshire. The Francis family have had a cabin cruiser on the Thames since 1957 and it has provided many, many weeks of solitude and relaxation in some of the most beautiful countryside in England. Even today, my parents spend a quiet week on the river each summer, nowadays taking their grandchildren to jump on and off the boat with the mooring ropes.

Traditionally, the first meeting of the new jump racing season takes place down in the West Country at Newton Abbot, Devon & Exeter and the (now-closed) Buckfastleigh courses. Dick Francis would always be present, either to ride or to report. Consequently, we would stay at a hotel in Paignton for ten days at the beginning of each August. Dad would go to the races while the rest of the family would build sandcastles on the beach. For Merrick and me, it was our summer holiday and we used to look forward to it eagerly. We stayed at the Redcliffe Hotel and, like us, other families would return there year after year providing ready friends for each visit. One incident that stands out in my memory occurred as a result of my father's liking for practical jokes. One morning at breakfast, with the hotel dining-room packed, he spotted a friend on his way in. Dad immediately stood up, banged the table, called for silence, and uttered the phrase that has become the Francis family motto, 'Quiet everybody, he's arrived!' Thereafter, grown men would crawl on hands and knees to get to their tables in the dining-room without being seen.

We still go annually to Devon, and still to the Redcliffe Hotel, although these days in a rather less embarrassing fashion. In 1992, my parents notched up their fortieth year at the Redcliffe and the hotel made no charge for their stay and also named the hotel conference room 'The Dick Francis Suite'. We now go for two weeks and it is the only time in the year when we are all together. It is our family Christmas, our birthday gatherings, our Easter and our Thanksgiving all rolled into one.

On another occasion my father's love of a quick quip nearly landed us in deep trouble. Some family friends were staying and six of us were returning from a restaurant in our friends' car. Dad was in the front passenger seat with the window down on a warm summer's evening. As we passed by the fish and chip shop in the town of Wallingford, my father noticed a man coming out carrying a great bundle wrapped in newspaper. 'Got your lemon, mate?' shouted my father with a laugh. The man was not amused. We drove on. As we left the town and started along the narrow, dark country road towards home we were overtaken by a car that proceeded to stop in front, blocking the road. Out stepped the man. To my childhood eyes he looked huge, and he was angry. He strode towards us flexing his fists. 'Drive on' said my father. Our friend needed no further encouragement and mounted the verge to get by. A hair-raising chase around the villages of south Oxfordshire ensued. We were in an old Armstrong-Sidley, strong being the appropriate part of the name. At speeds up to 60 or 70 miles per hour we rushed through the night with this idiot on our tail and nudging the rear bumper. We couldn't lead him home so we drove to Didcot where we stopped outside the police station. Here we sat with the car doors firmly locked as the man approached. Dad opened the window a crack. A moderately polite conversation took place in which the man questioned my father's parentage and then invited him to step out of the car and repeat his comment. The invitation was declined. The man was still not amused. It became clear that he was an ex-boxer, his cauliflower ears and flattened nose testament to some fearful beatings in the ring. Lemons were used between rounds to revive the poor man. Eventually he accepted apologies for any unintentional offence and departed. I suspect his fish and chips were cold.

September of each year sees the publication of the annual book and the hectic round of publicity that accompanies it. Dick Francis usually does an annual tour of the UK and one of the east coast of the States and, most years, one other tour to some other far-flung location.

November and December are months to plan and think, time to research and learn, ready for another start in January. And so it goes on, and long may it do so.

*　　　*　　　*

Having shown little inclination towards our four-legged friends, a life in the saddle was not for me. Add to this the fact that the only works of fiction I have ever written have been school reports and it has become clear that I will not follow in my father's footsteps. My brother Merrick had left home to become an assistant trainer and this took away any parental pressure to become involved in the equestrian world.

I went to London University in 1971 and graduated three years later with a Bachelor of Science degree in physics. I love physics. It is the study of the unseen world, of the great invisibilities of life: gravity, magnetism, sub-atomic particles, radiation, and more. The laws of physics try to explain *why* things happen in the universe but actually just throw up more unanswerable questions than they solve. Why does gravity act? Why does the sun burn? Why? Why? Why? How big is the universe? How do radio waves travel through the void of space? How? How? How?

I also love flying, and learnt to fly as soon as I could. I flew alone in an aircraft before I drove alone in a car, just a week or so after my seventeenth birthday. I resolved that I would fly for a living. The RAF unfortunately would not take me due to my hip operation, but l was told that no such problem would exist with British Airways.

In the end it was the actuaries, those financial risk assessors, who decided that I was not a good bet for the airline's pension scheme as my hip may not last the course to age 55. Having been previously accepted, these kindly folk gave me the news that the offer was withdrawn on the day before my final degree examinations. Bastards!

Hence, I found myself with a degree but no job. I resolved this situation within five days by applying for a job on Friday. On Monday I received a call inviting me to an interview on the following day. The post was offered and accepted. I was now a physics teacher.

'A WHAT?' exclaimed my father; 'You can't be a teacher. Teachers are the scum of the earth!' I am not often speechless. But what does one say?

I am pleased to report that I changed his mind about teachers and it was not long after that I heard him telling someone, with pride, that his son was teaching Advanced Level physics.— Since then he has even used a physics teacher as one of his heroes in a book!

I am no longer a physics teacher. Perhaps he would say that I have learnt the error of my ways. But I loved teaching. For seventeen years it gave me great enjoyment and satisfaction. Then I was made a better offer, but more of that later.

Throughout the 1970s, the Dick Francis books continued to sell in ever-increasing numbers and they regularly went straight to the top of the best seller lists on publication. By 1973 the weekly article for the *Sunday Express* had become more of hindrance than a help in his writing, disturbing his routine and concentration. After 16 years of not missing a deadline, my father retired from another profession.

In late 1974 Dick Francis was the subject of Eamonn Andrews's big red book in 'This is Your Life'. I don't know whether my father was pleased or not at the time, although later it gave him great satisfaction to have been chosen. He certainly did not like the idea that someone had been prying into his life without his knowledge and he was cross with himself for not having realised it. To suddenly have one's past dragged up and paraded in front of an audience of millions is a daunting prospect. So many old friends, some long forgotten (and often best left that way), are cajoled, or in our case scriptwritten, into saying flattering sound-bites about the poor victim. However, the party afterwards was great fun and a certain young physics teacher, just three months into his first job, gained no end of brownie points among his colleagues and pupils for appearing on TV. Not that they behaved any better towards me, especially my colleagues!

Anne and I married in March 1975. My mother took this as final confirmation that I had left home for good and she promptly remodelled the-house, which resulted in the complete disappearance of my bedroom. Was she trying to tell me something?

Mum and Dad were very proud of the home that they had created at Blewbury. My mother had personally designed the house as one to be ill in, with views from her bed through the house and out of the windows to the front drive. She had contracted polio in her twenties and was expected to be bedridden for long periods. Fortunately, this has not been the case. However, the ability to see what is happening meant that Merrick and I were installed in my mother's bed whenever we were ill as children. My father used to be a keen gardener and he would spend hours digging or mowing. On one occasion he was stripped to the waist busily tending to the borders at the front of the house when a white van pulled up and the driver asked whether he was interested in buying a carpet. Dad immediately replied that he was only the garden boy and that the master of the house was away. Thereafter he was always referred to as 'The Boy' whenever he was in the garden.

My parents enjoyed the fame and the financial security that the success of the books gave them. They travelled extensively and my father was invited to judge horses at shows around the world. In 1979 they spent a month in Penang with Lester Piggott and his family, discovering the delights of escaping from the damp and cold of an English winter. By this time my mother had begun to suffer from asthma and the warm weather of the tropics was a fillip to her breathing. Her asthma is not helped by a general weakness of her muscles, the result of the polio. She was becoming almost housebound during the winter as cold air in her lungs would trigger an asthma attack. Mum and Dad resolved to find a second home somewhere warm where they could escape to during the cold months in England.

Fort Lauderdale in Florida seemed ideal. The winters are warm and dry, there is easy access from London to Miami, and English is the main language. An apartment was purchased that overlooked the sandy beach and my parents moved in for the 1980 winter. Dad would walk along the sand before breakfast and a swim in the pool would precede a busy day with the pencil. Perfect.

The stays in Florida became longer and longer. The USA's rules concerning residence mean that one has to become a tax resident there if one stays for more than four months every year. In the UK the limit is three months. My parents decided that they wanted to spend more than

ake and Jennifer Edwards.

Dick and Felix Francis.

te Gayson and Pierce Brosnan.

Eunice and Kate Gayson.

Quincy Jones and daughters.

Dame Barbara Cartland and Ian McCorquodale.

John and Hayley Mills.

Hayley Mills.

four months per year in Florida and could survive with less than three in England. So, in 1986, they departed from 'home' to emigrate to the west, just as millions have done before them, just as the forefathers of that nation did three and four hundred years ago. They went a little faster, taking Concorde across the Atlantic in as many hours as their predecessors took months to complete the same journey. Over the past centuries it has become fairly commonplace for the children of a family to emigrate to distant parts — Australia or New Zealand, India or South America. Trust our family to be different.

A short episode at Easter that year changed my life for ever. My wife and I were staying with my parents in Fort Lauderdale and, as usual, we were sunning ourselves on the beach or at the pool. I went into their apartment for a drink and my mother said, 'Can you help your father as he is having some difficulty in getting his tax papers ready for the accountants?' This was a considerable understatement. He was sat at the dining-room table surrounded by receipts, bank statements, cancelled cheques, credit card slips, ledgers, record sheets and more. He was saying words to the effect that the Internal Revenue Service could 'go forth and multiply'. How could he be expected to sort out all his spending on three continents as well as all his earnings on five?

I joined him at the table with the words 'Can I help? It can't be that difficult'. How wrong one can be!

Hence started a change in our relationship. All my childhood, and into adult life, too, I had relied on my father and mother. For love, for advice, for guidance and for financial assistance. Here was a chance to repay my loan. I spent the rest of that holiday sitting at that table sifting through the information and making the tax return. I cannot describe the pleasure it gave me to do it — to do something for my father that he could not do for himself. Selfish? Maybe, but it had taken 33 years of my life to come about.

I started going to Fort Lauderdale often to help them with their finances. Not just with the tax returns, but also with their investments. I had appointments to meet with bankers and investment managers. I did not know much about mutual funds, equities, gilts, bonds, keogh plans and other investment opportunities, but I learnt fast. I worked out what questions to ask and I appeared more knowledgeable than I was. It is amazing how attentive an investment manager can be when one has a small fortune to invest, more so as the fortune grows.

Half-term breaks, when my colleagues put their feet up in front of the telly for a few days, were spent nipping across the water for a session at the dining-room table. I would return overnight from Miami in time to be back in school by 9.00 am for my first class. It was exhausting and I loved it. I once went for just one night.

I taught in a boarding school, which had classes on Saturday morning. I nipped off at eleven in the morning to catch a one o'clock flight from Heathrow. Merrick came too. We were on our way to surprise them for their 40th wedding anniversary. As we approached their apartment in a taxi from Miami airport, Merrick said that wouldn't it be funny if they had gone to England to surprise us. Not so. They were both so pleased to see us. Mum could hardly speak as tears welled in her eyes; Dad didn't even flinch as we gave him the bill for our air tickets! Merrick stayed for a week, but I flew back on Sunday in time for start of school on Monday morning. I remember walking up and down in a class thinking that if only these boys knew where I had been for the past two days...

By 1991, I realised that something had to change. As head of the physics and the science departments I had a seemingly ever-increasing workload — GCSE assessments, A-level coursework, teacher appraisals, new courses, new syllabus, new developments in my subject, new this, new that. Change, change, change. Work, work, work. Add to that the increasing reliance my parents put on my frequent visits to Florida, and life was becoming rather too complicated. I seemed to sleep less and less. I said to my father that I could not go on doing so much for him and my mother. It was affecting my day job. He would have to find someone else to act for him. He asked whether I would be prepared to give up the day job instead.

He made me an offer I couldn't refuse. It wasn't the money that attracted me, even though he was offering twice what I was earning as a teacher. He was asking me to be his manager, to do officially and by name what I had been doing already for the past four years. And more, he was offering me his trust to act on his behalf. It was, and remains, an honour.

All I asked of him was to write, as a minimum, five more books, and to agree that if in any circumstances I said 'No', then he should not go and say 'Yes'. Since then I have done far more than just prepare the tax return information. It has been a fine arrangement and I cannot remember us having a single argument.

In September 1995 the thirty-sixth Dick Francis book appeared. They are published in 33 different languages as diverse as Korean and Welsh. Together with film, TV, audio tape and radio rights there is plenty to keep me busy. In fact, I have the best job in the world.

I have never felt that having a famous father is a burden. Perhaps it has been more so for my brother who chose to enter the world of horse racing. For me, who took a path Dad would never have taken, I did not have an icon to live up to. I was not competing. However, it is important for *me* to know that I made a successful career outside of the 'family firm'.

I was offered a headmastership soon after taking the decision to leave teaching, but it was easy to refuse. I was pleased to have been asked and it settled any disquiet I may have felt about making such a radical change of career. In several friends I recognised some envy that I was able to leave a profession of which they, too, were becoming tired. I know that I was lucky to have an alternative direction to take. Perhaps I subconsciously created a job to escape into: first make my father dependent on me, then satisfy the need. Maybe so, but I don't think either of us is complaining.

At an age when most sensible people are settling down for a quiet twilight of their lives, my parents have upped and moved home again and are about to do so once more. In December 1990 they went on holiday for two weeks from Florida to the Cayman Islands. My father wanted to get away from the telephone and fax in order to think about the next book. My mother wandered up the beach and fell in love with the new apartments being built next door to their hotel.

In the ten years since they first bought a home there, Fort Lauderdale had changed from a medium-sized town into a large city and their Cayman holiday reminded them how much they missed the peace and quiet of rural England. Grand Cayman may not be rural England, but it is as quiet *and* it has better weather. They moved permanently to the Islands in 1993 and love it. So much so that they have sold their Florida home and are making plans to move into yet another new, larger, beachfront apartment just half a mile along the sand. I wonder where they will go next!

Dick Francis is a modest man who rates loyalty as one of the greatest virtues in his fellow human beings. Fame and success have not spoilt him. He is a man of great personal courage and I have never seen him afraid. He is as kind and considerate as any person I know and he is liked by everyone who has met him. Even hard-nosed reviewers seem to have a soft spot for his work.

We have always been a close family. Becoming my father's manager has strengthened the bond between us. Like all children, I am sometimes exasperated by the actions of my parents. I may work with them and for them, but I couldn't live in the same house. Visit, yes; live, no.

When my father and I greet each other or say goodbye, we shake hands. My mother always implores us to hug and kiss. I am more comfortable shaking hands; it is how I was brought up. It doesn't mean I love him any less.

What's it like to be the son of a famous father?

Great fun.

EUNICE GAYSON
ACTRESS, (1931–)

Eunice Gayson was born in 1931 and is a British leading lady of both stage and screen. She achieved a cinematic landmark by playing Sylvia Trench, James Bond's first screen conquest in the first Bond movie, *Dr No*. She repeated the role in the second Bond movie, *From Russia with Love*.

Her other film credits include *Carry on Admiral, Dance Little Lady* and *Revenge of Frankenstein*. Her extensive TV credits include *The Saint, Danger Man, Tales of the Unexpected, The Avengers, The Goon Show* and *The Dick Emery Show*. Her equally extensive theatrical career comprises plays and shows as diverse as *The Sound of Music, Into the Woods, Hobson's Choice, The Grass is Greener, The Little Hut, The Barretts of Wimpole Street*, as well as numerous pantomime seasons.

Kate Gayson, who is 27, is the only child of Eunice Gayson's marriage to actor/producer Brian Jackson. Kate is an actress, and appeared in the last James Bond movie, *Goldeneye*, and recently completed a year in *The Mousetrap* in London's West End.

KATE GAYSON:

My parents were separated before I can even remember. It was a very protracted and bitter divorce, which was not resolved until I was nine. There wasn't anyone else involved, and my mother has never remarried in all these years. I am no longer bitter about it. It was something that took place a long time ago. There are no siblings from my mother's first marriage, and I am her only child from her marriage to my father. He has had a 22-year relationship since the divorce. I have an elder half-sister to whom I'm not very close, and an elder half-brother with whom I've always had an affinity. I saw him the other day, and I felt a feeling I have never felt before. It felt like a rush of pent-up emotion coursing through my body — an accident waiting to happen. It was the sudden experience of seeing this person who is like a mirrored image. I have a younger half-sister who is doing her GCSEs, and I love her very, very much — she's so different from the rest of us.

I was born on 24 October 1969 in Brighton. For a long time after my birth I took it for granted that everyone had the same life as me. Ignorance was bliss. I only remember my mother doing stage tours; I don't think she's done any movies since my birth.

The early years of my childhood were completely different from the later years. We lived in the countryside, just my mother and me, in the most idyllic area outside Haslemere in Surrey. We lived in a wonderful manor where everyone had their own piece of land and their own house. Although it was very middle-class, it felt like a commune, and I spent more time running around the neighbouring farm with the kids next door and riding horses whenever I wanted, than I spent at home.

I was educated at the local village school, and although I was just with Mum, I had everything and everyone I needed around me. If my mother needed to go away to work, there were always people around to look after me. Those were my halcyon days, and I assumed they would never end. Yet, it was also a period in my life when I had very little contact with my father. Unfortunately for both of us, that was beyond his control.

When I was eight, we moved to London. Until then, I had had no contact with showbiz or with London. I've since asked my mother what brought the move about and she attributed it to two things — she got bored in the country, and she wanted me to have a better education, as I was approaching the age for junior school. Even now, a big part of me wishes we hadn't made the move.

When I was nine, and very shortly after moving to London, my mother bought a second home in Majorca, which meant that, as well as being hit by London for the first time, I did a lot of jet-setting, and spent time with — possibly — not the most suitable people.

Ironically, I was brought up in Richmond, which is where I live today. We had a beautiful house on the river. Maybe there is some Freudian connection that brings me back to this place as an adult, because my mother doesn't even live here any more.

I was educated at Vineyard School in Richmond, which had a village feel to it. So, although I missed the countryside, at least it was beautiful here, too.

It wasn't until we came to London and my parents' divorce finally came through, and things got a bit nasty in the Press, that I was aware that I wasn't like the other kids. It was probably then that I saw in other people's eyes that I wasn't a Jackson but a Gayson. However, I would say that throughout my schooldays I have always had the most incredible amount of support.

I wasn't born when my mother made her début in the Bond movie *Dr No*. It's strange that she is remembered as Eunice Gayson, 'Bond girl', when she has made around fifty other movie appearances. This has affected me, too, because I am known as 'Eunice Gayson stroke Kate Gayson, Bond girl'.

Accepting a role in *Goldeneye* put me in the same trap, although I did not see it as a trap. I thought of it as kudos, something brilliant, fantastic, which it is. But, when all is said and done, there is still a voice inside saying, 'this is just a job and you're not the same person in the next job as you were in the last.'

When the publicity for *Goldeneye* started, my mother and I appeared on all the TV programmes. When someone asks if you always wanted to be in a Bond movie, what do you say? I said 'yes'.

Being stuck with an image is something that my father recently experienced. He appeared in a TV advert for Del Monte oranges as the distinguished, grey-haired 'Man from Del Monte', as well as being involved in video production and video distribution, all of which help him to avoid becoming too 'pigeon-holed'.

When I was 15, I went to live with my father at his house in Marble Arch, where he still lives today. My mother's health was suffering at the time and she felt that she couldn't cope. She also felt that I needed discipline in my life — specifically my father's discipline. So this wasn't a suggestion, the decision had already been made. Equally, Dad had no choice, although I don't think he was against the idea. My mother is a very strong character, but then that's what has made her successful.

I had a bad adolescence. At the time, I didn't think that I was having any particular problems. Looking back, I must have been a worry, but whose fault was that? My mother must have felt that I was off the rails, as she felt the need to distance herself during this period. She genuinely thought she was doing what was best for me, but because it felt like rejection and punishment rather than guidance, I've come to think that people who are genuinely guiding me are in fact putting me down. I am only just starting to learn that there are people who you can completely trust. I have started to listen. I no longer just want to get my own way, or have people around me let me get away with things if I'm not right.

Looking back, I have been thoroughly spoilt. I mean this in the truest sense, not spoilt with money. I have never been spoilt as an actress, though. When I did *The Mousetrap*, I worked very hard, six days and eight performances a week for an entire year. No one could criticise my work or my talent, but I sensed that there was a lingering concern in others about my unsettled personal life. My response to that is that's my business. If I do the job and I do it correctly, then that is enough.

I started acting in school plays and was involved in the National Youth Music Theatre, and I was always encouraged and told that I wasn't just good, but I was *really* good. I began to think, 'well, it gives me a buzz and I enjoy it, so I'll pursue an acting career.' However, the whole business is image. Here I am, dressed in black, making some sort of statement, when the important thing is to know that it's all image. Now I'm not sure if I wish to pursue it any more. I don't know why it jars, but it does. Probably because nothing causes me more stress. Having to be something that someone wants me to be filters down to every other aspect of my life and I refuse to take myself, or anything in my life, too seriously.

I have been fortunate and professional work has come my way. Now I'm beginning to question it, because I find it quite stressful. Money has never been a big attraction for me. The year in *The Mousetrap* should not have been a stressful time, but somehow I managed to get caught up in family traumas, sadly to the detriment of my own personal life. I decided then that all this family drama rubbish was going to end.

Sustaining a role in a show for such a long run is very stressful, especially if you feel the need to keep moving on. I got on blissfully with my mother during my time in the show, because in her eyes I was being what I should be. However, when the run came to an end, we began to fight again. I don't see myself ever being what she wants me to be.

I use my real name, Kate Jackson, everywhere except for work. I had to choose another name for Equity, because I wasn't allowed to use Jackson, and I had about three minutes to make a decision. I could think only of my mother's stage name so I took that, which was a shame as it establishes another career association between my mother and me.

My mother and I have always had a volatile relationship. In recent times, we were beginning to forge a workable relationship of sorts, which I thought was better than nothing, but clearly I was wrong. Words were spoken, as they always are in these situations, and the lines of communication were closed.

It could be that our joint efforts on promoting *Goldeneye* indirectly led to our current situation. All the TV and Press interviews and being driven around together in stretch limos — it was thoroughly stressful and I maybe began to resent the ties between us, bearing in mind that my personal life was so traumatic.

One interviewer got very personal about my family's past but all the facts were wrong and the interviewer misquoted me and my mother. So, suddenly, I have to deal with upsetting people I care about, even though I had done nothing wrong. I had to explain myself, all the while thinking, 'No more, no more'.

Personally, I don't care what is said between me and my mother, because what gives people their talent is the passion they have within them. You destroy their talent if you try to quash their passion. So you have to make allowances for the silly things people say and do when you know that they're just expressing their personality. I am always ready to resume communications no matter what has been said. This applies to all my relationships.

I try to remain philosophical about things, and not take them too seriously. If I ever start to believe my own publicity then I can only hope and pray that I have loved ones around me I can trust and who will tell me the truth.

My mother does love me, but love can reveal itself in strange ways. I would like to think that there is light at the end of the tunnel in terms of our relationship, but that could be because I am a relentless optimist. Everyone wants a mother — everyone wants *their* mother. I wish I didn't, but I do feel incomplete while I am going through this rather unpleasant time of my life with, or rather without, her. I think emotionally she's still a child.

In a sense, I am a reminder of a tough time, yet it is only because she chooses to see it that way — it doesn't have to be so. Ironically, she's not a negative person and, as a person, I think she is a great friend to others. However, as is sometimes the case with people who have had the craziest of lives and have lived what they are on stage or film, actors tend not to be able to maintain relationships. After all, my mother has lived her life as Eunice Gayson, actress.

We have argued in the past for various reasons, probably reasons based upon familiar themes, but this last argument originated with her. I have never really been able to understand the way we behave together — there has always been a clash of swords between us. But I've always respected her for what she does and for what she has done in the past, and for her independence and guts — even just for being my mother and giving me life. Those feelings are there and always will be there whatever our relationship may or may not be. What I can't tolerate, though, is that if I am able to dispel all bitterness, to forgive and forget, I don't think it is unreasonable of me to expect to be met half way.

She sees herself in me, I'm sure. It's the old story of living through your child's youth — be all the things that I was and that I wasn't. The reality is, it's not possible. I wouldn't dream of criticising her for it, because I was never pushed into acting, although equally I was never discouraged. If I'm honest, I have never really been myself with either of my parents. I have tried to be one thing to my father and one thing to my mother. Although we are not talking at the moment, in a funny way she has forced me to accept myself as my father's daughter and to see who I am without her influence and without her presence.

Some time after our move to London, I attended Putney High School for Girls, which is a private school. I was making a leap not only from a childhood spent in the countryside, but from State to private education. Personally, I just wanted to go to the local comprehensive. My love for the countryside never diminished and I look back fondly on that time.

There were other factors that made the experience all the greater. I was witnessing some of the bigger dramas of life — I was starting to see friends die, to see friends go the wrong way. By this time, though, it all felt quite natural, because I lived in such a dramatic world.

Living at my father's house for two years didn't mean that I lived with my father. By now, he had left for work in Los Angeles, leaving me with my stepmother and stepsister. There was talk of us all moving out there for a time.

My father advised me to think about a career. If I wanted to act, then I must have a 'back-up' qualification — and he would not allow me to go to drama school. All this when I was in the National Youth Music Theatre, doing amazing things like going to Edinburgh and Sadler's Wells, and thinking, 'Wow! This is a great life!' However, just because I understood that acting was something I wanted to do from an early age didn't mean that I wouldn't consider being good at something else. That is where my father came in.

I fought Dad every inch of the way to the extent that, when he refused to give me money to go to Edinburgh, I took five jobs, including working before I went to school in the mornings and all weekends at McDonald's. It was the only way to save up the money to go to Edinburgh. Much, much later in life, he turned around and said, 'I knew then that you'd be all right as an actress.'

My father has never liked to be pigeon-holed. He has always been involved in business of one kind or another, as well as acting. He regards acting as a luxury. Also, he had experienced a lot with my mother and was just being the over-protective father. It's the age-old adage: 'Do as I say, not as I do'. Of course, as he has never turned his back on acting completely. I can say to him, 'Who are you to talk?' We struck a compromise — he insisted I do a degree, in addition to which I would do theatre studies.

Once you get used to being around people whose lives are not office-bound, it is inevitable that you will be affected in some way. When you are the child of an actor or actors, it is always a possibility.

The idea of being an actor yourself just comes as naturally as waking up in the morning. Those who have no actors in their family to consciously or unconsciously influence them are unlikely even to begin to consider it.

My father and I finally get along well. We have always talked, although rarely personally, and we have never really fallen out. I have a practical, business-headed side to me because of my father's influence. I still feel that, even now I am young enough and open-minded enough to not to be beyond his influence. I'm the sort of person who strives for the truth and I am not afraid of facing it. It sounds ridiculous, but in a way it would be easier to be me if I wasn't that type of person.

My father returned from America, and I continued to live with him in Marble Arch with my stepmum, who has been very important in my life. I think a step-parent can stand back and view all the problems and dramas in a philosophical way.

Even before I'd finished school, I left them to start doing my own thing. Prior to leaving for university, I was in a relationship that lasted four years. He was a difficult boy, but a great laugh and very loyal. I know I was not an easy person to get on with, but we've stayed good friends.

After a string of broken relationships, I have to ask myself, is it coming from me? Perhaps they haven't been able to cope with the fact that I have difficulty coping with myself. I get very stressed and I know that does not make me the easiest person in the world. I should imagine I'm difficult to live with when I'm stressed. I think they have found me trying to be someone that I'm not. I'm at that point where I'm prepared to admit that. I'm prepared to say, all defences down, I'll go and sit down and write and work it out.

Due to my father's influence, I took a degree in theatre studies, then a postgraduate course in drama and education because I was going to become a teacher. Then, out of the blue, my first professional acting job fell into my lap. Once I started acting, I thought I might as well keep doing it as it was a good life. I'm no longer sure that it is a good life. I do not want to spend my life hoping that I'm going to work with a great director or hoping that I will get a great script. That would be beyond me and I wouldn't want to have to cope with it.

When I finished school and went to Warwick University, I didn't know what had hit me. I don't know if I hit upon a particularly crazy bunch of people, or if people in these places are always like this. It certainly appealed to my sense of drama.

It was a period when, again, I wasn't talking to my mother and, like a fool, ended up with the first bloke I clapped eyes on and stayed with him for two years. I started my third year, then had a nervous breakdown. I cannot blame it all on that relationship. The catalyst was finding out about a betrayal. Betrayed by my boyfriend and by friends I had considered to be family. It really got to me and made me realise that betrayal is my biggest demon.

I believe that everyone should be prescribed one nervous breakdown in their life, as you come through it a far better person — or you don't come through it at all. Depression of most kinds is usually a prelude to change. Since then, I have had a slacker attitude about being totally and utterly committed to someone. Now I'm ready to make room for it again.

I still managed to make good friends during college, and my friends have always been soulmates, people who have had an unusual upbringing for one reason or another. Your friends need to bring out the best in you and forgive the worst in you. These are the people who I have stuck by and who have stuck by me.

None of my best friends is an actor or in showbusiness — for instance, I have never had a relationship with an actor. I think it's because you know that, whatever happens, eventually they will put themselves first. So what about me? Do I put myself first? No. At the end of the day, I won't. In terms of being an actress, I probably do, but if I fell in love with someone tomorrow and he was totally and utterly worth it, then I would amend my ideas and ways to suit that new and different scenario. My desire to write will take me away from the actress's lifestyle.

I can pinpoint the area of writing that I'm attracted to — screenplays and novels. I would like an outlet where, within the context of what I'm writing, I can release all the emotions that I need to express.

I had to get away recently — from home and from work. I sat down and wrote for four days and came back feeling complete again. Whether it's fiction or non-fiction, it's just me working out what I know. The answer for me seems to be right there.

I have been involved with a couple of writing projects over the last year or so and it is what I enjoy. I am going to pursue it, and take a short break from everything I have been and know and, it sounds awfully clichéd, escape to a farm and write.

There is, however, a side to me that needs to be around other people, learning from other people. I cannot deny that social side of myself, which contrasts sharply with the lonelier life of a writer. I also know that directing and producing will feature in my life.

Recently, I've been trying to get a club theatre operation (a similar set-up to a pub theatre) off the ground. The revenue from the club would bring in some money to run a small theatre company in the same venue. As the Arts Council knows, these things can all run in tandem because they run at different times of the day and different days of the week. I would be happy running my own theatre company, as it would feel like a return to my roots.

Having said all this, I'm off to York to do panto in a week's time, so there remains a real mix in my life at the moment. I suppose half of me is very practical — been there, seen it, done it, got the t-shirt. The other side of me is still a little girl, just learning what growing up means. I have always needed to be totally independent and, indeed, was encouraged to be so. I suppose I inherited it from my father — not wanting to be trapped in a role, because I have aspirations to do so many other things.

After accepting a small part in *Goldeneye*, John Gilby, a journalist who was taking care of my PR, said to me, 'You do realise that it's going to be "Kate Gayson, Bond-girl" for ever now.' But you always believe you can be the one to break the mould, that you can get it to happen on your terms.

I have always dreamt of being an actor, a director, a writer, and still do only the things I believed in. Or that I could strike a balance between working just for money and using that money to do what I want. Some people can do that. Willem Dafoe, movie star, is a completely different person from Willem Dafoe, experimental stage performer. Even people like Robert De Niro and Holly Hunter are joint owners of a fringe theatre project in west Hollywood.

My problem is that I'm seen as Kate Gayson, actress, and now Kate Gayson, Bond girl. That creates a dilemma. If the opportunity arises to appear in another Bond movie, do I take it? The answer, I feel, must be that I would take it if it gets me nearer to where I want to be, and I'm not going to compromise on that.

I feel happier as a character actress or comedy actress — warts and a wig — than glammed up. I've done Shakespeare and really loved it, for we all strive to do something really satisfying. I like to see myself as a dramatist rather than just an actress. That sounds demeaning to those who are actresses, but it's my interpretation of what I see myself doing. I would never disparage anyone for doing what they want to do. We all try to get from A to B, and in the end we can do no more than go with what we think is right for ourselves.

I'm not foolish, though. I know on which side my bread is buttered, and I'm eternally grateful for having had the opportunity to learn the pitfalls and the ins and outs of the business from my parents.

I do have the double-whammy, though — the acting in the family *and* the Bond girl hangover. I would add that it has probably been very tough for my mother, too. Her whole career has been associated with being the first James Bond girl. She no longer chases work. She's probably happier without the added stress.

The actress and writer Carrie Fisher has been a great source of hope and inspiration to me, and I often hear her words ringing in my ears. Carrie felt like jacking it all in and coming to live in England with her little girl. However, in the final analysis, she concluded that her mother, Debbie Reynolds, is famous; her own *alter ego*, Princess Leia, is famous; but Carrie Fisher is not. That struck a chord in me.

A very well-known producer/director once said to me during an audition, 'Yes, well, you'll probably have a right time of it; you'll probably end up giving up acting because your mother is an actress, just like my daughter.' Apparently, his daughter was sick to death of remarks at auditions, such as, 'Aren't you X's daughter?' She knew immediately whether or not they would give her a hard time or give her the job.

Although I'm a soft touch, I know I am very stubborn and strong-willed. I've always wanted to do just what I've wanted to do, but I think sometimes the things I have wanted to do have not been the right things for me. I've reached a point in my late twenties when I've started to think, 'Right, I've got the rest of my life to fill here. Am I going with what I truly need, or am I just going with it because it has always been something I could do?'

Whatever else you could say about me, whatever anyone may think I've done wrong in my life, I have an enormous wealth of experience from which to write. I want to feel that some good will come from it. I feel it's in me and it is going to hang over me until I get rid of it.

I'm not a child any more — that's a daydream that is totally removed from reality. I am only 27. I still have a career ahead of me and all that goes with it, just like millions of others. Also, like millions of others, at the end of the day I want a relationship and eventually a family.

QUINCEY JONES
MUSICIAN, (1933–)

S ongwriter and producer, Quincey Jones, is a legend in his own lifetime. Quincey Delight Jones Junior, born in Chicago on 14 March 1933, was one of ten children — seven sisters and two brothers. His upbringing was humble and problematic, but, finding his direction in life through music, he went on to transcend its many changing styles over period spanning some five decades. From playing with Lionel Hampton's band in the 1950s to scoring numerous films and TV shows, to producing and arranging music for artistes such as Frank Sinatra, Barbara Streisand and Michael Jackson, he has earned huge respect both within and outside the music industry. He was recently presented with a lifetime achievement award in Hollywood.

Martina, born in November 1966, is Quincey Jones' daughter from his second marriage. She lives in Los Angeles, where she works with young children.

MARTINA JONES:

My mother, who is Swedish, was my father's second wife. My older sister and my mother were modelling at the time and my parents met through that. They got married and then came me, the first of two born to the union of my mother and father. We were travelling when my brother was born. He was born in Wimbledon, England. Then we moved to the States and our first house on Lake Glen. After that we moved to a house on Deep Canyon.

My parents divorced after about seven years of marriage. My mother never remarried — my father was definitely her one and only. Once they got divorced she moved back to Sweden. I'd travel back and forth every summer and winter to visit her. For a while, between the ages of nine and eleven, I lived in Sweden.

While I was in Sweden, Dad had an aneurism, which is when a vein pops in your brain. He had about eight hours' surgery and they put a metal plate in his forehead. When I heard about Dad's operation from Mum, I just said with youthful innocence, 'Great, can I go and play now?' There were a couple of specific instances after that when I realised that I almost lost my dad. That really got to me later. When he received the City of Hope award he made a speech in which he talked about his aneurism and his operation and I just totally lost it. I had no idea until later about how serious it was.

After that, I came back and lived with my dad and stepmum, Peggy, whom he had married by then. We stayed in the States, at a house in Rockingham, Brentwood, for a couple of years and then I moved back to Sweden to join my mother.

I ended up being very close to my stepmum. We became more like friends than anything else. My mum had a little bit of a hard time accepting that, but there was nothing I could do about it — it was just the way it all ended up. She found it hard to accept that I was able to get along so well with Peggy, because she felt Peggy took my father away from her. As I was living with Dad and Peggy from day to day, it was always likely to grow into a close-knit relationship.

Discipline was tricky when sharing a home with Dad and Peggy. I was the first teenager — I'm older than her two daughters. I got the lecture: 'I was sixteen when I started to drive, so you'll have to wait until you're sixteen,' and so on. Although my father believed in discipline, he wasn't great at implementing it, mainly because he wasn't around that much. It was a seriously busy time for him then. All these projects came at him one after the other. Peggy did have a positive influence on me. There were lots of 'first-time matters' that I got to talk to Peggy about and she was the one who was right there in my life, as opposed to my mum who was overseas and removed from those immediate situations.

Mum and Dad don't really get on too well now, but I'm not going to get on to that one because I don't feel I want to be a deliverer of bad news. Let's just say that there's a lot of static there. A lot of the memories are very painful and I ended up in the middle of it. My mother would run out of money so it would be down to me to tell Dad that we needed more money. It got to a point where I didn't know what to do for the best — what was right. It gave me a whole lot of guilt trips. I've since tried to let myself know that you have to go forward and not allow things to hold you down. My mother, though, is very much a living-in-the-past kind of person. I try to let her know that if you live in the past, it won't help the future.

Dad met his first wife during his high school days. I suppose they were victims of youth. Inter-racial marriages just weren't the done thing when they got married. His third marriage, to Peggy, was different. Peggy was tired of showbusiness and wanted to settle down. Dad was also keen to settle down by then. Peggy came from a family where the parents had been together for 35 years. That was missing from Dad's life.

Dad had a tough upbringing. He was born and raised with his brother, Louis, in Chicago. His mother was in a mental hospital for much of the time and his dad had to work and work. They were 'home alone' kids. The word 'mother' didn't mean that much to him. Through us children he understands what it's all about, but in terms of his own life there was no real meaning, no relationship there. But he realises he lost something.

He doesn't talk much about his childhood. Basically, a lot of the past is blanked out. He can't piece it all together.

He was always curious about music. A teenage girl lived next door to him when he was five or six years of age. She played stride piano — the first 'live' music he ever heard. He was hooked. Sadly, his mother thought music wouldn't benefit him, so it wasn't encouraged.

Music really entered his life when he was twelve. He started to watch other performers like Duke Ellington, and watching their style. He began to realise that great things were happening out there in music.

His biggest break, and one of his happiest memories, came when he was at school in Boston and Lionel Hampton called him to come and join his band. They played at a club called Bird Land, and artistes like Charlie Parker and Miles Davis would join them. It was the mecca of modern jazz — artistes from all over the world played at Bird Land.

It was difficult being black on tour. Sometimes they couldn't get anything to eat, which was why they always had a white driver so they could maybe get some food. Occasionally, the racial pressures would get on their nerves — to the point where there would be violence. He has always stayed loyal to his culture and tries to help wherever he can. This nurtured a friendship with Jesse Jackson, which developed through a mutual effort to put things right after the riots.

As a child, Dad had a roller-coaster relationship with his parents. He was given a pair of boxing gloves that had belonged to Joe Louis. He swapped them for a friend's B.B. gun. His dad was furious and went to get the gloves back. Instead, he fell in love with this friend's mother and they married. His dad always did the best he could, but he had a real sad time with the women in his life.

His stepmum would tell him that his own mother was really messed up and that she'd kill him if she could. Dad's imagination had always been out of control, and he began seeing a mental picture of this. She came out of hospital one day and came running up to hug her two boys. They just ran for about seven blocks, they'd been made so afraid. That was the last time Dad saw her until he was about 15. He couldn't depend on her, so decided he didn't need her. That was how he dealt with it and, no doubt, why so much of his early years are blanked out. I'm sure that it affected his later relationships with women.

He has said that, if they'd stayed in Chicago, he was sure he wouldn't have survived. But they left when he was about ten, and there was nothing beyond Chicago that could surprise him after what he'd seen and experienced.

They moved to Bremerton, Seattle, in 1944. It was a different culture, far less violent. Six of them lived in a small house there. All the kids got along fine; it was the parent–child situation that didn't seem to work.

There was a tiny closet in the house where they would hide and spend most of their time. Dad used to go there and pass the time just day-dreaming.

Music was always his great escape. He could just climb into it and grab something beautiful. He was about 14 when he first went to jail, but once music had grabbed his interest, he no longer wanted to blow his energy on all that dumb stuff any more. He says that in a way he was lucky — he didn't set out to be rich and famous, just good.

From Bremerton, he moved into Seattle proper in 1948, and soon after ran into a bunch of kids who really wanted to play. He started playing for Billie Holiday — a dream of a lifetime. He would meet the likes of Ray Charles who told him that every music has its soul, and if you are really sincere and surrender to it and explore it, it's all soulful.

Dad always says that the whole jazz thing is like a big family, and that through it he was lucky as a young man to be able to get out and see the world.

His Rolling Stones and Beatles were Miles Davies and Dizzy Gillespie. They had an enormous influence on him.

Dad got into trouble with his own band in 1959. It wasn't so much the band as the timing of things and the places they were playing. He did everything he could to make the band work, but there were too many problems. Loving and living for music, he hadn't thought about the business side, and he had a pay-roll that had to be met each month whatever else happened. He lost a lot of money. He says it's the closest he's ever come to contemplating suicide.

I've become old-fashioned through the experience of my parents' divorce. A lot of people ask me when I'm going to have kids and I reply, when I have a ring on my finger. I'm not claiming that that's the ideal state because there's no guarantee that that person is going to stay in your life. But I know that I do want to be married first and know that someone has formally agreed to be with me. I feel strongly because I know I want only one marriage. Mr Perfect hasn't turned up yet. I've learned as I've gone on and I've thought, maybe I should have done this or that, but it gets tougher as you get older.

In 1988, I stopped travelling back and forth. Mum had moved back here again because she wanted to be closer to us. She figured it would be easier that way. I don't know exactly why she decided to move back to Sweden after a while, but she did.

I hadn't been to Sweden in five years, so it was weird going back there in 1993. It was one of those trips that, because you haven't been there in a while, you recognise people but age and time have made it possible for you to dodge anyone you weren't really into talking with, which probably sounds rude. They'd look at me with uncertainty and I'd have to choose how to respond. It was very funny.

We used to holiday a lot together, Dad, Peggy and me. Skiing in Aspen was always a popular annual outing. Dad had to look the part — he had all the right ski gear, which was amusing because his skiing schedule wasn't exactly punishing. He'd ski a couple of hours then wrap up for the day. 'What a hard day's skiing,' he'd groan. One and a half runs max.

I realised that I had an unusual parent at an early stage, because my godfather is Frank Sinatra — not that I see Frank all that often. But Sinatra, Michael Jackson, Streisand and anyone else you care to think of, all surrender to Dad's demands because he's an inspiration. They want to please him. As Dad says, when he gets them to leap without a net, that's when the good stuff happens.

His own biggest icon was Count Basie. Basie was like a mentor, uncle, friend and father all rolled into one. He was 13 when he first met Basie in Seattle, and they remained close friends for the rest of his life.

When I was about 11 and at school, people would come up to me and say, 'Oh, you're Quincey Jones' daughter; I want to be your friend.' I learned quickly and I made sure that telling people who my Dad was wasn't the first thing I said. When I was little I thought it was cool to introduce myself as Quincey's daughter, and I believed they'd like me because of it. But then I thought, wait a minute — they only want to come back to my house and meet my dad, they only want to know me because of my dad. I began to feel frustrated by it, so I played it down and if they found out then they found out, but that was much better. Maybe they'd come back to my house and see a picture of Quincey Jones. 'Who's that?' 'Oh, that's just my dad.' 'Oh right!' That sort of thing. That shouldn't be interpreted as my not loving my dad — I love him to death — but I avoided the connection because I was catching on to this whole thing. Of course, even when I stopped telling people, it still needed dealing with. 'Oh, so you're Quincey Jones' daughter. You're cool.'

It got worse when I became an adult. People would say to me, 'Can I give you this tape for your dad to listen to?' The way I was brought up, the direction I set myself in, meant that it was not my way to start lumbering my dad with their tapes. Sure, there were friends who I would certainly offer to help or guide, and that's fine. But it isn't my job to act as a connection or agent to my dad. I suppose I'm a kind of a rebel that way and I don't go along with it.

Once, I was at a 7-11 store and someone came up to me and said, 'Hey, you look like Quincey Jones' daughter!' 'Oh really, do I?' I replied. 'Yes,' he said. 'She's real pretty.' 'Oh, thank you!' Sometimes, if I admit who I am to some people, they won't leave me alone, and other times it's OK and I can cope with it.

Being the daughter of someone famous is normal for me — it's all I know. If, in conversation, I mention someone famous, I'm not doing it because they're famous but because I know them and mix with them and probably have done since I was very young.

My first tour with Dad was with Ray Charles. I naturally don't recall any of it, but as long as I live I'll like hanging out at studios — I grew up with it. The closest I got to being involved in music was dancing and modelling. Dad's passion was the trumpet, but I don't play any musical instrument.

I danced and modelled for about 12 years. I did music videos here and there, but it wasn't great. I was rather typecast by my agency — because I wasn't black or white I'd be sent to audition for hip-hop stuff all the time. I can do hip-hop, that's fine, but when I go to those hip-hop auditions everyone else would be black and I wouldn't get the job. Then another audition would be for a modelling job for black girls, but I wasn't black. I kept trying, though, and I worked as a waitress at the same time.

Before that, I worked at my dad's office inputting data into the computer, but I stayed in the same job for two years. I felt I wanted to learn about the music business, but what I was doing didn't have much to do with music. Basically, I was a glorified 'gofer' for two years. Then it started showing in my attitude. I turned up late because I wasn't into what I was doing, and all the time I was asking myself, 'why am I doing this? Why am I staying here?' You also have the added burden of knowing you're the boss's daughter. I was picking up lunch or the company's dry-cleaning, and wondering what it had to do with music.

I got out of it and did the dance stuff, and after that I worked in a recording studio. Then I moved to the job I have now, which is working with children. Not only do I love it, but I always felt that this was where I would probably end up. I've always been into child psychology. I assumed, wrongly, that I'd need a degree before I could do any work with kids and I am studying for a degree now, but the lack of a degree doesn't prevent you from starting out. Employers want to see how you react with children in a practical, everyday way. So now I work at a children's gym and get paid to be a big kid all day long. It's one of the few instantly gratifying jobs. You know where you stand with children. You come in to, 'Hey, your hair looks ugly today.' 'Thank you very much!' There's no hiding anything. They never cease to amaze me. Whenever I get to thinking of moving on, my boss seems to be one step ahead of me, which boggles me, but it's nice, too. It's nice feeling to know that he likes the way I'm doing my job.

I know I'm in the right place when my dad tells me people keep coming up to him and saying, 'Oh, your daughter teaches my kids.' Dad says he's starting to be known as Tina's father!

A lot of the parents know who I am and I did get some comments like, 'Why are you here doing a job like this?' But it's not a problem. I think they feel that I should be involved with music. I do love music, right across the board, but that's very different from having an active involvement in the music industry.

Naturally, I've come into contact with many people through my dad, and it's nice when you know that they can sense the love between us, and the whole thing of being his daughter and all that entails. Friends like Clarence Avon have expressed pleasure at seeing how close we are. It's unfortunate that, in this town, you cannot keep up with all the people you'd like to. There's the saying, 'It's the thought that counts', but I don't know if the people I would like to catch up with appreciate that.

Dad was at the studio at odd hours when we were young, which was hard. He'd be up in the morning when I was going to school listening to the stuff he'd worked on the night before, but he hadn't gone to sleep yet. It was like his day was never over. He'd have earphones on and I'd call out over the noise, ''Bye, Dad, see you later.' 'Oh yeah, 'bye, have a nice day at school,' would come the reply and, with the earphones on, he'd have no idea how loud he was shouting back. He's a workaholic. There are very few musicians who started out in the era he did and successfully transcended the decades and the countless styles. I think the tension and violence in his early life can be felt in some of his music, particularly in the film score for *The Pawnbroker*.

Dad has some good friends in the entertainment business, people like Steven Spielberg, Stevie Wonder, Alex Hailey and, of course, he's known Ray Charles for years. I enjoyed hanging out at the studio when Dad was producing Michael Jackson's albums.

There was a guy called Grady Tate, who was a drummer back when my Dad was playing in certain big bands. Grady knew I was tap-dancing at the time and he called me 'Tina the Toe-Tapper'. Dad wrote a song about me, and then he wrote one about my brother. 'Tina beana is a sweetheart, a love bug, a ladybird, and a kitty-cat', and basically that was it. One very small song.

Last year Dad received an award at the Oscars, this year he's producing the awards ceremony. We're not supposed to get tickets. Last year, through some silly logic, because Dad was receiving an award he got ten tickets, this year he's producing the ceremony and not getting any tickets. Very weird. To me, producing the show is kind of more important than receiving an award. So I was badgering him about this, and he said, 'I'm trying, I'm trying'. It happens that his partner, David Salzman, has a daughter who is hunting for a house with me. I've been hanging out at her parent's house so I've been able to badger them about it, too. 'I wanna go, I wanna go. You're going, I should be going, too!' Basically acting like a little kid, I guess. Anyway, the night before, I got a call from my sister to tell me I was going to go with them as their guest. That was late notice, but great all the same.

I have a separate life from my father, in so much as I have a job. I love my job, don't get me wrong, but it doesn't pay enough for me to be totally independent from my dad. I've been going through a bit of a spurt on the spending front recently, so now I need to calm down a little.

I've thought about setting up my own children's school, but that takes money, and my father wants me to do it on my own. I am trying, but I can only go so far, and I cannot talk about things when I don't know what the conclusions will be. However, there are directions I want to go in and we'll have to see what materialises.

There's been a lot of stuff that I've wanted to do in my life. I tried working at Dad's office, but that wasn't it. Then came the recording studio, which wasn't it either. So, in a sense, I've been the rebel in the family by not following a musical line, but I've found where I'm going through working with children. They are our future and that's very important to me and for all of us.

My mother's into styling clothes these days. She has some beautiful things — one-of-a-kind clothes. She buys clothes and redesigns them.

She doesn't do this for a shop or anything, but for a rock band in Sweden.

I have to say that I wouldn't want to change my situation for anything, so that must mean something. The hard times are all a part of growing up and forming the person you become.

Victoria (Sellers) is one of my closest, long-standing friends. When we were 13, she'd have parties down the street. She invited me to a boy-girl party, but my stepmum laid down the law on that one: 'No boy-girl parties,' and so on. I told her that no boys were going. She drove me down the street, even though it was only half a block away, just to make sure it was OK. Wouldn't you know it, I knock on the door and this boy answers it. 'Back in the car!' called my stepmum. I was heartbroken. The more repressed you are as a youngster, the more you rebel when you're set free.

Dad cannot stand still. It's impossible for him. He always has to search, to grow, to be curious. It's made it hard to be a family. He had this genius in him, the way I saw it, and it needed to be expressed. Everything else came second, whether right or wrong, in terms of the family. He continued to live his life like he was a single man, obsessed with his work. The life went right out of the house. You cannot have a career like his and also be expected to be the perfect father. It's just the way it was. He needed to fulfil his dream and, without question, he's done so.

DAME BARBARA CARTLAND
AUTHOR, (1901–)

D ame Barbara Cartland was born in 1901 and christened Mary Barbara Hamilton after her great-grandmother who came from Philadelphia.

Barbara Cartland published her first novel in 1923. It was a huge success, going into six editions and published in five languages. After this early success, she began writing seriously to make money.

She had 49 proposals of marriage before, in 1927, she accepted Alexander McCorquodale, a former officer of the Argyll and Sutherland Highlanders.

Barbara Cartland and Alexander had one daughter, Raine, whose second marriage was to the 8th Earl Spencer — the father of The Princess of Wales.

Barbara Cartland divorced her husband in 1935 and married another McCorquodale, Hugh, in 1936.

In 1963, she published her 100th book and started her fight against the fluoridation of our water supplies. That same year her husband, Hugh, died of wounds inflicted at the Battle of Passchendaele in 1917. As well as writing, she has pursued a lifelong interest in matters of politics and health. In 1931, she had the idea for an aeroplane-towed glider and carried the first Glider Airmail in her own glider from Manston Aerodrome to Reading.

In 1964, she began a three-year battle with the Home Secretary on behalf of gypsies, culminating in all Local Authorities being required to provide camps for their gypsies. She owned the first gypsy camp in Hertfordshire, which the gypsies christened 'Barbaraville'.

As a writer of romance, she has attained worldwide sales of over 650 million. In 1992, this earned her a place in the Guinness Book of Records as the world's best-selling author. As well as writing numerous other books, including on historical and biographical subjects, she is a Dame of Grace of St John of Jerusalem, Chairman of the St John Council in Hertfordshire, one of the first women in 1,000 years to be admitted to the Chapter General, President of the Hertfordshire Branch of the Royal College of Midwives and, in 1964, President and Founder of the National Association for Health. Barbara Cartland, author of over 635 titles, lives in Hatfield, Hertfordshire.

Ian McCorquodale, who is 58 years of age, is his mother's business manager. He handles all literary and merchandising contracts around the world and covering 30 different languages.

After leaving Cambridge University, he trained as an accountant before working in the family printing business. He left to join the British Printing Corporation, becoming Corporation Commercial and Export Manager. He became Chairman of Debrett's in 1980. He also originates and markets vitamins and food supplements, largely by mail order. Ian has published tourist guide books and has made videos of Great Britain and Ireland. His hobbies include fishing, gardening and tennis.

IAN McCORQUODALE:

My mother married two McCorquodales, which was very unusual. She always joked that she had the same in-laws twice. Her first husband was the first cousin of my father. He had a drink problem and the marriage wasn't a great success.She divorced him in 1935, at a time when people didn't get divorced so making it quite a celebrated case. She married my father a year later, and I was born in 1937, later followed by my brother, Glen.

My father was very badly wounded in the First World War. He was hit by a dum-dum bullet, which smashed straight through him and permanently damaged a lung, although it didn't stop him smoking for most of his life. When she married my father, my mother was told that if he ever got flu he would die. But they were both blissfully happy for 27 years. For the rest of his life my father would continue to have bits of shrapnel come out of him. It was a miracle he had survived at all, but he was very strong.

He had left Harrow at 17, did six months' officer training at Sandhurst, was commissioned and then sent straight to the front line, nearly killed straight away, spending the ensuing five years in hospitals. So, when he died at the age of 65 back in 1963, it was basically due to scar tissue on his heart. My mother has never remarried.

I had a very normal, upper-class upbringing, looked after by a nanny as one always was. I went to an all-boys preparatory school at the age of eight, then on to public school followed by university — an almost all-male, monastic upbringing.

I suppose it was when I was at preparatory school that I became aware that my mother was, let's say, different from the other mothers there. I was teased and bullied by the other boys because my parents were the only ones to own a television set and were therefore considered stinking rich. That seems very funny now.

It's true, we did have one of the first televisions and it was frightfully exciting. A tiny screen with a huge box around it. You could get only one hour of programming between half-past two and half-past three in the afternoon. It was a news reel that went on through a complete snow storm. We would gather with great excitement around the television.

Before my mother married, she was very sociable. She mixed with people like Winston Churchill, Lord Castle Ross and F E Smith, later Lord Birkenhead. By the time I came along they had all gone — well not Churchill, but he was committed to a few other things! My uncle was Ronald Cartland and my mother did a lot of political work for him when he became an elected Member of Parliament for King's Norton in Birmingham in 1933. He was a brilliant young man and sadly the first MP killed in the War. In fact, I lost three uncles within four days of each other — two on my mother's side and one on my father's. It was a terrible blow to my mother to lose both her brothers at Dunkirk.

My mother has always been interested in politics as, indeed, have I. I was not successful in politics, but I had a good try at it. I didn't get as far as standing for a seat because I found it hard to get adopted. In politics, like most things, a miss is as good as a mile. I wanted to go into politics because of a great family tradition, not only on my mother's side but also on my father's side.

My mother's social life was definitely interrupted by the War. When we moved to Camfield Place near Hatfield, where we've been ever since, we had friends such as Margaret Duchess of Argyll around for lunch.

I was allowed to join in, I wasn't kept to one side, but naturally I was away a lot, first with school and then with university. Camfield was the venue for all her social occasions. The tradition was that she would have a luncheon party on Sundays and we'd have Lew Grade, John and Mary Mills — sometimes with young Hayley Mills whom I always found very attractive — Trevor Howard, and Margaret and Dennis Thatcher — when she was just plain MP for Finchley. This coincided with a time when I was tremendously interested in politics. I was lucky because I used to sit at the head of the table and there would be Margaret on my right and Dennis on my mother's right, although I sometimes think my mother wished it could have been the other way around. Margaret came again for lunch when she was Prime Minister, although by then I was out of the political scenario. She visited us just before she was pushed out of power. I remember thinking that the last thing she would want to talk about would be politics, and I tried to discuss everything else under the sun, but within five minutes she was back to politics.

The same thing happened when we had John and Norma Major for lunch — all Norma wanted to discuss was politics, so I gave up after that.

I recall Fanny and Johnny Craddock, of television cooking fame, being regular visitors to Camfield. They lived outside Watford, which isn't very far away. They became great friends, although I always found Fanny rather intimidating. Johnny was great fun, particularly when he'd had a few drinks. She bossed him about in real life just as she did on television.

Lord Bath, as he is now, used to visit us quite often. He always had very pretty girls in tow — his 'non-wives' as he called them — and I always thought he was pretty nutty then but I think he's possibly even nuttier now. He was a lot of fun to be with, though.

My mother is interested in what goes on in the royal family and we all discuss them from time to time. As far as I'm concerned, though, they live in an ivory tower and are not part of my life. However, the Royal Family has impinged on my life to some extent because my sister married Princess Diana's father and they were happily married until he died a few years ago. He was terribly proud to see his daughter marry the Prince of Wales, but didn't live to see the break-up, which was a good thing. It would have been very upsetting for him.

As children, we went abroad every year to somewhere different, normally at Easter, for a family holiday. Seeing different places was a part of my education. I did the same thing with my daughters.

My first family holiday was to Le Touquet. You could fly the car over by air-ferry. Great fun. No one seemed to go abroad in those days. It was just unthinkable.

We went by train from London to St Moritz for a skiing holiday back in 1949. I really took to skiing and skating, but we never went back again. My brother wasn't very good on his skis and he fell over a rock and needed 27 stitches. That was an horrendous situation at that time just after the war and, after that, my mother announced we wouldn't go skiing again, and we didn't.

When my father was alive holidays would be just the four of us — my mother, father, my brother Glen and myself. My sister, Raine, was married when I was only ten. She married at eighteen and had two children by the time she was twenty. We're still very close. After my father died, we carried on with the family holidays but started going to more exotic locations when aeroplanes opened up the world.

The best trip was to Cambodia in 1966. Being prior to the Vietnam war it was just amazing to see the temples and everything in all their natural and unspoiled state. My mother was the most intrepid traveller. I once drove Mum and Glen from Beirut to Damascus and back again all in a day. Quite fabulous.

My mother and I went to India together in 1958, which was very exciting. Her great friend, Edwina Mountbatten, was stationed there most of the time and was allegedly having an affair with Nehru, although I've never believed that story. A lot of books and pundits have tried to make out that they were more than just good friends. My mother and Lord Mountbatten were good friends in later years. He was a big influence on her and she on him.

The last Viceroy of India was a great achiever and historically important whatever one's opinions are about him. As a small boy, my first ambition was to be an engine driver. A couple of years later my next ambition was to be Viceroy of India. Even at that age I was very impressed with history and was imbued with the concept and ideals of our Empire, which of course no one can remotely understand now.

The Indian Prime Minister was then living in Government House with its beautiful gardens laid out by Peter Coates. We had a memorable lunch there. There was myself, my mother, the Prime Minister, the Prime Minister's daughter, Indira (later Prime Minister, too), who said nothing throughout lunch but simply waited on her father (which I found rather charming), and Edwina Mountbatten.

I had a Sikh friend who was a Prince in the Punjab. He had been rather clever, because after independence most Princes had lost everything from land to money. However, he had seen the changes coming and got some of his possessions out beforehand. He was still living in great style and he gave a party for us at his house in New Delhi. There was a mob of people there and we all stood in the garden drinking whisky and sodas, which is about all you were offered to drink in those days. Suddenly I heard the sound of pipes and thought I must be dreaming. Into the garden came the Faridkot Pipe Band playing 'A Hundred Piper's', which has seemed vaguely incongruous to me ever since.

My royal friend had a palace in the middle of Delhi. My mother and I were invited there to meet his father, the Rajah, for tea. He was a lovely old boy. He'd arranged for his Palm Court Orchestra, all 25 of them, to play waltzes for us while we took our tea. Then he lent us his car so we could go on from Delhi to Jaiphur and Agra.

From that time my mother fell in love with India, and I went back with her on two other occasions. She continued to travel on many occasions without me, usually with my brother. Even up to as recently as last year, my mother and brother have gone on gastronomic holidays together in France staying in lovely châteaux and eating the most wonderful food.

I'm the extrovert of the family and have always enjoyed my mother's fame. My brother doesn't like all the publicity that comes with it, just as my father hadn't. My father would have been happier for his wife not to have been famous, not to have been a writer and not to have had people for ever making a fuss of her.

Being born in 1937 meant I was brought up during the War. We went to Canada in 1941 when Churchill was going to make England a fortress and evacuate the women and children. We took the ship to Canada as it was considered the best thing to do. Being a refugee in Canada was not a success and we came back on the last ship to England with German U-boats everywhere, as my uncle was declared missing at Dunkirk and my mother did not want any privileges during wartime. We had to go to bed dressed in life-jacket kits in case we were torpedoed. There was our mother and nanny, of course, and Glen and Raine. We were the only children on board. The rest were all airforce. Everyone was scared stiff. There was no way anyone could have rescued us if we'd been hit. They had only about three lifeboats on board. We were absolutely delighted finally to get home, and Mother threw herself into the war effort for the duration as a welfare officer. She was the only lady welfare officer looking after 20,000 troops, mostly in secret.

By this time we'd moved from London to a thatched cottage at Great Barford in Bedfordshire. We spent the rest of the War there, and I went to school in Bedford.

I have few memories of the war, having been so young, but I do remember sitting in the nursery with Nanny when I was about six or seven, and for some reason it stuck in my mind that I was surprisingly eating grapes. Funny thing to have in the war, but we somehow managed to get them. Suddenly, there was this screaming sound as a doodle-bug flew over. All the lights flickered indoors, then came the most thundering crash as it hit the earth about three miles away. We rushed outside and it was like watching the most amazing firework display where this thing had crashed harmlessly into a field.

My second memory is of VE Day at school where, with the tremendous celebrations that went on, we were given sweets and chocolates — treats we hadn't had for all those years. I suppose being disastrously sick afterwards is what makes it such a vivid memory.

We sold the house in Great Barford in 1949 and moved to Camfield Place. It's a very big house with an enormous garden and wonderful views — you can see for eight miles without seeing another house — and its own shoot. Unbelievably, it is 17 miles from Marble Arch as the crow flies.

Another interesting point about Camfield is that Beatrix Potter once lived there. It was where she wrote her first three books. Indeed, we have Mr MacGregor's garden as it appeared in the original Peter Rabbit book.

She lived at Camfield with her grandfather, George Potter, who bought the estate in 1867. He pulled down the old house, which was Elizabethan. He rebuilt it as a large, sprawling, Victorian mansion with large rooms and high ceilings, just as it is today.

My mother has very good taste and has made the house particularly beautiful. We call it her factory, for it is where she created, almost single-handedly, the romance industry. She has three secretaries at Camfield working on her writing and correspondence and the health movement that she started in 1948. She receives over 20,000 letters a year. Her fans usually ask for her opinions on health or love. Things like, 'My husband isn't paying me enough attention; what should I do about it?' Or, 'I've terribly bad rheumatism, what should I take for that?' Another type of letter is from someone saying their 13-year-old daughter has just started reading Barbara Cartland books. When you think of the sort of stuff they could be reading it's reassuring and my mother finds it very gratifying.

Even now she is writing at the rate of over 24 books a year — one a fortnight — and she has kept that up for an amazingly long period of time. Up until my father died, she hadn't actually written a great number of books. She would write four or five a year and that would be all. What with the War and its aftermath, there hadn't been time to write so many books. Also, she had to look after two children and my father and lead a sociable life, as well as becoming a County Councillor for Hertfordshire. Her writing up to then had been little more than a pastime, although all the books had sold very well.

The real difference to her career came in the early 1960s when the paperback revolution took off and publishers could produce cheap paperbacks. This process continued throughout the 1960s, and then what made Barbara Cartland and her romances really surge in the market was the advent of pornography. We saw the end of censorship in the late

1960s. The same thing happened in America a little later. The outcome of all this was that Barbara Cartland's pure romance took off like a rocket because women, generally speaking, are not turned on by pornography — it's much more a male preoccupation. The women, not liking what they were seeing, went to the opposite extreme and sought literary pleasure in romance.

A Barbara Cartland story has a brilliant structure with endless variations of plot. It's usually set in the eighteenth or nineteenth centuries. This makes the virgin heroine more believable. It is normally about aristocrats, royalty and nobles who live in beautiful houses with huge ballrooms and wonderful clothes. The story outline is boy meets girl and they fall madly in love. Then follows about 120 pages when they're being kept apart. The important thing is that she stays a virgin. The man is permitted to have had a bit of experience, so he's allowed a mistress or two, until he meets her and falls madly in love because she is sweet, innocent and charming. The heroines are usually religious and love children and dogs.

At the last moment the hero saves the heroine's honour by rescuing her from the clutches of the villain and in the last chapter everything falls nicely into place. They get married, the ring goes on the finger, and he's then allowed to carry her away to the bedroom at which point the story finishes. There are stars in the sky and they live happily ever after. That is the great moral message, which is, undoubtedly, as relevant today as when my mother first started writing. Basically, the message is that people shouldn't go to bed with each other at the drop of a hat. Wait until the right man comes along. In my mother's books, they all get married first anyway.

She has always written in this way, except once when she wrote an unhappy ending. The hero rode off into the night on his white charger and the girl went into a convent. Her readers were furious. She had letters and calls from all over the world. In fact, so great was the reaction that when the book was eventually reprinted she changed the ending.

She has always said that she writes the story of Cinderella over and over again. People identify with the characters and it becomes their real life. It is why she has been such a successful writer. She writes a very good story and the women who read them identify themselves with the heroines. All of them basically want to put back the clock and be young again and swept off their feet by some youthful Prince Charming and live happily ever after. Why was everyone so excited about Prince Charles and Princess Diana? It's all the same thing. The royal couple were, not surprisingly, a great disappointment to my mother because they should have lived happily ever after just as they do in her books.

She firmly believes in the message she is trying to get across in her books — that romance can be beautiful and should be beautiful. That romance is not sex and that love is not necessarily sex, although the two go together you need one before you have the other. That message, which she first started writing about at the age of 19 all those years ago, is still as strong and as relevant today. The world is back to love now. People want escapism, they want to read about beautiful people doing wonderful things and falling in love.

There is an infinite variety of themes in her books. Although the message and the way it is delivered remain the same, each book is different. Just the basic formula remains the same. Agatha Christie was a formula writer and so is Barbara Cartland. They say there are only seven stories in the world and each new novel is a variety on one of those seven themes. What she has sustained is the talent to amuse and give enjoyment to millions. That is because she is a wonderful storyteller.

You can write the best book in the world and make it incredibly boring, or you can write like Barbara Cartland, taking a very straightforward storyline where you know the ending but can't quite see how she's going to get you there. That is the excitement. She ends each chapter on a cliffhanger to make sure you have to read the next even though you know, if you've read enough Barbara Cartland, the predictable outcome because you're familiar with the formula. I've found myself reading through her books at half-past two in the morning thinking, 'How the hell's Mum going to get herself out of this one?'

She's had many imitators over the years, but there's been no one quite like her. In the 1980s, American publishers would say to their authors, 'Write like Barbara Cartland, but put in lots of sex.' They did, and these books became known as 'Bodice Rippers' or 'Hot Historicals', although they still call themselves romance.

Now you have in publishing the interesting phenomenon of women's erotica written by women for women and which is still called romance. I read one the other day and even I learned a few things from it! I was quite amazed.

She writes very good English. In fact, she's been studied in schools as an example of writing a good story using the minimum of language and making each point succinctly.

Her first books were published in America in 1966 by a small publisher. Then, around 1972, the books started taking off in a big way. By then I was handling her affairs and the publishers Bantam made us an offer we couldn't refuse. I was able to negotiate a particularly good deal with them, although Bantam then said my mother wasn't writing enough books. By that time she'd written about 150 books. So then, at the age of 71, she doubled her output. She wrote up to ten books a year at that time and it became 20 a year. In her best year she wrote 25. That's basically one a fortnight. Between 1972 and 1996, she has written over 400 books and broken her own world record over and over again.

My job is to sell the books around the world — I can't sell them as quickly as she writes them and no publisher could publish them as quickly as she writes them, but it does give us a good backlog. The interest continues to grow even today. Last week I was contacted by someone who wanted to publish her books in Armenian. In the last last year we have published in three new languages: Slovene, Croatian and Lithuanian.

One has to be careful with the religious elements of the country where one wishes to find a publisher. Arabic has proved one of the more difficult areas. They like Barbara Cartland because they want their girls to remain virgins until they marry, but at the same time they don't quite like it when they kiss if they're not married.

America was the impetus because at that time there were only two romantic lines in existence — one was Barbara Cartland, the other Harlequin, which is Mills and Boon in Britain. Before that everyone said that Americans don't like romance, which is why it took so long to get Barbara Cartland books into America.

When we first went over to promote the books back in 1967, we took what we could get. One of the shows she appeared on was the Merv Griffin show, who became a great friend and she always went back on his show thereafter. The really big success was in 1974 when she went on every big show there and book sales soared. She was number one and number two in the Dalton bestseller list. That's never been achieved before or since by any author — American or foreign. To date, she has sold well over 120 million books in America alone.

Normally with a paperback, like an Agatha Christie, you throw it away or give it to a friend. Interestingly, with Barbara Cartland, women tend to keep her books and make libraries of them. If a woman is feeling unhappy because of a bad relationship, or simply because it's raining outside, she will pick up and read one of her favourites again — or she'll read the last chapter or two again and feel happier.

Although I've worked with my mother for over quarter of a century I have never been involved with the actual writing of the books. There was never a question of me wanting to be a writer. I wanted to run the business side and get the best deal I possibly could from every aspect of her work. Due to her huge sales figures, it is something that needs to be done on a full-time basis or money can be lost and opportunities missed.

There was a time, however, when I'd come up with some of her titles, my favourite being *A Duel with Destiny*. My mother's brilliant at titles herself, but when you've written about 640 books, you can do with a little help sometimes.

I remember discussing a title for a new book once and saying to her, 'I hope you're not going to give it some awful title like *Love Forbidden*?' She paused and said, 'What a brilliant idea!' And that was that.

I, personally, have only one book in me that I want to write one day and it's a specific idea for a history book. That will take time to research and write. I have genuinely never wanted to compete with my mother. I write very good romantic literary contracts and dealing with advances and royalties is enough for me.

I think I've been reasonably successful at my work. We haven't allowed ourselves to stumble into the pitfalls of having too many agents, accountants and solicitors take over. I've made it my task to be knowledgeable on copyright laws. It's been very useful because I can negotiate with American publishers, whom I've found don't always know their own copyright laws. Copyright was enormously complicated in America before it changed. In point of fact, it came about that we had 40 or 50 Barbara Cartland books in the public domain over there despite the fact she is still alive and kicking, which is all rather absurd. Slight alterations to the books, such as title changes, small text changes or cover illustration changes all helped because it created a new copyright. You have to register it and the new copyright appertained only to the changed bits — the original books remained in the public domain. No publisher in America would ever pirate any of those books because, although one could not attack them under the copyright law, one could do so under the law of fair trading, which in the States is a very strong concept.

There was never a problem with film deals. American television, which was what the Barbara Cartland films were made for, beams into other countries that have always been signed up to the Universal Copyright Convention.

We've had copyright problems in other countries like Japan, indeed her books are being pirated extensively in the Far East. Indonesia is a big problem. Some 15 years ago I sold four Barbara Cartland books to an Indonesian publisher. I received a rather pathetic letter from them about a year later saying they published them and they sold very well, but that they couldn't take any more because every other publisher in Indonesia was also selling Barbara Cartland books!

The books are very successful in India. They love the stories of virgin heroines and the innocence of it all, as do the Japanese. The Japanese men see themselves as very macho and when they get married the girl has to be a virgin. The women have it in their mind that they must keep themselves pure for when the right man comes along. Therefore, they read and relate to Barbara Cartland, which is very good news for us.

I always accompany my mother on her trips to do television shows. Recently, she was invited to France for such an appearance. I dealt with all the Press and television and told each one that they had five minutes, then after ten minutes I dragged them out and let the next ones in. I think I've become very good at the organisational side of the business. Mind you, my mother is very good at handling the Press and they are for ever ringing her up to ask damn silly questions like, 'What are your New Year resolutions?' 'What are you going to give your dog for Christmas?' That type of thing. She always gives them something to take away and they appreciate that, and I believe as a result of it she gets very good press. She says herself that it's so easy to lampoon her, she can do it so much better than most journalists. If they ring up about Prince Charles and Princess Diana, she never says 'No comment', but just explains she's not in a position to say anything about it and moves quietly on to a different topic.

Back to French television. Not speaking any French, she was supplied with an earpiece to receive simultaneous translation. Unfortunately it didn't work and, as it was live television, there wasn't much anyone could do about it, so she chatted happily away anyhow, saying what she wanted. Afterwards we asked someone who was fluent in French what they had made of it and he said she'd made an awful lot of sense but didn't actually answer the questions in sequence. She had waited for a phrase that she recognised, like 'Princess Diana', then chatted away.

What's nice now is that my younger brother, who used to work on the Stock Exchange, joined the family business about two years ago and I'm now teaching him the romance industry. Actually, he deals with the financial side and I handle the business side, and that works very well. We both have our own area of expertise. Indeed, the family is a close-knit team, which is why it continues to work so successfully.

I'm based at Camfield, but my brother has a flat in London. I sold my flat when I got divorced. Working from Camfield is ideal. If I want to go to a party in the West End any time after 11pm it takes no longer than 35 minutes to drive home, yet at the same time Camfield is set in the heart of the countryside.

My mother has always been a very strong influence on my life. We have an amazing rapport and can discuss myriad subjects. We can also totally disagree and have tremendous rows, but they never last very long. Five minutes later, we have both forgotten what the row was all about.

Living in the same house as my mother and working for her does mean we see a tremendous amount of each other. If I don't see her on a certain day, I'll ring two or three times and we'll go through everything. The most I see of her is at weekends. I'm a bachelor now who doesn't cook and it happens that she has a wonderful chef, so we have splendid meals together. We discuss current affairs, history, politics and the Royal Family. We don't talk much about sport. 'Oh no,' she'll say when she sees what's on television, 'not another football match!'

A mother's hold over her son is always very strong and my mother is a particularly strong personality. I have always been attracted to strong women in my life, possibly because of my maternal influence.

That is the major influence that my mother has had on my life. The fact I'm still there at Camfield and we still work intimately together on the family business, speaks of how successful and strong our relationship has proved itself to be.

On the current work-front I would say it is an ambition to get Barbara Cartland books on television in 50-minute slots — story after story after story. Beautiful unknowns would play the young heroines and all the big stars would play the bit parts, which Lew Grade did so successfully with the feature-length films he made. Putting such a series together is proving difficult as it is currently a difficult climate out there.

Another big deal I'm working on at the moment is a Barbara Cartland comic that will be produced in Japan. Comic culture is huge in Japan. We have one of the top Japanese comic illustrators, Riyoko Ikeda, and whatever she does will sell.

My mother and I will probably go back to Japan together for the launch of the comic. She's very game and she loves travelling with me. We have a wonderful time together — lots of jokes, lots of laughs. We get on terribly well. She's 94 now and I'm quite sure she'll make 100. She's an institution — a legend in her own lifetime. Definitely a one-off.

SIR JOHN MILLS

ACTOR, (1908–)

International film star and stage actor John Mills has won many awards in his long and active life from Best Actor for *Great Expectations* (1947) to an Oscar for *Ryan's Daughter* (1971). He has appeared in scores of films, making his screen debut in *The Midshipmaid* in 1933. Many of his films have become classics of the twentieth century: *Goodbye, Mr Chips, Scott of the Antarctic, Hobson's Choice, The Colditz Story, Round the World in 80 Days, Dunkirk, Swiss Family Robinson, King Rat, Oh! What a Lovely War, The Wrong Box* and, of course, *Ice Cold in Alex*.

John Mills has also appeared in over 40 stage productions including *Charley's Aunt, Cavalcade, A Midsummer Night's Dream, She Stoops to Conquer, Of Mice and Men, The End of the Day* and *Separate Tables*. He received the CBE in 1960 and was knighted in 1976. He lives with his wife, Mary, to whom he has been married for 55 years.

Hayley Mills is the younger daughter of John Mills and writer Mary Hayley Bell. As an internationally acclaimed 'child star', she worked with her father on five feature films, the first of which was *Tiger Bay* (1959). One of her most memorable films is *Whistle down the Wind* (1961), which also starred Alan Bates and Bernard Lee and was directed by Bryan Forbes from a screenplay based on the novel written by her mother, Mary. Hayley has recently finished appearing in a highly successful run of *Dead Guilty* at the Apollo Theatre in London's West End, where she co-starred with Jenny Seagrove. She has an elder sister, Juliet, who also acts and a younger brother, Jonathan, who writes and makes surfing videos. Hayley, who is 48, has two children, Crispian and Ace, from two previous marriages, and lives in London.

HAYLEY MILLS:

It is hard to picture the actual moment when I realised I was part of a family known to the public at large — it was always a part of my existence. As a small child it seems to me that, whatever type of parents you have, whether ghastly or otherwise, you still look up to them. That's the way things are, that's the way things are done, and for the early part of your life you just assume that there is no difference between your upbringing and any other's upbringing.

When I was very small, maybe seven, I went to a village fête that my father was opening somewhere in Sussex, where he bought a farm and I spent much of my childhood. At my mother's suggestion, I entered into a running race at this fête. I remember I was wearing sandals and socks, certainly not proper running gear. The gun went off and me and these other children went tearing off down this grass track and I suddenly became aware that an awful lot of people were staring at me. I couldn't understand why, but the attention being paid on me threw me completely. Was it because I was running in a peculiar sort of way? As soon as I thought that, I really did begin to run in a peculiar sort of way. I ran along this track staring at my big sandalled feet plopping down in front of me and eventually came in last. A shame, really, as I was a very fast runner. It's about my earliest memory of being influenced by my father's fame.

My mother, when she kissed me goodnight, would always leave the door slightly ajar because I didn't like the pitch darkness. She'd say, 'Just that much, just this much,' and finally we'd get it right. Then I'd hear the noises downstairs of people arriving for dinner and curiosity would finally get the better of me.

I'd slip out of bed and take forever to squeeze myself through that gap in the door because that's how she'd left it, and there was no other way that door could be because it was kind of sacred now. I have always adored my mother and father and have continually been inordinately proud of them. I'd look down on all their guests and the sound of grown-up laughter and talk — it was usually very theatrical — and it was such a wonderful spectacle because everyone dressed so beautifully in the 1950s.

Sometimes we would do our 'party piece' as it were — sing a couple of songs around the piano — but on the whole we were not 'performing' children.

I went to boarding-school in Camberley when I was about eleven. My second night there, I was told to clear up the dirty plates and take them to the kitchen, which I did. As I came back this big kitchen door swung gently shut leaving it just ajar. I put my hand up to push it open when I heard the house-mistress say my name. And she went on with, 'Just because her father's John Mills, I don't want to see you behaving any differently with her. I don't want to see you sucking up. She's just the same as everybody else.'

I stood there transfixed. Then she went on to talk about other things, so I gently pushed the door open and walked in thinking that it had been a rather extraordinary thing to say. It hadn't occurred to me that anyone would be bothered about me. In my own mind, I was just dealing with getting on in a new environment.

For weeks after — and it seemed for ever — no one spoke to me, for the worst thing in the world at school was to be accused of sucking up to someone else. I wandered round feeling very lonely and rather sorry for myself. I spotted a pretty girl with short black hair and introduced myself. She said her name was Jane and then I asked her if she'd be my best friend. She said yes, and she's been my best friend for life.

The truth is, the girls during my schooling couldn't have given a toss who I was, it was the teachers. 'Just because you're John Mills' daughter you think you can ...' this, that and the other. And you think, 'What are they on about?' The problem was definitely theirs and not yours.

As I mentioned, I wasn't a child who performed for the family very often and I have an elder sister, Juliet, who was much better at doing things than I was. There were the plays at school, of course, and I went to ballet school and I've always enjoyed hearing people laugh. I always had a desire to send myself up because it made people laugh.

I was very clumsy, which I soon realised could be very useful. People like to be amused. I did a show early on when I was at school. I played a bedraggled fairy on top of a Christmas tree and sang a little song. It got a great laugh and I loved it.

The movie *Tiger Bay* came round when I was 12. I can't say it was difficult, despite my lack of experience. I don't think it is difficult for any child to act — it's something that is natural to them.

I grew up with the studios so it wasn't an alien experience. We lived at Richmond in Surrey and Shepperton Studios were just up the road. I remember my father going to the studios on a Vespa motorbike with me tied to him by a leading rein. If he'd come off that thing we'd have both gone flying like Siamese twins.

I always enjoyed being around the studios, although I was never as crazy as my sister who would go up into the gantries. She was six years old when, on one occasion, she did this and the height scared her so much, she wet her knickers.

My father was always very trusting of me as an actor. He didn't, thank God, give me line readings or anything like that. If he had done, it would probably have made me doubt my instinct, because he would have imposed his way of saying it on me and I wouldn't have necessarily understood it, because that was where *he* was coming from, not me.

Tiger Bay was with my father and he did the screen-test with me at Beaconsfield Studios. It was the scene where a police inspector — the part he played — was trying to get this girl to admit she'd seen this man and she's procrastinating because she wants him to have time to get away.

We played this scene on the set of a church. My father played it for real so I did, too, and the help he continually gave me was always to be real, to be true about what you are doing.

I remember walking through Mayfair in London, with him going through a scene with me. It demanded he grab me and shout at me insisting I'd seen this missing man. Of course, people in the street began looking askance wondering if they should involve themselves or maybe smack him around the head with their handbag. I was terribly lucky to start when I did because I was still in my own make-believe world anyway, making up games that stayed with you all day. Even when you came in to have tea, you were still in your imaginary world, and at bathtime, and at bedtime — endless, wonderful games.

I'm sure children still have their make-believe life, but I suspect it is slightly different now because there's so much bombardment from television and external stuff, like computer games. I'm grateful I had the childhood I had because it's a different kind of world today. I was very lucky. I had a priceless, happy childhood. It helps with later life; helps you get through your problems and other people's problems. How many times do events in a day trigger a very old memory? If you haven't had a happy childhood, how many times are the memories triggered unhappy ones? And if you've had an unhappy childhood you have really to reinvent yourself, or allow it to destroy you.

I think growing up is easier for girls than for boys as girls don't have to quite make the break from the family as boys have to. Girls always go back to Mum, dragging their baby and husband with them. Boys have to break away from their mum and form their own nest. They come back, but it's different.

The world I was brought up in was a privileged one. We had staff, which was great for my mum because she's always loathed cooking, and we always had nannies. I never felt deprived of their love and attention because they didn't bathe us every night and what have you. But I'm a very different mother myself.

My father was invariably working when I was a child. By the time he came home we'd had our bath and tea, and in our dressing-gowns would go into the study to spend a bit of time with him — perhaps watch *Sunday Night at the London Palladium*, or *Dixon of Dock Green*, and then we'd go up to bed. It was a very ordered life.

I was never able to provide that sort of life for my children and I never really wanted to. I had a cook and a nanny for a short time when my eldest son, Crispian, was born, so I didn't have to do too much of the domestic things, but then I grew very unhappy *not* doing them. Although I needed a nanny, and always employed nannies, I did much more with my children as time went by. And I love cooking.

My parents had a marvellous collection of friends — Larry Olivier and Vivien Leigh were perhaps their greatest along with Rex Harrison and Lilly Palmer, who was Rex's first wife and my godmother. Rex then married Kay Kendall. Rex and Kay had a beautiful little villa in Portofino. And David Niven, with that wonderful home of his in Cap Ferrat, was a good friend.

There was always a lot of people flowing in and out of our house, particularly at Richmond where we lived for 14 years in a beautiful Georgian house. In fact, my parents sold the house after seven years and moved to Sussex, but they missed it so much they bought it back again. All the furniture returned to the same marks on the carpet. Quite extraordinary.

I remember being terribly smitten with Kay Kendall when Rex brought her to the house. She was so beautiful. I never heard her swear. The worst thing I ever heard her say was 'ladies' knickers!' That's about as far as her swearing ever got as far as I was aware.

The Boulting Brothers came around when I was about six.

Apparently I sat on John Boulting's lap and looked at his hand and said, 'You've got disgusting nails.' Extraordinary that they used to visit us during my youth, then I ended up marrying one of them!

I remember one of those Sunday parties in Hollywood at Jimmy Grainger's house, Jimmy also being a great friend of my parents. He was then married to Jean Symonds, but his first wife was Elspeth March who was my other godmother. She was at school with my mother and they've remained friends all their lives.

I was in the swimming pool at Jimmy Grainger's, and suddenly he stopped everybody in their tracks and roared in that very loud voice of his, 'Hayley Mills has peed in my pool!' I was transfixed with embarrassment. 'I haven't, I haven't,' I cried, nearly drowning in the process — and I really hadn't. 'Yes, you have,' he said. 'I've got a special chemical in the water that shows me when anybody's peed in my pool.' Everyone silently stared down at me. Unfortunately, I had filled the top of my bikini with kleenex to make it appear that I had a pair of boobs, and the kleenex was floating out in long, disgusting threads to the surface of the water like scum.

My parents had a wonderful life — a wonderful lifestyle. I think as children we understood that their life and each other came first, but we certainly didn't feel deprived — it was just the way it was and the right way as far as we were concerned.

They always took us with them wherever they went. When we came out of school we'd go on these wonderful trips. If Dad was filming in Australia or filming in Tobago in the Caribbean, we'd be there. He probably spent all his money on travelling expenses. Then I did the same thing with my kids as far as was possible.

The fact that I've gone into the same business as my parents and my sister has kept us very close. My sister paved the way for me in many respects and that's also the case in terms of acting — it made it feel even more like my life was mapped out. It was simply a case of going into the family business.

What one picked up about the business through the family was what most budding actors go to drama school for. People go to learn what went on around me as a child. The technical aspects of filming I'd automatically absorbed by watching my father. Not by focusing hard because I was thinking, 'Yes, this is what I want to do,' but just by casually watching with that vacant look of childhood and yet taking it all in.

My brother became involved with the industry. He was a 'runner' then became a 'third', then he did get to be a Second Assistant, but I don't think it suited his mentality. Let's say, he didn't like being a minion. Now he's a writer.

I never really had the problem of living in my father's shadow because I was so young when I started making films. And it depends how much you want to do it. It's tougher for boys I think if it's their father who is the 'big cheese'.

When I did *Tiger Bay*, the notices I had, this child had, were wonderful. The media couldn't resist saying things like, '*Hayley Mills acts her father off the screen — John Mills should look to his laurels.*' Not to be taken seriously, of course, but I read the papers that morning before anyone else did and was appalled by the idea that my father might be upset, so I hid them and wouldn't admit to where I'd hidden them for hours. They rang the newsagents and gave them a hard time, until finally I showed him. The thing I then discovered was that he was absolutely delighted. He was always too sensible to be worried by perceived threats of competition from within the camp. Whether he disappeared into the toilet and sobbed I don't know, but I somehow doubt it because we went on to do lots of films together.

Not working with our father is one of the things my sister regrets. I hope she still may have the chance, but in the past they never really had the opportunity. He appeared in one of her TV series of *Nanny and the Professor*, and we all did a *Love Boat* together, but that's not quite the same as jointly getting your teeth into a good part.

I never confused my personal feelings towards my father with the man I was acting with. Indeed, I'd like to work with him again because, of course, as you travel through life you learn more and more and keep changing and when we last worked together I was a child.

After *Tiger Bay* came *The Family Way*, *The Chalk Garden*, then a film my father directed me in called *Skywest and Crooked*. That last film was harder for me than the others. I think it was to do with being seventeen and therefore more involved with my developing life and sexuality. My mind wasn't on the work as it should have been. Also, my weight kept fluctuating during that time. I didn't get as much out of making that film as I should have done. The last film we did together was *The Truth about Spring*, in which we not inappropriately played father and daughter. A total of five films with each other.

My father is a very instinctive actor and there is a great truth in his work. He has that ring of truth about him and a very emotional centre to his being. I find him very moving whatever he is doing. It was good to work with him because you knew there would be no worries. I found it easy to take direction from him, although I confess I preferred to act with him. The director is your audience, sounding-board, conscience — who else do you have? It was more fun to work together as actors — it's a different relationship.

Beginnings are so important. I started by playing the part of a tomboy, which was fun to play, and my parents were very much around. J Lee Thomson directed me and was brilliant and sensitive and never said the wrong thing, and he could have. It was a wonderfully easy process.

I've been lucky to have met so many amazing people. When I was fourteen I attended a Hollywood dinner and sat between Edward G Robinson and Boris Karloff. Quite an interesting occasion, especially as my sister and I were hooked on late, late television and these two were permanently on at that time. We must have seen Karloff in *The Bride of Frankenstein* about 25 times.

Robinson had a wonderful voice and, to my delight, was the same height as me. Sadly he was terribly deaf, but he was unbelievably warm. Karloff was very tall and possessed wonderfully old-fashioned manners. A true gentleman.

At another party I met Mary Pickford, who became America's sweetheart via the film *Pollyanna*. *Pollyanna* was the film that really got things going for me in terms of creating a worldwide public.

There always seemed to be lots of tiny people around when I was in Hollywood. I remember being introduced to a very short lady who was the same height as me. We talked for ages and she was quite enchanting. She turned out to be Lillian Gish. What an actress! She lived to 90 and was acting right up to the end.

I knew Noel very well because he was a great family friend and an enormous influence on my father's life. I first met Noel Coward at the Savoy Grill when I was fourteen. In fact, it was Coward who gave Dad his first big job when he came back from touring in the Far East. Coward had seen him in a theatrical company in Singapore. They were meant to be doing *Hamlet* that night, but couldn't because Hamlet had got terribly drunk and had such a bad hangover that he couldn't go on.

My father was in the leading role and made his entrance on roller skates. He rushed at it too fast and hit a knot in the stage, flew up in the air and landed on his thumb, breaking it. The poor chap had to do the rest of the play in excruciating pain.

Afterwards, the great Noel Coward came backstage to the dressing-room and all the actors gathered round thrilled that he was there. When he met my father he said, 'A wonderful entrance.' My father truthfully replied, 'Well, actually, I broke my thumb.' Noel patted his shoulder and said, 'Keep it in, keep it in.'

He did go on to tell my father that when he got back to London he should contact him and he'd give him a job. It was months later when he returned from this tour, but Noel was true to his word and gave him a part in *Cavalcade*. That was the start of Dad establishing himself in the West End with the 'master' as his great friend and mentor.

I was very fond of Walt Disney, or 'Uncle Walt' as I came to call him. He led an enchanting life. I visited him many times but the first time was at The Dorchester Hotel in Park Lane, London. He wanted to meet me because he was interested in my playing the part of Pollyanna in the film of the same name. I was accompanied my parents and brother and this white Pekinese dog given us by Vivien Leigh. Larry Olivier had originally given it to her, but it had peed on her pale green carpets and she quickly gave it to us. Our carpets had already been peed on so often that it didn't really matter.

The little dog, Suki, promptly peed on the carpets in the Dorchester's Harlequin Suite. A great first meeting with Walt Disney, all of us taking it in turns to clean up the mess from this dog.

I've always resented the stories that have come out about Disney being so ruthless. This man created an empire of entertainment and joy, laughter and love, that generation after generation carry with them through life. It was done on such a gargantuan scale and has continued to increase even after his death, so that if he was a ruthless bastard at times then he probably had to be. There's a lot of jerks out there who are going to screw things up for you.

When I worked for him he always seemed to be available, wandering around the studios always impeccably dressed in a grey suit and he knew everyone's names. That's what studios don't have any more. They don't have 'big Daddy' — the boss who knows everybody by their first name.

He adored my mother. He found her so funny, which she is. So we visited Walt and his sweet wife Lilly a lot, even went to Disneyland for the first time with them. He employed so many people, some of whom didn't recognize him, that when we tried to jump the queue he'd be told to go to the back. When we tried edging in on the Matterhorn Ride, the guy there said, 'Who do you think you are, Walt Disney?' Walt said, 'Well, yes I am.' This guy had white zinc on his nose and, in his shock, threw up his hands spreading it all across his face. Then he stumbled back and fell into a load of geraniums.

Like many out there, Walt had a viewing theatre in his own house. Beside the reclining seats you'd find your hand could just gently nestle into a bowl of liquorice allsorts. All during the film showing you'd hear the sound of Walt Disney making ice-cream sodas from a machine in a huge juice bar. The other thing I recall vividly was his model train set that went right round his garden.

I find spiritualism an interesting subject. I've read all of Shirley Maclean's books. She's been a big influence on me. Actors are given more opportunity to investigate the less earthly aspects of life because it is all a part of the job that we're doing — to investigate our own inner depths and understand things on many levels. I think it goes hand-in-hand with creativity. If it's not so relevant to what you do then the opportunities for such self-investigation are more occasional. But in everybody's life, someone gets sick, or some dreadful drama stops you in your tracks, and you have to ask yourself questions that you know have got to be answered.

Drugs seemed to be considered a short cut to finding what you were looking for, but in many cases that just led to permanent brain damage from which you can never recover. The positive side of it was that it kicked open that door of opportunity and you suddenly saw the many levels of your being — the 'doors of perception' — although while that's very valuable it's not the answer.

It's the same with dope. Marijuana is a valuable tool to release the subconscious and the creativeness in us instead of just living in the left side of our brain where our spiritual and creative side, and contact with our spiritual nature, is so often neglected.

I'll just have to see how things work out, but I'd love to visit India. Out there spirituality and love of God is in the air. It's lived and breathed. Every minute of their lives is influenced by their spiritual philosophy.

A very fortunate aspect of our business is that you work terribly hard when you're working, then you've suddenly got a long break during which you can disappear and lead a completely different life if you so wish. Mind you, the downside is you can never make any real plans as you never know when you're going to be working again, when you're going to be earning any money again. That limits your spending because your future's uncertain, but despite that insecurity I wouldn't change any of it if I could. I just wish it hadn't taken me quite so long to understand the life I lead and appreciate it all. It's taken a long time for me to have a sense of control over the life I lead. I sometimes felt it was controlling me for much of the time. I suppose that up until a certain age you are too busy doing it to step back and question it.

When I was young, I used to think, It must be boring being old. I wasn't looking forward to it because I knew I wouldn't want to be doing the things that I was enjoying doing then, but of course life gets more and more fascinating as you grow older.

Turning 30 was a nightmare — suddenly you are saying goodbye to your youth. But I thoroughly enjoyed turning 40 and saw it as being a great achievement.

My father was 89 this year. He's just had his fifty-fifth wedding anniversary. 'We had a marvellous day, it's all gone like clockwork,' Dad said, 'and we're having supper after a show at the Savoy Grill.' They enjoyed the champagne and everything. 'But you always have a wonderful anniversary, don't you?' I said. 'Yes, but this is the best ever,' he insisted — and he meant it. A great philosophy to life. There's none of the negativity about it being hard work because they're old and having to deal with all the problems age brings. Now is all you've got so make it the best ever, is essentially how he's always approached life. And it would be so easy to turn to nostalgia and think, 'Oh, how I remember the old days when I came to the Savoy Grill before they lowered the ceiling,' and so on. You could spend all your time thinking about what has gone and what has been.

Dad is great when you consider that he cannot read because his central vision has gone, so he has to rely more on his memory, which has got better. He has a marvellous friend who comes and reads all his scripts for him. In fact, he has a lot of good people working for him.

I suppose if there is something left that I would like to do in terms of acting, it would be a Shakespearean role, simply because I haven't ever done one. There are many wonderfully talented people around I'd like to work with.

I love working in theatre, although I discovered it later in life. I'd been making films for 12 years before I did any theatre. It's grown in my life, in my heart. It's a hard taskmaster, but it teaches you so, so much. One's fretful spirit having to channel itself into a character, night after night after night, while real life is going on in all its turbulence at home and in your head. You are two people. The part becomes the defined person, the understandable person, the person where you feel effective and powerful. Your self, your true life, is this total shambles where it's full of the unknown and unpredictable, the endless choices and decisions that need making all day long, and are they the right ones? So you feel like this defined 'being' of the theatre is sort of syphoning you off. It's a weird feeling that at times makes you feel completely schizophrenic. Difficult experience if you're not used to it. It can make you emotionally volatile at times and totally drained, but it's a wonderful learning process. As a soul, you learn a lot. After a year of doing *Dead Guilty*, I'll be quite happy to stop 'learning' for a while and put my feet up.

ROGER MOORE
Actor, (1927–)

R oger Moore was born in 1927 in South London. The son of a
police constable, Moore trained as an artist but was soon drawn
to an acting career. After studying acting at the Royal Academy
of Dramatic Art (RADA) and serving his National Service in the army,
Moore worked as a model while developing his acting career. He
appeared as an extra in 1944 in *Caesar and Cleopatra*, starring Vivien
Leigh, but his first major film performance was in the 1954 Hollywood
melodrama *The Last Time I Saw Paris*, which starred Elizabeth Taylor.
Other Hollywood films that Moore appeared in during this time
included *Diane*, with Lana Turner, and *The Sins of Rachel Cade*, with
Angie Dickinson and Peter Finch.

One of the first major stars to emerge from TV, Roger Moore
established his leading man credentials in *Ivanhoe* (1956-58). He then
replaced James Garner as the star of *Maverick* before becoming,
arguably, the definitive Simon Templar in *The Saint* (1961-68), one of
the most successful TV series of all time on both sides of the Atlantic.
One more TV series — *The Persuaders*, co-starring Tony Curtis —
followed before Moore succeeded Sean Connery as James Bond in *Live
and Let Die* (1973).

After 12 years and seven Bond films, Moore retired from the role
after *A View to a Kill* (1985), having starred in some of the most

financially successful entries in the series. His non-Bond films during his decade-plus as agent 007 included *Gold*, *The Wild Geese* and *The Sea Wolves*.

Roger Moore's three children, Deborah, Geoffrey and Christian, are all from his third marriage to Luisa Mattioli.

Christian Moore, who is 23 years of age, works in the film industry. His work has been varied, and he's gone from 'runner' to Second Assistant. He is currently a production executive. He lives in London with his fiancée.

CHRISTIAN MOORE:

I was born in London in 1973. My father was working on his second Bond movie at the time, *The Man with the Golden Gun.*

As a family, we moved around quite a lot when I was very young, although I first went to school in England. That was at Denham, near Pinewood Studios. We moved to America, and I went to school in Los Angeles, and then we went to Paris for a brief period while my father was shooting *Moonraker.*

Basically, wherever my father did a film, I went with him and I would be enrolled in a school there.

Accompanying my parents stopped when I went to boarding-school at the age of ten. That was a Canadian school in Gstaad, Switzerland, where my parents have based themselves since I was about seven years of age. I remained at the school for roughly nine years on and off. There were occasions when I still travelled with my father, but it was my main base in terms of education.

Other celebrities' children would enrol at the school for a time then disappear. I was one of the few who stayed.

I then moved to a college in Switzerland, which introduced me to the English educational system, having until then been on the American system. That was also a boarding-school, and I was there for four years.

I wouldn't describe myself as academic, but I didn't do too badly at school. I had interests in other things, which I felt would be more beneficial. I had artistic interests, and I painted a lot, just as my father does. When it came to sitting down in a classroom and learning about geography, I would do very well, because it interested me. The trouble was trying to do well at things that didn't grab my interest.

At school in Switzerland, I always went up for the lead parts in the plays and usually got them and I used to sing a bit as well, but that was about the closest I ever came to an acting career.

After school, in the late 1980s, I went to Oxford — not the University, I hasten to add, but to one of the crammers. I enrolled at one of the art colleges while I was there and did a few other courses with the universities just as a fun thing.

It was a whole new experience — the first time I'd been unleashed on the world after spending so much time being strictly regimented in boarding-schools. Other than my grandparents, who lived in Frinton, I was alone in England, but I had a great time in Oxford.

I didn't make too many friends there and, funnily enough, it was because it still lingered with me, as much as it had earlier on, who my father was. Even now, I have only three friends in the whole world. I keep everyone else at arm's length. Maybe I tried too hard when I was young to break away from my father and that has stuck with me.

I had a slightly frightening experience in Oxford, one that rationalises just why my concerns about having a famous father still lingered with me. I was sitting in a pub with a group of people I was at college with. We hadn't met properly and we were still getting to know one another. One of them said he'd heard that Christian Moore was in town — Roger Moore's son — and he was a prick and a 'this, that and the other'.

I sat there looking at him, and the thought crossed my mind, Should I hit him now? But I got up and walked away and never felt so bad before in my life. I'd thought it was all behind me, but apparently it wasn't. From that moment on, I've never announced who I am. Theoretically, it's no big deal, but the strange part of it all is that it is a big deal to other people.

I used to be able to have a talk and a laugh with my local grocer, then one day I walked in and he picked up the *Hello* magazine having spotted me in it. It's changed between us now. He looks at me differently and talks to me differently and I absolutely hate it.

My thoughts during those years in terms of thinking of a career, were geared towards finding something in which I didn't have to do very much. The film industry seemed a very suitable choice. You don't need credentials for it.

I'm striving to be a producer. Earlier on, I had an interest in becoming a director, but now it's a lot clearer to me that being a producer is more my thing. I'm more comfortable in that role. It's probably a security thing. I would direct if I was producing the project, but I wouldn't want to be put in the position where I was responsible to someone above me.

I seem to have shot ahead from being a 'runner' on films. This scares me a bit, when I look at guys who were fellow 'runners' and they're still there doing the same thing, but I've always felt the need to jump around. If you stay a 'runner' for too long, you get labelled as being a 'runner'. I haven't made the mistake of staying in one position for too long. For instance, on the new 'Saint' movie starring Val Kilmer, I was video play-back. Mind you, I was taken off that job due to a burst appendix, but that's another story.

I'm certainly eager to get on in life. Yes, I'm ambitious, but it's a slightly diluted ambition as, and I know it sounds big-headed, I expect I will get what I want in the end. Whether that means becoming rich, fat and sitting by a pool smoking Havana cigars, or skinny as hell sitting in a bathtub, I don't know. I guess it's being in control of what you want to do that excites me, and I want to remain in control.

My father has always said something very true. A lot of people say money doesn't bring happiness. But he always says, 'I'd rather be rich and unhappy than poor and unhappy.' I'll stick by that one and see what happens.

I do feel I might have had it easy, that being Roger Moore's son has helped to push me up the ladder. I've also found that it's had its disadvantages. I've met with the heads of television and so on, and thought that things are really moving, and then, nothing. I think people are very frightened. They seriously consider employing you, but worry that if you screw up they're left with an embarrassing situation because of who your father is.

Anyone who in any way is different, people either find intimidating or curious and will act differently towards them. That applies to everything. If you have an arm missing, people look at you differently. If you have a stutter, people will notice that. In the same way — and it shouldn't be considered special — if you have a famous parent, people will look at you differently.

It definitely gets easier as I get older. I think that's because I don't really care any more.

I've talked to friends who have said, 'God, you've really had a bad life, haven't you?' And I've replied, 'Well, no, wait a second. I haven't had a bad life. There's been a lot of advantages as well, like getting a private tour round Disneyland, or being ferried around in a limousine, and a great lifestyle.' Anyone's problems can be put at the same level as anyone else's. Mine might be different to the guy who is worried about paying his mortgage, but viewed independently, they are still problems. I can't say if the pluses outweigh the minuses — I reckon it tallies itself.

I had seen my father working crazy hours, but never 9–5, and that had some bearing on how I saw my own life developing. Sitting behind a desk 9–5 would drive me mad — I could never do that. Although I'm lazy as a person, I don't mind working 16 hours a day as long as I know what I'm doing and it's pretty straightforward. Not too many jobs in the film industry require anything more than that unless you're on the talent side.

The first realization I had that my father wasn't your everyday dad came early on. Unfortunately, it came to me through being badly bullied at school. I still don't understand why — I guess it was envy. One sadist broke my finger in the hinges of a door. In those days, you didn't run to your teachers or parents and complain. It was still the era of the very English 'stiff upper lip' thing. My parents knew that there were problems, but as Deborah and Geoffrey had come through school all right, they assumed I would.

Although my father had been doing Bonds when Deborah and Geoffrey were at school, they were that much older than me and better equipped to deal with the pressure of a famous parent. They didn't get bullied.

At first, the bullying was harmless. It was mainly based around taking the piss out of Dad being James Bond and, in a way, I must have thrived on it as it's a lot of fun having people know who you are.

But when I changed to another boarding-school, it became a lot more malicious. That was when I altered my own attitude to my father. I became very embarrassed by who he was. I couldn't stand him visiting the school, because by then I didn't like being considered any different.

It wasn't my father's fault, of course, but I came to hate him for it — to direct my anger at him rather than those doing the bullying. It really hurt and it made me a bit more afraid of things. It wasn't all bad times, but I do recall having four or five years of total misery.

Even today, I still cannot be in public with him. I'll walk down the street with him, but if it's to a function where there are photographers, I'll keep well back and get out of the car last to disassociate myself from him.

From the age of ten right up to when I was 18, my father was right at the top of the tree. Wherever you went, someone knew who he was. There was always that fear of being recognised.

The John F Kennedy School in Switzerland wasn't a problem. That was a much smaller school — maybe 40 students — and everyone was much friendlier with each other as all the kids came from an acting or a wealthy family, so you couldn't really have a go at each other as you were all in the same boat.

My father and I are much closer than I thought we ever would become. We are more friends than anything else. We have so much to chat about. A day doesn't pass without us touching base with each other to talk about work, my problems, his problems. We just love to keep in touch. Some mornings, he sends me a jokey fax just to get me out of bed and on my way for the day. He's based in Monaco, but wherever he is, I can always get hold of him. I find that reassuring to know.

Deborah works in the film industry as an actress. Geoffrey used to be in the industry, but he is now a singer. I was always more into grafting. I've always enjoyed getting into the mucky bits of the business, to involve myself in all the dirty work. That brought me closer to my father, because I started meeting so many people he'd known down that particular route.

Much of my interest naturally developed from hanging around the big sets when I was a kid. Whether it was on a Bond movie like *Moonraker* or a movie like *Sea Wolves* with David Niven and Gregory Peck, I just loved interacting with movie people.

Walking on to a 'Bond' set when you're about ten years of age, seeing all the gadgets — some of which I'd be able to take home — was a unique experience.

In terms of the end product, my father's favourite Bond movies were his early ones: *Live and Let Die*, *The Man with the Golden Gun* and *The Spy Who Loved Me*.

Moonraker was very pleasing, because it was the highest grossing Bond movie at that time. Then the films grew a little silly which, perhaps contrary to popular belief, wasn't the direction he wanted to see them move in.

My personal views, and those that I believe my father shares although I won't speak for him, is that the stories became too far-fetched or weak. That made it lose the Bond feel that the others had. It became increasingly more difficult to convince the audience that what they were doing on screen was believable. In the earlier Bonds, you could pick up a pen and say it was a laser gun and that would be accepted. But now you would do the same thing and the audience would say, 'No, it's not a laser gun, it's a Bic.' Expectations made it become more difficult.

I suppose I must have talked to my father about the Bonds from time to time, but not in any great depth. He wasn't someone who got lost in his character to the extent of bringing it home with him. He doesn't really like talking about the films that he's done. Also, he can't watch himself. He'll watch the 'Saint' films, because it's interesting to watch something from so long ago.

I can sit and watch my father's 'Bond' films either on my own or with a friend. I don't find that a problem. But if it's something new that no one has seen, like an interview on Clive Anderson, I'm first to walk out of the room. He does tend to come out with some things that, as his son, I frankly find a little embarrassing.

His last Bond movie was *A View to a Kill* back in 1985. His contract ran out and he didn't want to renew. I guess the producers didn't, either. In terms of playing that role, he was getting a little old. I also think he was getting bored by the end. It was becoming tedious. After the last movie, he couldn't wait to get out. He had become labelled after umpteen years of Bond and it was time to move on.

A while back, Dad rang Eon Productions, the makers of the 'Bond' movies. The person he wanted to speak with was out. The girl on the phone said she would take a message, and asked who was calling. Dad told her he was Roger Moore. 'And how are we spelling that?' she asked. Dad replied, 'I'm sure if you look on the posters in the office, you'll see how to spell it. If not, then maybe you can find someone working there who knows how to spell the fucking thing!' I was standing next to him, and I had to smile.

I was assistant studio manager on *Goldeneye*. Pierce Brosnan was fine, and through the way he conducted his interviews, you could see he was stepping into a larger shoe size than he was used to, so to speak. He had experienced fame, but nothing so international, and nothing that had brought him such media coverage. For my father, it had been gradual. He was 46 and an international star before he even stepped into the Bond role. I think Pierce has had difficulty not believing his own publicity. It's quite understandable — everyone is suddenly on their hands and knees for you, and *Goldeneye* was such a big success. I dragged my father down on to the set to have a few pictures taken with Pierce, which was a lot of fun and something that I knew would be good for Dad.

Family holidays were taken in Switzerland, the South of France and Los Angeles. The family home was in Switzerland, and we had second homes in France and Los Angeles.

Two or three weeks of my Easter holidays would be spent in Los Angeles, summertimes in France, and winters in Switzerland. This was ideal.

Switzerland is my home. I grew up there and love the place with a passion. I was three when I learnt to ski. I started racing for the local Swiss team after a time. We're all skiers in the family. Being in Switzerland is a whole different ball game. I've come to understand, you have to change your attitude when you go out there. Everyone is so money and style obsessed in Switzerland. I actually feel very uncomfortable when I visit after living and working in London. The first four days are usually a nightmare, because it's difficult to put up with all the mink coats and the ridiculous amounts of money floating around. But you get caught up in it.

My father has always put a few months of the winter aside for skiing. It was very much our shared interest, as Deborah and Geoffrey, being that bit older, were getting on with their careers. Dad has become great friends with a former restaurateur in Gstaad, who is also a ski teacher. It was always the three of us skiing together. We would go off in the morning, ski for a few hours, then stop somewhere on the slopes for lunch. We'd ski a little more in the afternoon, then drift home and relax. But all this was done through constant joking. My father's not someone who says, 'Right, let's tear down this mountain as fast as we can.' We would always go slowly down, taking in all the scenery and stopping to talk.

Indeed, the days spent skiing were the time we did much of our talking. We've asked each other some of the most intimate and personal questions during these moments. He feels more comfortable now about answering my personal questions than at any time before.

It's great to bond that way. I remember that if I ever got into trouble at school — caught smoking or whatever — I would with no hesitation or fear go up to him and tell him. He was never the sort of person who, if you went to him because you'd done something wrong, would whack you across the ear. It was more a case of, 'Well, it's done now. I'm not going to scream at you, but you're going to have to accept the consequences of your actions.'

Switzerland must seem a slightly unreal place to have been brought up, especially when you consider we had neighbours like Niven and Sellers. But if that's all you know from childhood, it doesn't seem unreal — you treat it as being normal.

I've had a lot of people come up to me over the years and they always say, 'What's it like being the son of a famous father?'

I've thought long about this, but I can only reply that I've never been anything else, so how can I answer that? It's like someone asking me what it feels like jumping out of a plane. I've never done it, so I don't know.

I do know what reality is, and one thing I'll say about my family is that we aren't — my father especially — dreamers living in La-La Land. He doesn't have this delusion that he's a star and that people should worship him. He's very down to earth and we were brought up to be that way.

When I started work, I had it in my head that my training would probably mean being a tea-boy for the first two years. I understood and accepted that that was the way life worked and I didn't expect to all of a sudden go in as something special. It made it very easy for me to be just one of the lads. As long as no one knows the Moore connection, and I try to keep that very private now, I get along fine.

If I've known someone a year or so and then they find out who my father is, I find it very uncomfortable. Their attitude does change. It's the way they look at you and invariably questions crop up that were never there before — as I mentioned earlier with my comment about my local grocer.

My father has surrounded himself with a lot of business-minded people. In a clever way, he knows that he doesn't like that kind of thing. He likes making money, but he doesn't like having to think of how, other than through his acting. My mother has definitely been the strong arm behind him.

As my father is at a time of life where he is not frenetically hunting work, he can get involved in other kinds of things. He's been an ambassador for UNICEF for the last seven years. This is something he takes very seriously. He finds he won't do any films that will look bad on his role within UNICEF. His work for them is non-paying, so I think that shows how seriously he takes it. After college, I spent six weeks in Central America with him on one of his UNICEF visits. I went as a photographer. I've done a lot with my father that has helped forge our relationship.

My father's always tried to be involved with businesses. For ten years, Dad a co-Chairman of the Board for Faberge, which gained him much on the business front. In the near future, I hope we will have a joint business interest. What I would like to do with him is get involved with some films. I want to encourage him to direct, because he's a very talented director, although he's frightened to do it. Something that surprised me a short while ago, was learning that he had directed a number of episodes of *The Saint* and *The Persuaders*, as well as having produced them and owned the company.

My father still retains a great sense of humour and has never lost his ability to shock. When on set, he would wait for the word 'Action', and appear with his trousers around his ankles. He wouldn't do that now, it was more a part of how he was then, particularly in the Bond era. He hasn't grown more eccentric as he's grown older, just a lot wiser. He used to tear down the road in his car at about 220mph, now it's more like 10.

For me, he's the wisest person I could ever speak to if ever I had a problem. I could turn to him for anything and he'd give me the best advice he felt he could, and I would respect it to the full. That's a part of why we've become such good friends.

I think Deborah and Geoffrey are also close to our father, but probably in different ways. I think Dad and I are closer as characters. We look quite similar and have very similar personalities. Deborah and Geoffrey take more after my mother. I'm a joker, I can't really have a serious conversation, which is how he is, and I know my brother would get a bit angry if I was like that with him.

My mother is a more serious character. She's also extremely intelligent and strong. Being Italian and, with no disrespect to her, not fully *au fait* with the English language, she doesn't appreciate half of our comments. This does cause problems. In any mixed relationship, I think it would.

Sometimes I've come out with things that are supposed to be light-hearted and fun, and she's taken them completely the wrong way. It's not her fault, simply that she does not fully understand. When she entertains, she's hysterical. She threw a lot of parties at home over the years when she and Dad were together.

Nowadays, it's different in view of their separation. Dad has just bought a place in Switzerland, but it's in the neighbouring village from where we all used to live. A few mountain-tops separate them. This is the first year, so we don't know how it's going to unravel itself. The separation has most definitely affected the family. Being very close to my father, I do understand the reasons behind it. It's not my choice or place to judge him, because I wouldn't want him to judge me and thankfully he never has. He's always supported my decisions whether they've been misguided or not. He's allowed me to find out the hard way. But he's never said, 'This is really wrong, don't do it.' It's live and learn. What's done is done. If my father felt that way in his own marriage, then so be it.

We, the children, are caught in the middle and we have to be very neutral, particularly while there's a lot of hate going on from one side. I will not hate my father for what he has done, because I know that if I was in a similar situation, I would do exactly the same thing. I have to do things the way I feel and I wouldn't do anything in my life if I didn't feel it was right.

I still communicate with my mother. She doesn't agree with my train of thought, but she's come to terms with the way I am and my own individual character and I can't and won't change that, no matter what anyone says.

You have only one chance at life, and you've got to go with what you think is the right thing. That's my father's philosophy and he brought me up to think the same way.

ERIC MORECAMBE
COMEDIAN, (1926–1984)

E ric Morecambe was the comic half of a double-act with Ernie Wise. They met in 1939 and began working together as a double-act in 1941 at the Liverpool Empire as a young discovery act for impresario Jack Hylton.

They found increasing success on numerous variety bills during the 1940s and 1950s. They started in radio in 1943 and, in 1961, had their own TV series for Lew Grade at ATV that brought them to the notice of a national audience.

In 1968 they moved to the BBC and began an historic decade for them, culminating with an entry in the *Guinness Book of Records* for achieving 28 million viewers for their 1977 Christmas Show.

As well as countless shows for TV, they made three movies for the Rank Organisation: *The Intelligence Men* (1963), *That Riviera Touch* (1965), and *The Magnificent Two* (1967), In 1978 they moved from the BBC to Thames Television where they would remain for the following six years. As well as making TV shows for Thames, they made a movie, *Night Train To Murder* (1983).

The following contributions are from Eric Morecambe's eldest son, Gary, who is 40, and Eric's only daughter, Gail, who is 43. Gary, who is a full-time writer, is married to Tracey, who runs a property-search company. They live in Somerset with their four children, Jack, Henry,

Arthur and Dereka.

Gail is married to Jonathan Stuart, who runs a printing business, and they live near Kimbolton, Huntingdon, with Gail's two children from her first marriage, Adam and Amelia. Gail is a volunteer for Victim Support, and enjoys painting watercolours and horse-riding.

GAIL MORECAMBE:

It was just after 4.00am, Bank Holiday Monday 1984, when I received the second phone-call from my brother, Gary. The first call was about 11.00pm. This was to tell me that Dad had collapsed in the wings of the Roses Theatre at Tewkesbury, immediately following a performance on stage for his old showbusiness friend, Stan Stennet.

Deep inside I knew that this time he was going to die, but it was still a devastating shock when Gary phoned that second time and said, 'I'm afraid he hasn't made it this time, Gail.'

I sat down on my bed trying to take the information on board, trying not to scream and trying to think clearly to plan and reorganise the next few days.

At about 5.00am both my children walked into the bedroom. The radio was on and, with awful timing, a voice announced that 'Eric Morecambe is dead.'

My daughter Amelia, then aged five and a half, looked at me with alarm and said, 'Do they mean Poppa?' I explained as best I could that they did and that Poppa had died, after which my three-year-old son Adam took his thumb out of his mouth and said, 'Does that mean there won't be any more magic?' Of course, he meant tricks — magician's magic, but it completely summed up my own feelings. Dad had died, the magic had gone.

I had an acute sense of loss, a deep knowledge that this was the end of a special and unique relationship. I'm sure many daughters would talk in similar terms about the death of their fathers. But how did mine manage to establish this relationship with me in the first place? I ask this question because, unlike many other daughters, I shared my Dad with thousands, millions, even. During my younger years he was away for long periods, yet when I think back and my mind plays over family scenes, he is always there at the centre. Apart from his genius as a comic, he also had another great gift. Put simply, he had the gift of communicating love. In spite of his absences and pre-occupation with work, I always knew he loved me. I knew it was important to him that I was happy.

In many ways he was a wonderful father to have when we were small because he could very easily get in touch with the child in himself.

I have many happy memories of him playing with me and half a dozen friends from the neighbourhood. If a couple of friends turned up on their bikes to play, it wouldn't be long before he'd have the football out. His shouts of 'Goal!' would soon summon another friend or two.

In our first home in Harpenden we had two saplings ideally planted as goal posts — I'm sure this was not entirely unintentional.

Cricket was another one of his passions. Now, I have to tell you that this man, my father, was extremely competitive and had to win at all costs. No matter that Gary and I were only six and eight years' old respectively. If this meant cheating, then so be it. This also applied to card games. If he lost the first hand it would be 'Best of three'. If he was still losing, it would be 'Double or quits'. If this failed he would blind you with science and cheat that way.

I went to the local grammar school, St Georges, as a day pupil from the age of eight. I was very happy there. I don't believe the teachers treated me any differently because of who my father was. I think the same could be said of my fellow pupils. I do think, though, that I was someone to be spotted in assembly or Chapel by the younger and older years.

Morecambe and Wise were just beginning their rise to stardom as I started at St Georges. This meant that initially the other children didn't take any particular notice of me, which was great as it gave me a chance to establish myself. By the time I was ten years old, I was definitely more of a curiosity. After a *Morecambe and Wise* show there would be comments at school. Children are very direct about what they think is funny or unfunny. These comments could sometimes feel like a personal criticism of Dad and I did have to find a way of dealing with this so as not to fall out with my friends.

Of course, there was the usual question of what's it like to see your Dad on TV. By the time I was 12, Morecambe and Wise were almost at their peak — where they stayed, much to their amazement — so I'd grown accustomed to seeing them regularly on television.

I wasn't academic, but I was quite good at music and sport. I don't think Dad ever saw me perform in anything, but I do remember he came with my mother once to a school sports day. I took this day very seriously, as I was head of my school house and probably as competitive as he was. I remember that Dad found this rather amusing, much to my irritation. It was quite a day for me as I won all my races and my house won overall, Gary won the invitation race and my parents won the parents' event. Now I don't think the school knew that Dad was going, but the event couldn't have been more suited to him. As I recall it, one parent stood at one end of the one hundred yards track with a pen and paper (my mother), while at the other end of the track stood the other parent with a passage to dictate. At the sound of the starting pistol, they had to make themselves heard by their spouses down the other end who had to jot the passage down. It was fairly frantic. I think Dad's years of pantomime and summer season gave him a slight advantage!

I started riding horses at the age of eight. By the age of twelve I had well and truly caught the bug and, after some persuasion, my parents bought me my first horse. I don't think Dad came within 50 yards of it, but he did a little better with my next horse and I have some Press photos as proof.

What started out as a basic disinterest with anything to do with the equine world became a much more hostile attitude towards horses — mine in particular. This change was entirely due to two riding accidents I had in quick succession.

The first and worst one happened the same day Dad was returning home from a trip to America. I was fourteen years old and I was riding with a friend. We were looking forward to a gallop down a track aptly named 'Mud Lane'. Just as we were setting off we caught a glimpse of some other horses disappearing around a bend ahead, so we decided to wait. Unfortunately my horse, Melody, had also seen the other horses and she did not like giving them a head start. After much jogging on the spot and doing her impression of the Spanish Lippizaner, we set off — rather faster than I'd intended.

I wasn't too alarmed as it wasn't the first time I'd been totally out of control at speed, hardly able to breathe with the wind blowing in my face.

However, seeing the hindquarters of the other horse again, Melody decided to stop dead from a flat-out gallop. I, of course, continued. I remember hanging round her neck facing her hindquarters and fleetingly thinking, as she was picking up speed again, that I should let go as I couldn't do anything like this. Unfortunately for me, as I did let go her front leg hit me full in the face. By the time my friend had caught up with me there was a lot of blood and no horse.

We decided she should try to find the horse and take her home and I would knock on someone's door for help. By now I was in quite a state of shock. I wore a dental brace at this time, and although I was still aware it was in my mouth, I no longer had the teeth it was supposed to be straightening. In fact, I had also fractured my nose and upper jaw and my split lips and gums had bits of shattered tooth in them. I did have an operation to remove all the bits, but that was some weeks later.

I had grown up with an instilled sense of not causing trouble, of not making a fuss and, in particular, of sparing my father from any of life's little problems. As a family we tried to protect him from stress outside of work. So all I cared about as I arrived at some poor couple's house seeking assistance was the effect all of this would have on Dad.

I let them drive me home rather than to hospital. It had taken me some time to decide which would be the lesser shock for Dad, a call from hospital or me actually showing up.

Dad, fresh back from America, was brilliant, and I discovered that on these sort of occasions he surpassed himself. It was over silly little things like the dog coming in the house with wet feet that he would get very stressed. My mother at once called the doctor, and my father, who badly needed to do something useful for me, made a pot of tea — the only time I can recall him ever doing so — and I was unable to drink it!

That night when I went to bed after seeing the doctor and the dentist, Dad came in and sat on my bed in the darkness and said he would stay there until I was asleep. The next fifteen minutes or so were extraordinary. It was very dark and I was aware of the pressure on the bed where he was sitting. We didn't speak, but I knew I couldn't go to sleep while he sat there, so I shut my eyes and pretended to be asleep. After a few moments I became aware of a sound in the room. Then I realised it was Dad crying. Another few moments elapsed when he squeezed my hand, kissed my battered face and quietly left the room closing the door behind him. In those few moments he had communicated all his unconditional love and support — nothing was spoken yet everything was said.

I was reminded of that incident years later. It was the first night after he had died. I had gone to stay with my mother in Harpenden. It had been a truly ghastly day and it wasn't until I was in bed and alone that I felt able really to cry and grieve for Dad. I was not in my old bedroom, but in a spare bedroom I hadn't slept in before. Suddenly, in the darkness, I felt the pressure of someone sitting on the bed and my hand being squeezed. For the first time in fifteen years, I had a very vivid memory of the night of my accident. Maybe it was just my imagination, but I like to think it was Dad's way of telling me he was OK, and comforting me.

A few months after Dad's death, I experienced another 'strange' incident. I was tidying up my living-room, in one corner of which stood my piano. I bent down to pick up some music from the floor and as I stood up I could smell my father's pipe tobacco. Nobody else in the house smoked anything and I had had no recent visitors who smoked pipes, cigars or cigarettes. It was very startling, as one moment there was no smell and the next it was as if Dad had just entered the room puffing his pipe. I sat in a chair half-expecting him to appear.

Since then I have moved house and now have a small office-cum-music room. Over the piano is a lovely portrait of Dad and every once in a while the tobacco scent returns. It also happens on the landing, half way up the stairs, where I have two portraits of Morecambe and Wise. In case you are starting to feel sorry for me and wondering if I'm being treated for delusions, I am not the only one who can smell it when it happens. Both my children and my husband can. I suppose I wasn't surprised that Amelia and Adam can experience this, although I was slightly taken aback the first time they casually said, 'By the way, Mum, Pop's here.' I find it more extraordinary that my husband, who never met my father and who is not given to being fanciful, can also smell it.

Back to my horseriding. When I broke my wrist in a second riding accident only weeks after going out on the same horse again, Dad's reaction was to say absolutely nothing about it, ever. He never even referred to the plastercast on my arm. At first I was quite hurt, but then came to understand that it was because he was upset that he'd chosen to react that way. My mother thought he'd say that the horse must go, but he didn't. However, I don't recall ever having another conversation with him about riding.

I think my early teenage years were the toughest. I suffered from exactly the same sensitivities as every other teenager. All teenagers find their parents are a constant source of embarrassment, but imagine what it was like to be the adolescent daughter of a comic genius who seemingly had never understood the word embarrassment, let alone experienced it himself.

I can recall many moments of excruciating embarrassment, but the following two examples do stand out in my memory. I had been hoping that a certain young man would call me on the phone. I'm quite sure that phoning and visiting me must have been a daunting prospect for any of my admirers. If ever a group of friends came round, Dad couldn't stay away. I sometimes felt they looked as if they had just been in the eye of a storm having been greeted by my father. He would hold out his hand to shake with them and, with perfect timing, take it away and push his glasses up leaving a red-faced teenager with outstretched hand trying casually to recover his dignity. To no avail, as by then Dad would be firing questions at them, not pausing for them to answer: 'Do you always dress like that? Oh. Well, who poured you into those trousers? Are they leather? Is the jacket leather, too? You look like a very large wallet! Is that an earring or do your parents hang you up at night?' And so on, full speed, no pause for breath. Hilariously funny, but not exactly my idea of greeting my friends, although I'm sure they loved it.

Sometimes I'd ask Mum to try to keep him with her in one side of the house while we sat in a room in the other side. But he couldn't stay away for long.

That particular evening while I was awaiting the phone to ring, it did so when I was not in the room. Dad answered. Then he called me. 'Gail, it was for you.' I was momentarily confused by the use of the past tense. Then he chuckled and said, 'It was a young man, but he's hung up.'

'What do you mean he's hung up?' I asked.

'Well, I answered the phone,' said Dad, 'and a boy asked if he could speak to you, and I said, "I'm sorry, there's no phone here," to which he replied, "Thank you," and hung up.'!

Like many teenage girls of that time, I thought Gene Pitney was rather gorgeous, so when he was to appear on a Morecambe and Wise show, Dad invited me along to the studios and said that I could probably meet Mr Pitney afterwards. I should have known better.

After performing his song, the producer informed Gene Pitney that, due to a technical hitch, he would have to sing it again. Unfortunately for the poor man, he had to sing it five times in all. After the third time, Dad joined him on the set to help him deal with the delay while the recording was checked. After a few moments of banter with Pitney and the audience — which Dad was brilliant at — Dad suddenly announced, 'My daughter is in love with you!' I think poor Mr Pitney said something like, 'Oh, that's nice.' Then Dad said, 'She's in the audience tonight, would you like to meet her? Stand up, Gail. Where are you?'

Many thoughts flashed through my mind at this point, some of them murderous, but I decided it would be better to stand up quickly, smile and sit quickly down again. Once standing, rows of heads turned around to see where I was. Mr Pitney kindly said, 'Oh, she's lovely,' to which my father replied, 'Yes, we call her sparrow legs.' I was very self-conscious about my skinny legs and now I'd wished I'd worn trousers and hoped I wouldn't meet Gene Pitney afterwards.

At about this time, I did find being Eric Morecambe's daughter quite a heavy load. The Press became interested in me for a while and I didn't like this interest. I felt it was the journalists' way of getting to Dad via the backdoor. I had far more attention than my brother, Gary, at this time and this annoyed me, too, as I was quite aware that it was because I was female and they hoped for a glamorous picture.

My father knew how I felt, but I don't think he really understood why I felt it. He did try to help matters by not being at home himself if the Press asked to interview me. As it was, they wanted only to talk about Dad (understandably) and they would always ask if he was around — sometimes the moment they walked through the front door. If he was in, they'd ask if he could just join us for one of the photographs. The few moments of chat with Dad were what they used for the story and the interview with me would feel like a total waste of time.

Dad and I managed to remain very close during my teenage years, despite it being a notoriously difficult time whoever you are. Probably because of this I did start to resent not being able to go into a restaurant or anywhere public and just be ourselves. Due to the warmth of his nature, which leapt at you from the television screen, and his generosity of spirit, which made him so approachable, people really felt they knew him. Indeed, sometimes they seemed puzzled that he didn't seem to recognise them — he was an old friend, a member of their family, even. I don't remember him disappointing anybody meeting him for the first time, and he would always sign an autograph, even when he was lying on a stretcher at Leeds hospital having his first massive heart-attack! He gave of himself unstintingly to work, colleagues, the public, the Press and his friends, which meant that by the time he arrived back home he was often drained.

Luton Town football club figured large in our household and I went through a phase of going to the matches with Dad. I did this not so much from any love of football, but to be with Dad, sharing something he clearly enjoyed. As soon as we arrived at the ground he was public property again, but I enjoyed the car journey, for the most part it being just the two of us.

We also went birdwatching together on a few occasions. The first time he took me he gave me a little 'pre-walk talk' about keeping still and keeping quiet. He took his binoculars — just the one pair between us — and said that we'd need rations. These rations turned out to be a packet of jelly cubes and a raw carrot each! We found our spot a short walk from home, and almost immediately the jelly cubes were produced, quickly followed by a rather fluffy, tobacco-flavoured carrot. Having eaten our rations, he quickly became fidgety and it wasn't long before he said, 'Well, Gail, I think it's time to head home.'

I always liked the fact that the name Morecambe was a stage name. It meant that when I met people for the first time, I could feel confident that their reaction to me was not coloured by who my father was. I would go to great lengths to avoid this discovery. This did cause quite a conflict of emotions in me as on the one hand I really loved my father and felt extremely proud of him, but on the other hand, I didn't want people to know he was my father.

An example of this happened when I went to college at the age of 17. I had been there a couple of weeks when one of the girls came up to me to say excitedly that there was a rumour going round that Eric Morecambe's daughter was one of the new students. Who did I think it was? I quickly changed the subject. A couple of days later, she said she really couldn't work it out as she'd now asked almost all the new girls what their fathers did for a living. I remained vague and silent. That evening we were both on the college bus on our way into town when yet again she brought up the subject. I think my lack of interest baffled her. Then suddenly she blurted out, 'It's you, isn't it?'

About six months later, I was with a group of girls in the room I shared with three other girls at college. One of them asked me something about Dad and as we were talking I became aware of a totally stunned look on another friend's face. It transpired she had missed all the preceding gossip and had no idea that Eric Morecambe's daughter was at the college and furthermore was a good friend of hers. She'd actually thought my father worked in a bank. She had this mental picture of my life at home and had pigeon-holed me as we all tend to do when we meet new people. The shock of this revelation was so great that she had to go and lie down quietly and get used to the idea.

Part of me always felt I was rather a disappointment. Comments like, 'You're not a bit how I imagined ...' did much to promote this feeling. I have now decided to take this comment as a compliment.

Once I had left home, my relationship with Dad subtly altered. This was probably due more to us both getting older than to my leaving home. In my teens I really wanted long, deep, meaningful conversations with him, but he found it quite impossible to be serious for more than two minutes. On my visits home in later years, I think the roles reversed.

He was always pleased to see me, in fact I sometimes felt he had just been waiting for me to arrive. Then he would follow me around the house, up to my bedroom, back to the kitchen asking questions like, 'How's things, then?' Having failed to get my undivided attention, he would disappear leaving me to talk to Mum. But after a few minutes a voice from somewhere would call, 'Gail ... Gail ... Come and have a look at this ...'

I imagine that, had he lived, now would be the time for those meaningful talks — now that I'm in my forties and he would have been approaching 70.

He would definitely have wanted to spend time with his grandchildren. I will always be grateful that they did at least know each other for a short time. That is not the case for Gary's four children.

It is incredibly difficult to get across to my children a sense of who and what Morecambe and Wise were in this country. Recently, when Comic Heritage mounted a plaque over the door of our first family home that commemorated the fact that Eric Morecambe had lived there for a time, my son casually said, 'He must have been quite famous then.'

On Saturday 26 May, 1984, we went together as a family to a friend's wedding. On Sunday, Dad went to Tewkesbury and by Monday morning he was dead. I will always be extremely grateful for that wedding.

When I arrived at the house, Mum was still upstairs getting ready for the wedding. Dad came into the kitchen to greet me, and as soon as our eyes met, somewhere in my subconscious I knew he was very ill and I think he knew, too. A very strange few moments passed when we seemed to be communicating on two levels — one was ordinary chit-chat, the other didn't use words. The impact of this was so great that I left him as quickly as possible to find my mother and ask her if he'd been all right. It was very difficult for me, because I didn't want to alarm her unduly. None the less, something had to be said. Unfortunately, our conversation was cut short because, true to form, Dad followed me upstairs.

The time came to leave for the church. Mum was always the last out, double-checking everything and locking up. Dad and I waited in the car. I was sitting immediately behind him studying the curls on the back of his head, when something he used to say if I was obviously exasperated with him, came into my head. With a mischievous backwards glance as he left the room, he would say, 'You'll miss me when I'm gone.' As I fondly studied his curls in the car, I said, 'I'll miss you when you've gone.'

The questions people ask now have changed slightly. Now I'm asked, 'What's it like to see him on TV, or hear him on the radio? Does it upset you?'

It was actually very important to my father that we, the family, continue to watch Morecambe and Wise after his death. On one occasion when I went to visit and was called to go and look at something, he suddenly said that he didn't want lots of tears when he died. I wasn't to miss him and I was to look after Mum, as it would be very hard for her. I told him that was easier said than done. He replied, 'When I'm gone, I'm gone. No point worrying about me, you know. But you will still watch the shows, won't you? If you don't, then it's all been for nothing.'

Oddly enough, shortly after he died, I had no problem with seeing him on TV. For me, there was a very clear distinction between Eric Morecambe and my father. After a few years this distinction became a little blurred. I found myself really watching him, exclusively, taking in every mannerism, listening intently to his voice and feeling very empty when the closing credits moved in to replace him on the screen.

The most chilling incident of this sort happened about six years after his death. I'd been out, but had left the radio on in the kitchen. As I came in through the back door, I could hear Dad talking in the kitchen and the hairs on the back of my neck prickled. It was actually a recorded interview, which is why it had sounded so natural.

It is now over 11 years since he died and I'm completely comfortable watching him on television or hearing him on the radio. In fact, I like it!

Ironically, because he died when I was only 30, I am left with the feeling of not having had enough of him, very similar to the feelings I had of sharing him with everyone when he was alive.

My father was a very moral man and doing the 'right thing' mattered.

He had been strict about our behaviour, but this had been achieved more by expectation than any formal discipline. He expected good behaviour, so we behaved well.

Neither Gary nor I ever went 'off the rails'. I've never smoked a cigarette in my life, let alone anything stronger. I have only been totally, leglessly drunk once and luckily for me Dad wasn't there, only my mother and grandmother. Considering his profession, I think this is fairly remarkable. I didn't want to let him down — I was proud of him and I wanted him to be proud of me.

What I miss most now is his humour. It ran through his veins and oozed out of every pore. It was infectious and made you feel good. Although I may feel I never had enough of him, I did have more than most people and for that I feel blessed. It is a privilege to be his only daughter.

GARY MORECAMBE:

When I think of my relationship with my father and, indeed, my whole general upbringing, there is a tendency to create two independent areas. First and foremost is the rather private, highly amusing man who was the male parent, and second is the magnificent comedian who won a nation's love and respect.

It interests me that I should see it this way because, ironically, Eric Morecambe the performer and Eric Morecambe the private man had very few noticeable differences. I imagine the main reason for this was due to my father having been a totally natural performer. Although he worked desperately hard on the Morecambe and Wise shows, particularly behind the scenes, the actual task of being consistently funny and making people consistently laugh came with remarkable ease to him, and always had done.

My relationship with Eric Morecambe has grown complicated in recent years through transmutation from my personal, everyday involvement with him during my childhood and youth, to my working involvement in adulthood. For example, I've co-written a biography and a play on him, and there are several further 'Eric Morecambe'-linked projects in the pipeline.

What with the continuing business side pertaining to Eric Morecambe, which is carefully monitored by the family, in conjunction with Billy Marsh Associates, I have suddenly in recent times become aware I am very much a part of a not inconsiderable cottage industry. This has, however, served to make it far simpler to discern the man from the comedian.

As a father, it was his sheer personality and eagerness to entertain us and everyone else that I reflect upon most. His own father, George, had been a cheery and amusing fellow, prone to mischief and odd sayings. His mother, Sadie, the woman who believed her only child had talent and did her bit by suggesting Eric and Ernie form a double-act, was also an amusing character, but forceful with it. 'She knew I had to be pushed and encouraged,' said my father. 'But she only ever wanted the best for me, to give me the opportunity to rise above my station.'

There are no memories — not even one — of my father's practical role as a parent. He never cooked for us, bathed us, and our homework was beyond his own limited formal education. If the telly had a faulty plug, he wouldn't have changed it — probably wouldn't have known how.

He would have left it not working until someone, usually my mother, Joan, took care of the problem. My mother was aware of his shortcomings in this area from day one and it certainly hasn't blemished my own opinion of him in any way.

During my early years, he was away so much of the time that I imagine it became increasingly difficult for him to slip back into the domestic scene. Yet, somehow, it didn't matter in the least. We became accustomed to his absences and my mother went beyond the expected role of any good parent to compensate.

The most repetitious question I was and am asked is, 'What was it like having Eric Morecambe as your father?' To be honest, knowing no different and having no other father, it was relatively normal. I suppose the mere fact I use the word 'relatively' suggests life wasn't *totally* normal, and it wasn't — it couldn't have been. Eric Morecambe was arguably the greatest post-War comedian this country has had. He was totally unique, a complete one-off, a man who could generate laughter unscripted — in fact, without even having to open his mouth. How can such an individual be cast as a normal parent? He can do his best to give that impression — and he did — but that isn't quite the same thing.

To balance that, one must consider my upbringing as a whole. No big parties, very little rubbing shoulders with the stars, few fancy toys, no palatial mansion. I went to school with the other kids in the area and in the holidays we took a fortnight in Spain or Portugal — and quite often in England, too, because for many years Eric and Ernie were working summer season at bog-standard resorts. My parents moved to Hertfordshire in 1962 and my mother is still there now, so there was none of the unsettling travelling that can accompany a star's life and definitely no outrageous high-life.

Life wasn't mundane either, but there was routine and discipline, and the combination of these intangibles meant security. Allied to that was the fact that my parents deliberately kept showbusiness as a business and it rarely clashed with home life.

The media — in particular the tabloid Press — has often tried to make me appear the hard-done-by son who is in some way bitter about his upbringing. One prominent headline read something like: HE MADE THE WORLD LAUGH, SO WHY DID HE MAKE MY LIFE SUCH A MISERY? Nothing could be further from the truth. My father was neglectful at times, irritating on occasion, but the mere fact I wouldn't want to change who I am and what I went through for the world speaks volumes. I've been lucky. I've had it both ways — the star parent, yet the normal upbringing. There are no skeletons in the cupboard, no angry words to be written to right any real or imagined wrongs. Life was and is great, and my world — maybe yours, too — is a quieter, sadder place without Eric Morecambe. It wasn't for nothing that the 'sunshine' tag — originally associated with their signature tune — should become synonymous with Eric Morecambe the man.

I suppose there were moments I wished my father was anything other than famous, but those moments were rare. Most of the anguish I experienced during my youth was at my having to share him with his public and that's something I think my sister and brother both felt. We couldn't go anywhere in Britain without him being recognised and the total professional within him made him feel obliged to deliver the whole Eric Morecambe rigmarole. He hated to let people down, hated them to go away thinking he's either not well or not funny. This made it difficult for him to have his quiet moments. He dared not shut down completely. Even on holiday — perhaps especially on holiday — a part of him was as electric as a live wire, for he reasoned that if he totally switched off he may never switch on again — not even *want* to switch on again. His attitude to comedy, you see, could be very love/hate at times.

Yet, somehow, he did manage to relax. Not always. Occasionally, he would leave the dinner table mid-mouthful, nervous and fidgety, unable to settle. But there were other times — summer days sitting by his own swimming-pool on a lounger, drink in one hand, Cuban cigar in the other, brown and smiling and relaxed — when he appeared not to have a care in the world and not to give a jot about Morecambe and Wise, or anything. This was deceptive because I believe he cared about Morecambe and Wise almost more than all else and perhaps even more than he chose to allow himself to believe — not unnatural when you've created something that has taken three decades to reach its zenith. There's something of the 'Frankenstein's Monster' in such a rags-to-riches tale. From his mother's idea to form a double-act came this huge success, this comic machine, which was always larger than either of its two components and which without strict and strong guidance could easily have gone berserk and destroyed those two components.

He thrived on being Morecambe and Wise and could talk about them incessantly. Strange that to me he spoke of them as something disassociated from his own life. 'The great thing about Morecambe and Wise ...', he'd say, and never, 'The great thing about me and Ernie ...'.

One of his greatest pleasures was watching his own TV shows, especially *The Morecambe and Wise Christmas Show*. He would sit back with a glass of port and a huge cigar and smile and laugh all the way through. We soon learned not to talk during the whole 60 minutes unless it was to make a pertinent point and even that could be expressed only during a guest star's song and not when Eric and Ernie were on the screen.

People have often asked if he was a bit tetchy on Christmas Day, while awaiting the culmination of what amounted to six months' work. Well, it wasn't that he was so much tetchy or anxious as filled with an air of expectancy. Indeed, we all were within our household. First, he adored Christmas and all the traditional aspects of it, and so would hardly even make a reference to his own show being on until about half an hour before it was actually transmitted. Second, he knew in advance roughly how well the show would or would not be received by the public from when it was recorded some weeks before in front of a live audience. It is almost certain he would then have seen it screened at the studios with the producer and director after the editing was over. The only unaccountable area, therefore, was the Press. Would they continue, year after year, praising something that had become as familiar as the turkey? The overall answer is, yes. The worst reviews the Christmas Shows received were remarks that perhaps there was a certain sameness about them — surprisingly enough, a criticism that Eric himself had directed at their shows as far back as 1973. As he went on to say, 'If the viewers want Morecambe and Wise, then we'll continue to give them Morecambe and Wise.' Once they the public no longer demanded them, he claimed they would stop. Christmas Day still has that same Morecambe and Wise feel to it in my household.

My wife and I watch the show and I still have the same sense of expectancy that I had in my youth, only now I can no longer turn to my father afterwards and say, 'Great show, Dad.' I confess I feel a sense of momentary emptiness after watching their Christmas re-runs, no doubt brought about by his absence.

Memories of Christmases past and an era gone for ever, come flooding back. Then I usually ring up my mother and we commiserate along the same lines, while also agreeing how truly 'great' those shows were in the true sense of entertainment. I may phone Ernest Maxin, who produced and directed many of those shows and I feel better and more business-like about the matter as we discuss the editing of the piece and the material still awaiting an airing in future years, with which the BBC has been sensibly parsimonious.

One of the ironies concerning my father and Morecambe and Wise, is he never lost the fear that they might one day fail. It didn't haunt him on a daily basis, but it was always lurking somewhere deep inside, usually rearing itself in comments like, 'You've got to be seen regularly on TV to be a star. And you have to be a star.'

That the Morecambe and Wise act was indeed a living legend undoubtedly crossed his mind, but I sense he never really took the information on board. He felt that their being at the top of the light entertainment tree was always going to remain a transient and unstable situation. I suppose the cliché, once you reach the top there's only one way to go, crossed his mind on many an occasion. At one time, this could have been, and probably was, the case. After all the years of success, the years of wonderful series' and Christmas Shows, they were beyond such uncertainty. As national treasures, which they certainly were and are, unless they really blew it, Morecambe and Wise could hardly fail.

I agree with the late Roy Castle, who pointed out that Eric had a serious side that he permanently suppressed. Whenever it began to show itself he would go quiet, almost afraid to be seen as anything but a clown. This was even the case in the privacy of his own home. At the same time, though, he was generous with his humour, quite happy in social situations for others around him to crack the jokes and get the laughs, be it a Jimmy Tarbuck, Frank Carson or Michael Caine. He particularly loved listening to other comics. He never felt the need to compete, perhaps because he never had anything to prove. I recall a trip to Florida culminating in a visit to Disneyworld. We walked around the Hollywood Hall Of Fame, where stood mannequins of John Wayne, Humphrey Bogart, James Cagney *et al*. He was like a child in a sweet shop. There was no hint of envy, or that he should be remembered with the same glorification.

Holidays with my father are where I derive my favourite memories, simply because whenever I visualise him, nine times out of ten it is the image of him abroad that comes to mind.

Usually he would wear a pair of baggy shorts to cover his spindly legs — used as a brilliant working device, but which were the cause of much private grief — a vest, a straw hat, and invariably a pipe would be clenched between the teeth leaving a trail of aromatic smoke in his wake.

My parents had a house built in the Algarve when it was still possible to see locals instead of tourists and the roads were dust tracks used by donkeys and carts, not strips of smooth tarmac overflowing with Mercedes taxis.

My mother and us, the children, probably got more out of Portugal than my father. He didn't swim, wasn't keen on extreme heat, which, if you don't swim, is all the more extreme, and didn't have the temperament for the *mañana* attitude to life out there. Truth be known, he would have been happier in America where you clicked your fingers and things happened. Indeed, some years later, he was to buy a condo in Florida and he really took pleasure in visiting it. No language problem, no Third World mentality that he just couldn't abide. Actually, I think he took more pleasure from those summer seasons in resorts like Blackpool, even though he was working. The only benefit he could see to Portugal was the short flight.

We sometimes had dinner with friends who had a villa almost opposite ours. They often invited their German neighbours. My father found accents contagious as, I assume, most comedians do. I can still picture him as we left the party fumbling in his pockets to find a small coin that he inserted in one eye like a monocle. He barrelled his chest and strode back to his own villa with a stiff left leg, mimicking a German general from a 1940s 'B' movie. 'Who is this English swinehunt visout zee sense of humour, ya?' and that sort of thing. Totally over the top and all great fun.

His holidays in Portugal were paradoxically the source of major ideas for shows. I remember him developing the classic Shirley Bassey and Tom Jones routines while sitting on the verandah. He would fall quiet for half an hour and you could almost hear his brain working. Then he'd disappear indoors and start scribbling notes. He'd recite the words over and over, then change them around a bit. He'd never volunteer information about what he was doing, but if you showed interest he would go through the whole thing.

I vividly recall him finding a record at the villa that had the track on it, 'Exactly Like You'. He must have played it 20 times. 'What do you reckon?' he asked seriously. 'We get Tom Jones singing this for real, and Ernie and me are his backing vocals just singing the "Yeah-yeah-yeah" bit?'

'Sounds like a good idea,' I told him, which, in all honesty, Gail and I said to just about all his ideas, because no one — perhaps with the exception of Eddie Braben (writer) and Ernest Maxin (producer/director) — fully understood what was right for Morecambe and Wise except Morecambe and Wise themselves.

I occasionally look back on my father as someone who was his own worst enemy. He would complain of recognition yet do something very 'Eric Morecambe' to get attention. This continual contradiction unduly irritated me. I couldn't fathom why he wished to be anonymous then disliked it when he actually succeeded in being so. I think he was torn by a need to be the extrovert performer and the introvert private man. He was capable of being both, though inevitably the former won out and possibly to the detriment of his own health.

The only difficulty in living with him was that at times it was like living with a live Morecambe and Wise show. That could be debilitating for the family and, also, for himself in the final analysis.

He was a man who saw everything in black and white. There were no grey areas, a definite failing as most of his arguments were 'For' or 'Against' and there was little space for compromise. I suppose by that way of thinking he would have made a diabolical diplomat, but an excellent Fascist dictator. This was the man whose idea of explaining the facts of life to his son was to take me to his bedroom, whip out his penis and say, 'These can be dangerous things, son — be careful what you do with them!'.

He wasn't a particularly volatile person, but his lack of tolerance would give out that impression. Shortly after passing my driving test, I smashed my car up. He was furious. He ranted and raved for ages. After this outpouring he then became composed as if satisfied his point had been duly made and his parental role fulfilled on the matter, and went calmly on to say how relieved he was that it was the car that had been damaged and not me.

For years I misread his moments of temper. It wasn't the mad hot temper I had read it as being in my sensitive youth. On closer inspection, when he exploded one came to sense the anger was directed at himself rather than anyone else — his inability to deal with his own shortcomings, perhaps an airing of frustration at thinking he couldn't turn his hand to anything outside his own natural creative field. Therefore, when the inevitable domestic crises — major or minor — set in, he didn't have the answers. And he liked to have the answers. Being in control was perhaps his greatest strength. As Eric Morecambe, star, he wasn't the remotest bit pretentious, weak or unreliable — indeed, he was the opposite of these things. The Morecambe and Wise 'monster' grew out of all proportion — way beyond his wildest dreams — yet, save for a period of back-breaking demands during the late 1960s which gave rise to his first bout of bad health, he never lost control of it, not even for a moment.

He never succumbed to the by-products so prevalent in showbusiness. The wine, women and song of it all was carefully kept at arms length, himself choreographed by his own choosing as a non-partaker in such debauchery. He was a strong-minded man of basic Victorian principles. He had been brought up understanding you were either one of the good guys or one of the bad guys, black and white, no grey areas, again. He always had the right answers to keep the act not only on the straight and narrow, but miles ahead of the rest of the field in terms of sheer quality and brilliance. I admired those qualities in both him *and* Ernie.

It is definitely his humour and all-round sense of fun that we all, in our family, recall most vividly, for that permeated our lives more than any other factor. He was always so mischievous. Even when in the company of the late multi-millionaire pianist, Liberace, he couldn't resist a gentle jibe. Liberace told him, 'I wish I'd had the foresight to buy more land in Vegas when it was still desert.'

'Yes, you should have done,' replied Eric. 'You could have been a rich man!'

I have a signed copy of the *Eric and Ernie* biography, published in 1973. It says: 'Lern to spel and you could rite a best cellar, like wot I have.' Though a minor point, it sums him up nicely. He couldn't have signed it: 'To Gary, love always, Dad'. That would have been far too straightforward for the natural comedian within.

Being only fleetingly interested in a diverse array of hobbies and fishing not being a sport that is practical to pursue on a daily basis, meant my father had plenty of time to drift around and see what I was up to when I was in my early teens — something I sense fascinated him.

His own youth had been spent on the road working, often facing hostile audiences. There was little glamour, little real life, beyond the travel, the meals the work and the laughs — both professional and private.

My generation of teenagers was always going to be different from his. This was the end of the comfortable swinging 1960s. Sex and drugs and rock 'n' roll, and all that. Passing concern over alcohol and drug abuse and the sort of people related to it underscored many of our conversations. One could sense his fear in guarded remarks of the time that were designed to be a fatherly warning, but also became a father eager to learn more about a world of which he knew so little, for he was surprisingly naïve and misinformed on certain subjects while acutely knowledgeable on others.

In my very early teens, he was a constant source of fun. If I put on any music he would appear at the window and start impersonating the singer. If it was one of John Barry's James Bond scores, he'd rush by the window holding a toy gun. Hilarious stuff, but sometimes overpowering.

Five young school-friends — all girls — turned up on our doorstep one day. He opened the door and said, 'Look Gary, two and a half each!' I was embarrassed by his carefree abandon — inexplicably, when I recall such moments, I still am and I'm 40. If he sensed embarrassment, he played on it until you sometimes wanted the ground to swallow you up because this man did not have the capacity to experience personal embarrassment.

One of the most vivid images I have of him is his darting around the drive of the family home kicking a football. The wrought-iron gates, miraculously still standing to this day, was the goal. He'd been quite a good player in his youth, at one time seriously considering a professional career. His father, who had had a bad injury playing football that had nearly led to the amputation of a leg put him right off the idea. He was so happy kicking a ball around while keeping up a running commentary that included such names as Charlton, Eusebio, Pele, Matthews. He enjoyed being a part of what was happening around the home. He wasn't someone who gave kids an angry look and retired to the seclusion of his study. His way of coping was to join in and take over.

The more unsettled years in my own life were not surprisingly my earliest ones, because back in the late 1950s, although they weren't exactly struggling, Morecambe and Wise weren't exactly stars, either. Most of their work other than occasional radio shows was theatre based. That meant travel on a regular basis. My father would be home for a while, then he would be gone for weeks. We grew accustomed to it —

you grow accustomed to anything if you have to — but it distanced us at first. I was nervous of him, much more dependent upon my mother who had naturally geared our routine around herself as she was the constant adult presence in the house. I don't know how my father quite felt about all this. I suspect it saddened him a little. Anyway, he won us around in the end and the irony is that once the variety halls started closing and he found himself breaking ground in TV, he was consistently at home. Even when rehearsing and recording, he made sure he was back for dinner. It was a much healthier family environment.

My time at home was limited by the fact that I was sent to boarding-school. Aldenham School, Elstree — overshadowed by its more illustrious neighbour, Haberdashers — was a run-of-the-mill public school and, from what I see and hear, still is. On reflection, I did enjoy the latter part of my four years there, 1969–73. I was quite homesick at first, an indication of how comfortable things were on the family front, but when I was a fully settled senior, returning to the bosom of my family wasn't quite so enticing. Home became a place to wear old clothes, play records and get a great meal.

The biggest and best role my father played as a school parent was turning up and being Eric Morecambe and everyone loved it. One prize-giving day, he agreed to do the honours. One boy's face he slapped like he would Ernie's and when all the trophies had been handed out, he proceeded to hand out the table they had been standing on.

I stood watching all this from a distance quietly proud. It wasn't pride based solely on his being so well known and well loved, which he was, but because he had the pure talent to amuse people just by being there. He hardly said a word the whole ceremony — he didn't have to. Yet he was indefinably funny. What a gift for any mortal to have.

I am also grateful to the staff and students at the school, for not once did I detect any jealousy or unpleasantness through having such a famous parent, something that I know has proved a nightmare for other sons and daughters of well-known parents.

With my father being home far more frequently, we naturally forged a stronger bond between us and, indeed, were very close. Had he lived, I think we would have grown closer still — there was room for that. Alas, I was still unsettled and uncertain about my own future at the time of his death and, although married, didn't have even one of the four children I now have.

I would have liked him to have been around for his grandchildren. He would have been brilliant with and for them. He had certainly been that way with Gail's two children, Adam and Amelia. Instead, they see him only on telly and call him, 'Our granddad, Eric Morecambe,' and ask impossible questions like, 'Was granddad built at the same time as Stonehenge?'! It must be strange for my children to have such a well-known and talked about grandparent that they have not personally known.

My wife and I took the children for a daytrip to Parnham House a couple of summers ago. In the gardens were giant statues of Eric and Ernie. That sort of thing gives you a jolt and it's particularly difficult to explain to your own children why, exactly, granddad is standing there in this garden that has absolutely nothing to do with us. Mind you, I'm still not quite sure myself.

Because my father and I cared about each other we cared about what became of each other. For me, it was concerns for his health. For him, it was what I would do with my life. I think he'd be surprised, though hopefully not displeased, at how involved I've allowed myself to become with Morecambe and Wise down the years, simply because for the most part all of us in the family remained divorced from the act during its working lifetime. I think he would be proud of the part I've played in perpetuating their reputation, which has become something of a personal crusade.

During his life I wish we'd shared more common ground. He loved fishing, bird-watching and, for a time, photography — all those bored me to death. I liked cycling, tennis and model-making, and still do. Thankfully, we did share a passion for Luton Town FC, which came about following his first heart-attack in 1968. We would spend many a Saturday afternoon at the ground, and many a Sunday either celebrating victory or holding a post-mortem on the reasons for their defeat. They were priceless moments for us. It was our own private world — a man's world — which as a football-mad 12-year-old, I simply adored. I think the football interest was the foundation of our relationship and it certainly entered most of our conversations.

I didn't leave home until I was 22, and then it was to become immediately engaged to be married. At the time, I reflected with a certain guilty conscience that I'd hung around the nest too long. 'You should be paying rent,' my father would say — and quite rightly, for by then I was working in London for his own agent, Billy Marsh, and commuting to and from town each day.

The obvious thing would have been to rent a flat in town, but somehow it just never happened and it wasn't only from a lack of effort on my behalf. My mother was keen I stayed around and, conversely, although my father discussed the benefits for all concerned if I moved on, he did admit that he enjoyed having the male company.

It was during my last years of living at home that he was to introduce me to drinking scotch and smoking large cigars, both habits that I have never shaken off. He liked to share his habits, as if by doing so it gave him companionship. Funnily enough, other distant relatives that I've come across lately claim the same thing. I think he enjoyed a bit of devilry. I know he disliked seeing me smoke cheap cigars — they had to be Havana. I'm not certain he ever considered the financial implication — he could afford to buy them, I couldn't!

When he wasn't busy himself what he liked was listening to me prattle on about everyday life at the office, for in a sense the office was *his* office as it represented his business affairs. Friends and colleagues such as Frankie Vaughan, Bruce Forsyth, Arthur Askey, Harry Worth and others, would have meetings at the office, so I found myself in the bizarre situation of updating my own father with the latest on his friends and his business.

One of many visitors to our house in the mid-1970s was a young Oxford graduate called Rowan Atkinson. I'd already known Rowan a few years by then and he was keen to meet my father, and I — as perhaps one of Rowan's first 100 fans — was equally keen to introduce them. Rowan recently said I embarrassed him with my opening line, 'And this is Rowan Atkinson — *he's* a comedian, too.'

I remember the occasion vividly because there was my father in one chair telling Rowan he must have a go at being a comedian, and Rowan seated opposite explaining that he wasn't totally sure it was the career he wished to embark upon. 'You've got youth on your side,' went on my father. 'Just think how disappointed you would feel if, at 50 years of age, you look back at the comics of *your* time knowing damn well you could have been better. Frustration alone would be enough to kill you!' The rest, as they say, is history. Not that I'm claiming my father influenced the young would-be — I don't think anyone truly influences Rowan — but it amuses me that this uncertain comic has gone on to become arguably Britain's top comic, so underlining my father's sentiment.

Eric wouldn't have had much time for today's comedians — not because he had grown particularly embittered towards anything new or outside his own generation. He just simply wouldn't have understood today's comedians. His black-and-white attitude is perhaps at its most apparent when dealing with comedy. If comedy was hard or crude, he couldn't bear it, any of it. I have to say that with the exception of, maybe, Victoria Wood, there isn't a comedian today he would have admired. He liked pure entertainment from comedy, not trends or intellectuals. He would certainly have considered comedy in serious decline.

By the end of the 1980s he was often remarking that we would eventually be a nation of sitcom programmes and watchers. I suppose he wasn't too far wrong.

Another memory that almost rivals that of our football outings in Luton, would be trips to the studios to watch Eric and Ernie recording their shows. I don't mean the final recording, which usually took place in front of an invited audience on the Sunday evening, but the Saturday recordings — extras to be inserted into the main body of the show the following day. Some of the best dance routines were recorded on these Saturdays and I'd happily sit behind the cameras and technicians with a school chum or whoever, watching it all happen, oblivious to the fact that I was witnessing the making of British entertainment history.

For some inexplicable reason — maybe it was because he was in the environment in which he felt most at ease — my father was even more fatherly during these recording sessions than he was at home. He'd drift over between shots to have a joke and chuckle — usually at my expense, for the family always played Ernie's straightman when the cameras weren't rolling — then get back on with the job in hand. And Ernie, too, would be ever so chatty and bubbly and inquisitive.

Eric and Ernie had a remarkable relationship. Unlike so many comedy pairings, they actually liked each other. I can only think it relates to the fact that they were childhood friends before they embarked on the double-act. There were clearly foundations in place, which put them in good stead for the struggles and joys that were to follow. There was never any unpleasantness behind the scene — they shared everything 50-50 on the strength of a handshake.

It's likely that Eric would have been better suited to a solo career than Ernie, but the combination of the two was better than anything either could have achieved and sustained as an individual. He always told my mother that he had no regrets, no thoughts that maybe if he'd gone on alone from the beginning he would have had *all* the glory and *all* the riches. He rated Ernie as the world's greatest straightman and, in his own words, would say, 'I'm not part of an act called Morecambe and that-fellow-he-works-with.' In terms of professionalism and conduct, theirs was the ultimate double-act. What I find so fascinating is that Eric Morecambe never told jokes — not even in the *Morecambe and Wise* shows. He made humour out of conversations and situations and out of Ernie's fallibility — the greatest writer 'wot' England has ever seen, and so on. That was his gift, and a rare one by half, for it is that much harder to force a reaction in this way than by reiterating a funny story that will always retain some of its humour whoever tells it.

The biggest strain on my relationship with my father surprisingly emerged from a mutual interest — that of writing. Since reading Alistair MacLean's *When Eight Bells Toll*, at the age of 15, I knew I wanted to be a full-time writer, come what may. My first published work was, no prizes for guessing, a collection of anecdotes about my father entitled *Funnyman*. He was a great help, not only giving me his time and effort, but accompanying me on the promotional tour, the highlight of this being a joint appearance on the late Russell Harty's show, transmitted live from Manchester. We went for a stroll past the Odeon cinema near the studios, originally a theatre where he had seen Ernie — though not to talk to — for the very first time. Surprisingly, he didn't show any sense of nostalgia — he was never an over-sentimental type. It was more a case of, 'And that's where Ernie and I first saw each other,' then on to the next thing. The minor conflict or rivalry regarding writing books was that he finally got his first book published in 1981, pre-empting my first publication by just one year. In many ways that was fine and it gave us a whole new subject matter that we would spend hours debating. The down side was that I'd seen it as my one creative avenue, one that wouldn't clash with his. Although always creative, I'd never had the genuine desire to perform, certainly not comedy, and so I figured that I would be the writer in the family. Of course, from a publisher's point of view, a comic legend handing them a couple of manuscripts a year is more viable than his young son doing likewise. It was second fiddle time — most frustrating. Entirely *not* the fault of my father I must add, who had to do what he had to do, but an unfortunate finale to the culmination of a happy-go-lucky upbringing, for a definite mood developed and lingered between us on the subject and what had begun as a mutual interest became something to be discussed competitively or, better still, avoided in conversation altogether.

In a general sense, he remained supportive of my writing career. It was his publishers, Methuen, who had, after all, taken on my first book, and my father himself who, interested or not, was willing to be my subject knowing it would help both on the sales and promotional fronts.

He also made the book a good deal more exciting than it would have otherwise been by allowing me to include some letters we'd written to each other at the end of each chapter. These appeared in the final manuscript for publication.

For the most part he kept the mood jokey, but occasionally he would turn serious, giving a clear example of how important it was to him that he retained an untarnished image:

13, Hardluck Street,
C/O Leaveoff, Leggo, Shurrup & Stoppit
Strangeways.

Dear Son,
Having read your first chapter, I can see that the million and a half pounds I spent on your education wasn't entirely misplaced. I was thrilled to see that you could spell 'Morecambe' the right way. Most people spell it wrong, these are just a few ways 'Morecombe' 'Morcom' 'Morecomb' 'Morkum'. As a matter of fact, in America, they pronounce it 'Morycamby and Wise'. And in an African paper they called us, 'Eric More — Camby and Erine Wise'. Another paper called us, 'Eric Morcum and Rene Rice'. But we've learned to live with it. The late Ed Sullivan once announced Jewel and Warriss as 'Jewels and his Walrus' ... honestly. However!
I liked most of what I read, already I've become very fond of the hero. But you must be careful what you say about other people, you mustn't hurt anyone's feelings, after all, it's supposed to be a happy book, not a 'True Britt'. Some of the people you mention are my friends, and I would like

them to stay that way.

Yours. Etc. ...

I recently read in an article that there may have been a Hancockian streak within Eric Morecambe, a morbidness, an innate sadness. This is utterly preposterous. I can honestly say I've never known anyone as self-assured and as continually effervescent as my father. But then, as time goes by, people like to scrutinise their icons and cannot settle for the simple truths or explanations. They have to engineer a dark side, some inkling of pain, the flawed genius type of thing. The truth was that, even when worried or uptight, he still retained a positive frame of mind and an air of control, such was his inner strength and self-confidence. Much of this would relate to the fact that Morecambe and Wise, the act, was on a steady upward rise from the mid-1950s — the time I appeared on the scene — so, although huge stress would accompany the success, it was hardly the stress of where the next meal was coming from. His career was positive, so he could be positive.

Ironically, it was in his last year, 1984, that I witnessed one of the lowest points in his working life. Morecambe and Wise had long wanted to make another film, something that was better and went further than their previous three outings for Rank during the 1960s. Part of the reason they left the BBC for Thames Television in 1978, was because Thames could offer them a film deal. That film was to be shot in 1983 and entitled, *Night Train to Murder*. It was a dire effort due to several reasons, not least the script and lack of pace. It was almost a parody of their own music hall days, all wrapped up in a Hammer House of Horror-type murder package.

Morecambe and Wise had always worked best to a live audience. Much of their humour was based on their audiences' reaction. On the big screen there are no natural laughs, just pauses.

When he saw a preview of *Night Train* in 1984 — just prior to his sudden fatal heart-attack — it brought him down so much that one was left wondering if Morecambe and Wise would continue.

There were two further ironies to this sad episode. First, my father wasn't alive by the time it was transmitted later that year (during Childrens' programming). Second, it did rather better than expected, selling quite well in Europe.

By the 1980s, shortly before his death, he was expressing boredom and exhaustion with the effort and commitment of being Britain's top funnyman. In particular, he was bored with carrying the burden of being the one who, in the final analysis, made or broke each show. One or two cracks were beginning to appear.

There was a paucity of outstanding material in their latter work for Thames Television and a lack of enthusiasm even to work on the scripts and go to rehearsals. The 1983 Christmas Show, their last recorded work, was a mish-mash of their BBC routines. They couldn't hope to score well down that particular avenue with material that wasn't wholly original and with two guys performing it ten years older than when they had first performed it. All they were achieving was to accentuate the cruelty of the ageing process. On top of all this, my father's health had been worsening for some time. In almost any other profession he would have retired five years prior to 1983, when he'd had his second heart-attack.

Tired of the demands of comedy, he wanted to turn his hand to writing novels. He had certainly verbally expressed that much to me and on more than one occasion. After 43 partly gruelling, partly glorious years, it was as simple as that — he'd just about worn himself out and there was virtually nothing left to give to sustain the act. The most he would eventually consider would be Christmas specials.

During his final months, he was back to his perky self again, looking for new challenges, making public appearances, and he was making a serious effort to improve his health. He stopped the pipe and the cigars, gave up alcohol — which was something he had done on and off quite successfully over the previous three years — and went on a remarkably strict diet that I, for one, didn't anticipate him sticking to, but he did. Maybe it was a case of too much too late.

The moment of ultimate tragedy came when I received a phone call from Tewkesbury at about 11pm on the Sunday of that May Bank Holiday weekend. It was his chauffeur, Mike Fountain, saying my father had suffered a heart-attack and this time it looked really bad.

I knew at once how bad it was because my father had told me that one more attack would kill him. He had a tendency to be right when it came to matters pertaining to himself and/or Morecambe and Wise, so I had little to comfort me during the long night ahead. He died shortly before 4am, and so began a long period of mourning, enhanced and made public by the focus of the media. Even in death we were having to share him again.

It's strange to hear myself say it, but I didn't grow up, become my own person, until he died. Both he and I hadn't been conscious that I'd been living in the shadow of his comic legend, but I suppose it was inevitable that I should have been — after all, he himself was living in that shadow to a large degree.

Although I was 28 at the time, the day my father died my childhood ended. That may sound odd, but I was a 28-year-old going on 18 in many ways. I'd never had to struggle or fend for myself. My simple analogy is to explain my situation as someone with a gun pointed to their head knowing it's only loaded with blanks. I was never going to be in any serious discomfort while his actual presence was there.

Once he'd gone that metaphoric gun had become loaded with live ammo, and I went from 28 to 40 overnight. My final ascent into adulthood came when I moved my family to France in 1989. This was, in part, a deliberate move to escape everything associated with Eric Morecambe. Our two-and-a-half years in France gave me breathing time. It gave me the rare opportunity to assess and mentally relive parts of my childhood and, in a calm, methodical sort of way, examine what the long journey had been all about so far and what, if anything, it amounted to. At the same time my wife and I were expanding our own family, building our own independent unit that again was further establishing an identity away from just being Eric Morecambe's son.

How paradoxical that it should all have culminated in my return to England in 1991 and my active involvement in Morecambe and Wise. But then, I suppose, I'd had the sabbatical I'd so wanted — and needed — and returned a wiser and sharper figure, with a bizarre and inexplicable desire to perpetuate and control Morecambe and Wise.

The greater part of the good-old-me had most definitely died in France, but I'm not so sure that's such a terrible thing. I needed to become focused. Right up to my father's death, he had been concerned about my lack of focus, my glum lack of certainty regarding almost everything. I always remember what my father said about his own father. 'The reason no one ever had a bad thing to say about him is because he never put himself in a position where he had to rock the boat, where he had to be judged.' I'd always thought that a harsh thing to say about kindly George, but now I understand what he meant.

Living with Eric Morecambe, I had been much the same. If he said jump, then I'd jump. I simply smiled and said the things that people wanted to hear. I wanted to please and I wanted to be liked through pleasing. Then, surely, I would be a success in my own right? Of course, all that inevitably achieves is that you become put-upon by just about every single person you come into contact with.

People tell me now I'm the double of my father, and down the years I've certainly tended to take on his looks more than my mother's. Even today, countless are the times my mother calls me Eric, before quickly correcting herself, which I don't mind at all. In fact, I'm flattered.

However, I think my father and I differ as middle-aged adults. Not so much from the humour stand-point — I think we laughed at the same things for the most part. But I'm the grey area to complement his black and white. Also, I know for a fact that I couldn't have endured those years of board-treading struggle or, conversely, being the focus of attention as he did and reflect back on it all as being wonderful.

I think that I'm a marginally angrier person than he ever was, although I tend to keep it bottled up somewhere deep inside, and I've honestly never felt the urge to be a 'star', which to him was everything. Being a star meant all other aspects of his career were in working order, which is why you will find Morecambe and Wise turned down so little during their entire, long career. They thought it prudent continually to remind the public they were still there, joking around.

I know for sure that I'm better on the domestic front than my father ever was, particularly when it comes to looking after my own children, but then that's possibly a reflection on how society has changed as much as anything else.

I think the greatest thing my father left to his family is his popularity — the 'feel-good factor' as it's fashionable to call it. What had once had been no more than a mere way of life for him is now a terrific testament to the talent of a very funny gentleman.

I think Ernie Wise sums up his lifelong partner very nicely in the following comment: 'You could depend on Eric to get that audience laughing, because it just flowed from him. I don't know what one would say, it was almost like hyper-super tension inside him, and when he went on he was transformed and he was magic. And if in doubt, he fetched out the paper bag and did his trick with that, or he'd grab me and say, "My little fat friend," and, of course, the more nerves and tension he had, the harder he used to slap my face. I think we lost a person that, when you looked at him on television, you relaxed, smiled and felt everything was all right with the world. And that applied to the whole family. He actually was part of everyone's family.'

My father admired longevity as though it were a decoration to be won and worn, and when he therefore joked that his ambition was to be at the next centenary Test at Lord's, it was in reality only a half joke. Although he had doubts about his health, I do believe he felt he would live through to old age.

It saddens me that my father died when he did. Whatever possible benefits that came my way as a direct or indirect result of his passing, are vastly outweighed by the sense of loss for a great father and comedian. He never for a moment stopped loving his family and we, in return, have never stopped loving him.

In my entire life, I have yet to meet a single person who doesn't still cheerfully recall something from the comedy of Morecambe and Wise, and surely that, along with his family's love and respect, is the greatest epitaph he could honestly wish for.

ROBERT MORLEY
ACTOR, (1908–1992)

During his long and active life, Robert Morley appeared in numerous films, stage plays and television shows, and during his later years showed a talent for writing highly amusing, anecdotal articles and books.

His first film appearance was as Louis XV1 in *Marie Antoinette* (1938) and co-starred Norma Shearer. His last film was *The Lady and the Highwayman* (1991).

Robert Morley was the first actor to play Oscar Wilde on stage and screen. His major movies include *Major Barbara, Beat the Devil, The African Queen, Gilbert and Sullivan, Around the World in 80 Days, Marie Antoinette* (Oscar nomination), *An Outcast of the Islands, The Doctor's Dilemma, The Young Ones, Those Magnificent Men in Their Flying Machines, Theatre of Blood, When Eight Bells Toll, The Human Factor*, and *Who Is Killing the Great Chefs of Europe?*

Long-running stage appearances include *The First Gentleman, The Man Who Came to Dinner, The Little Hut, Hippo Dancing, How the Other Half Loves, Banana Ridge* and *Halfway up a Tree.*

As well as being an acclaimed international actor, he was also renowned for his delightful wit and all-round ebullience, and often seen as a raconteur most ably equipped to extol the virtues of good food and drink — a passion equalled only by the racecourse and the roulette wheel.

The following contribution is from Robert's eldest son, Sheridan, who is a drama critic. Sheridan, who is 54, started out as a newscaster for ITN and as an interviewer for *Late Night Line Up* before going on to *The Times* and then *Punch* where he was arts editor and drama critic for twelve years. He currently hosts ITV's *London Stage*, and the *Radio 2 Arts Programme* every Saturday. He has written many biographies including the first of Noel Coward, *The Other Side of the Moon*, of David Niven and, more recently, of Audrey Hepburn. He is literary adviser to the Coward Estate, and is currently working on the authorised biography of Sir John Gielgud. He has three adult children, Hugo, Alexis and Juliet, and lives in Chelsea with his second wife, Ruth Leon.

SHERIDAN MORLEY:

People always assume I was called Sheridan because of the eighteenth-century playwright. Although I became a drama critic, the real reason for the name was that the night I was born in December 1941, my father was opening in a play called, *The Man Who Came to Dinner*, a Broadway hit comedy by Kaufman and Hart. The character in the play is called Sheridan Whiteside, based on a very famous American journalist called Alexander Wolcott who was a sort of combination of Baz Bamigboye and Malcolm Muggeridge.

Thirty years later my son, Hugo, was born when Robert was opening in another play called, *Half Way up the Tree*. The character in the play was called Sir Hugo, and so two generations were born on first nights of Robert's plays and took their christian names for that reason.

I had a very comfortable childhood. Robert was very easy-going. There's a great fashion now for 'agony' books by actors' children. Everyone in the Redgrave family does it, a lot of American actors' children do it. Apparently, Bogart's son has just done likewise in America. I can't claim any of that. Robert wasn't that kind of actor. I think if you're the child of an actor who is very intense or very narrowly dedicated to the business, or very neurotic or nervous, then it must be pretty fair hell being an actor's child.

I had an easy ride, as Robert was the kind of man who would have been equally happy running a big hotel or a casino. He didn't regard acting as intensely intellectual or personally traumatic, the way actors nowadays appear to in describing the agony of the business.

I believe, however, that Robert was a wonderful actor, although it was more a job that he enjoyed hugely and did to his best ability. He was an instinctive, natural actor and, what's more, he came from a generation where the actors were very much in charge. It was he who would hire the playwright, the director and the theatre. So he was much more in control and in charge, and therefore more secure than the actor now who is constantly at the mercy of being hired and fired by difficult people.

Robert's career was often a mystery to critics, but never more so than to himself. It was guided not by any theatrical, cinematic or intellectual principle, but by the ring of the telephone and the offer of a job. On the racecourse he tended to side with the trainers, but to understand the jockeys best — after all, they, too, had to get on whatever horse came down the track and ride it as best they could, if not always to victory then at least seldom to total defeat. If his later career did degenerate into a catalogue of minor movies, the trick, as he understood it, was to hang on and keep going.

He had few pretensions about himself or his work. In later years he tended to view the theatre as having got rather too solemn and certainly very introverted.

To Robert, the public was always right. As far as he was concerned they could arrive late, they could eat cheeseburgers through the first act, they could talk among themselves, they could leave and never come back, they could cough or lay out their shopping on the floor — they were his customers and they could do no wrong. If they chose not to come, it was in no way their fault — it was the fault of the play, or of him, or of the theatre, but never the public.

It is very different today. Now every actor complains about the audience. They're too small, or they're too unintelligent, or they don't understand, or they aren't sympathetic.

Actors hardly ever tour now. You base yourself in London, you work at whatever, you may go to Stratford or Chichester, but basically it's a London life. Robert's life was quite different. He would start a play in Blackpool or Manchester and he would travel to virtually every town that had a theatre. I'm talking about the 1930s, 1940s, 1950s and into the 1960s. He would often do a year on the road before he got the play to the West End.

Consequently, he was away quite a bit during my childhood. In those days, though, the man was the breadwinner and not particularly expected to be involved with the domestic side of changing nappies, and so on. One has to be careful because the world has changed. I'm 54. Robert was about 30 when I was born. So people say, 'Was he a caring parent?' and I tell them that the phrase hadn't been invented. It's like saying, 'Was he good with microwaves?'

In that sense, the modern sense, he wasn't a caring parent. But he was an immensely loving father and the idea then of a father being home with a baby, even in my own generation I have to say, just wasn't expected. Having said that, if we were on school holidays he would always take us with him. The truth is, we were at school much of the time so we were conditioned for long spells of separation.

He wasn't into parenting. He believed that his children were indeed his responsibility as far as clothing and feeding and providing a roof over their heads until they were about 18. What they went on to do with their lives wasn't his problem. He was interested — it wasn't as though he was irresponsible. Indeed, he was intrigued by what we did, but he had absolutely no interest in conditioning us to be or to do something specific. If I had said I was going to be a market gardener or an astronaut or an actor, he would have said, 'Very nice, dear. Get on with it, good luck.'

In much later life, he summed up his own parenting in a piece he wrote: 'I'm not sure how I'd rate myself as a father nowadays. Not good, perhaps; much too wrapped up in myself. Loving, certainly, but never much of an influence. My son in Australia once told Alan Whicker on a television programme that he'd really only gone to escape his father and his elder brother, which shocked us both a bit when we saw it, but I suppose we have both been rather noisy. I also have a daughter now living in Sydney. I'm afraid that if you're an actor and an egomaniac and a show-off, as I am, then perhaps you don't make a perfect parent. But my wife has been a wonderful mother to them all, still is; I think perhaps I was a bit of a bore to them.'

On the contrary, he seemed to me a wonderful father, generous and funny, and supremely undidactic. But he never really had the faintest idea what a father was supposed to do, which in my view is what made him so marvellous and such a great companion. He was the most unpaternalistic but most genial of parents, and one cannot ask much more than that. At least, I hope my children cannot either.

Robert had come through the 1930s during which he'd had a big success on stage with *Oscar Wilde*. He had gone to Hollywood in 1937 when he was only about 30 to make *Marie Antoinette* with John Barrymore. While at sea on his way to America to make that film, Robert was to have one of his few premarital affairs, this one with a married lady who seems to have initiated him into some of the mysteries of sex, according to a piece he wrote many years later: 'It's a club, you know, and a sort of secret society. Either you are a born member or you are not, and somehow I don't think I ever was. I was scared of disease, conception, involvement, retribution and above all else my own physical incompetence. To be a member of the club one must have no such fears, one must believe in sex as a way of life, just as some people believe in fame or money. I never could, and if it is not your way of life, then it's not the faintest use trying to understand the rules of the sex club. You can either thank God you never joined, or wish to heaven that you could. After a time, you get to the age when there's not much you can do about it either way.'

Having never made a film before, he got the Oscar nomination. They asked him if he wanted to stay and play the Hunchback of Notre Dame, which Charles Laughton did. Robert said, 'I don't think so; California's not really for me. I'm English and I want to work in the theatre.' So he came back to London, met my mother and married.

My first big trip with my father was almost immediately after the War. I was about six; my sister, Annabel, was barely born and my brother, Wilton, wasn't.

After the War, he had a huge success with a play called *Edward My Son* which he wrote, played the lead and virtually directed. Because of this he got the offer to go to Broadway, and us, the children, went along with our parents.

We lived in a New York apartment for the year of 1947. A great friend I made there and still have is Johnny Lahr, who is the son of Bert Lahr, the cowardly lion in *Wizard of Oz*. He's the drama critic of the *New Yorker*. He lives in London and is married to Connie Booth, John Cleese's former wife.

I was educated in New York for that year and we had a nanny who looked after us, although Ma was, and is, very domestic, so Ma really looked after us.

We led there, as far as I can remember, a very domestic life. I know I was thrilled by the sight of falling snow — it simply hadn't snowed much at home during the war.

I was brought up in Wargrave, Berkshire, where my mother still lives today at the age of 85, and having not been to London, probably because it was the War, arriving in New York and seeing all those flickering coloured lights was indescribable. Then, a year on, Robert got the offer to take the play to Australia, so it was decided that rather than going back to England and ending up in Australia that way round, we would go the other way and via Hollywood, too, so that we could stay with my actress grandmother, Gladys Cooper.

We spent a wonderful three months with Gladys in California. I'd never seen that kind of sunshine. I'd never seen a swimming pool. And I'd never seen Greta Garbo who came for tea, and whom I found fascinating. That's one of my earliest memories — Garbo coming for tea, and Gladys saying, 'Such a useful little woman; she always does the washing up.' And then Dietrich came, and David Niven lived next door. That was a wonderful summer.

Then we moved on to Australia. We had about a year and a half there and in New Zealand and I went to school in every town. In those days, you would do six months Sydney, six Melbourne, so we were able to settle down for a bit. I'm glad we had the opportunity to travel and live abroad.

We returned to England in about 1950. My brother, Wilton, was born that year. My parents had to find me a school and my father famously put an ad in *The Times* saying that a parent with terrible memories of his own schooldays wanted somewhere for his son where the food was more important than the teaching. The people who answered ran a school at Sizewell, now better known for its nuclear plant.

Robert so hated school he could hardly bring himself to talk about it. It was like a pathological illness. He wanted only to talk about his views on the subject and couldn't bear having to speak with headmasters or deal with reports, so he just never mentioned it to us. Going away to start a new term was treated like having a bad dose of flu that had to be got over. Whenever my sister was unhappy at school she simply changed schools. It didn't actually help because she was just unhappy, so moving her around probably caused more upset.

He didn't have any alternative solution to school. He would reluctantly make the occasional appearance and give a speech at prize-giving day in which he'd always encourage the children to run away while they had the chance and generally lambast the place. At first this caused a bit of a stir, but as the staff grew used to him they came to expect the rhetoric.

Robert had been educated at Wellington. Wellington in the 1920s he'd found really barbaric. They made him do marching and join the military band, the sort of things he couldn't bear. He couldn't bear the food or the teaching or the people. He swore he'd never send his son to a school like that. So he was looking for an unorthodox school, and Sizewell was just that.

Sizewell was unusual but it was very, very friendly. I still have friends I made there. It was clearly easier than Wellington had been for my father, who had been a shy child. By the time I had got to know him he had become very outgoing and I had seen and learnt that so was never really shy myself. I think in some ways I'm not very emotional and I'm not very sensitive, so as a result wherever I am I've always been very happy.

From Sizewell the headmaster got me into Geneva University because I really wanted to go to Oxford and read French, and I had only about two 'A'-Levels and three or four 'O'-Levels. The headmaster brilliantly said that if I went to Geneva for a year and got a kind of diploma, that would so impress them at Oxford they wouldn't notice my lack of Maths 'O'-Level or whatever. So I did just that — went to Geneva at 17.

Geneva is about an hour away from England by plane, so I didn't suffer any homesickness. I think being at boarding-school from the age of eight had accustomed me to being away and I knew it was only for three terms.

As for going to Oxford, Robert thought it was a terrible waste of time, but he had no resentment at all. He would put his view across and it was down to you to say yes or no. If you disagreed he would say, fine, that's your own choice. He would say to people, 'I can't understand why Sheridan wants to go to Oxford; it's a really bizarre thing to do.' But we rarely had any animosity between us. He genuinely felt utter amazement that I would have chosen to go to Oxford. He was a benign man, though. I never really saw him angry as such. He visited me at Oxford from time to time and there was never a sense that, because we disagreed over the matter, contact would temporarily cease.

I think, too, that once we were 18 we were more or less considered as being off his hands. It's a rather old-fashioned belief, but he saw his parental duty more towards Annabel. Being a girl he felt he had to make sure she didn't get into trouble and that she got married to the right person and had a flat of her own to live in.

If I'd got into trouble or been arrested or something, certainly Robert would have been the first to be there and help, but I think it would literally only have been in that type of situation that he'd have thought, 'My God, I have to do something to help.'

After Oxford, I started in television. First, I went to Hawaii and ran their student theatre for a year. I met my first wife, Margaret, got married, and also met Bette Midler who was my star pupil. I taught her when she was 16 and what little she knows I think came from me. Then I returned home and joined ITN as one of their first-ever trainee newscasters. There was me and Peter Snow, and the newscasters were Andrew Gardner, Reggie Bosanquet and Huw Thomas. I was a newswriter for a while then they asked if I would like to be a newscaster, which I did. That lasted for about three years.

All during this time I was, of course, in touch with Robert, but I never announced I was his son and because I was thin in those days — well, thinner — they never asked.

It wasn't until I'd gone to *Late Night Line Up*, which I started with Joan Bakewell on BBC2 in 1967, that the connection was made. Robert was promoting a film or play, so we had him on as a guest. I did the interview and wrapped up at the end by saying, 'Well Pa, thank you very much and goodnight.'

People wrote in saying they'd had no idea. What was nice was that I had partly established myself beforehand, so I didn't have the problem of being Robert Morley's son Sheridan.

During Robert's run of *Halfway up the Tree* at the Queen's in May 1968, he decided to celebrate his 60th birthday in grand style. The idea was to charter two small planes and fly out from White Waltham airfield across the channel to Le Touquet. It was the time of the student uprisings and France had chosen that month to hold a national strike. However, undeterred, we flew into Le Touquet and had the entire town to ourselves for one magical Sunday, safely, if fadedly, recorded on some old home movies.

This was the last great gathering of the whole family for Robert and included four generations. Gladys was still very much in evidence for some reason, appearing on the film driving a go-cart at full speed through deserted French streets. There, as well, is Gladys's sister, Gracie, deaf from birth, but already a redoubtable old lady, and Gladys's daughter Sally, with her actor husband, Robert Hardy.

It was a strange and miraculous day and I'm glad it never occurred to me at the time that we'd be unable to repeat it. Within a few years two of the party were dead, and within a decade it would have been hard to assemble more than about half of us.

Briefly back to my career. I knew I wanted to write about the theatre because I knew the theatre and I'd worked at the Oxford Playhouse and the student theatre in Hawaii.

I don't think I could have trodden the boards in the manner of my father. I'd flirted with the idea, I suppose, when very young. There is also the point that Robert had beaten me to it. I was keen to do something where I could make a name for myself, bearing in mind my family had its fair share. My father, naturally, and my grandmother, Gladys and there was Robert Hardy who had accompanied us to Le Touquet — most vividly remembered for his role in the James Herriot series — who was married to my mother's sister.

I did work with Pa briefly. I played the little boy in *Edward My Son*. Not quite the same as my brother and sister who both appeared in films with him.

In truth, I don't think it was because of Robert or Gladys that I didn't act, but because I didn't think I was going to be very good. Also, I felt there was a kind of Catch-22 situation whereby if you're somebody's son and you go into the same business and do very well, they accuse you of nepotism and if you do badly, they are equally dismissive.

I won't mention any names, but there are some fairly frightening examples of actors' children who have gone very wrong, usually with drink or drugs, because the pressure was too great and they failed. When they fail you hear, 'Funny he's not doing better considering whose child he is.'

I couldn't see how to win, so I chose not to get caught up in that mess. I was lucky, too, because I knew from very early on that I could write, talk and broadcast about actors. I grew up with them. I'd been going to plays with my father from the age of ten.

I'm a critic now in my fifties and most of my generation of critics began going to the theatre in about 1960 when we were all at college. I began in 1950 so have had the opportunity to see more than them. That was my good luck — because of Robert and Gladys, I was able to have this extraordinary education in theatre. Anyway, I'm fairly sure that Robert wouldn't have wanted his son to be an actor like himself. Mind you, becoming a critic wasn't the greatest step as far as he was concerned. He said, 'It is like being the head of the Israeli army and waking up to discover your son's an Arab.'

Having said that, my father and I grew closer and closer as the years went by. I would say that overall you will find more of Robert in my brother, sister and my children than in me. Pa and I were so physically and superficially alike in so many ways and ambitions that we often tended to keep a wary distance as if afraid of crashing into each other. In our own rather inchoate and offhand way we loved each other very much and in later life took to hugging each other, often to the amazement of passers-by who would watch these huge men in a bear-like embrace and wonder what on earth was going on.

I think what was going on was the realisation, perhaps a little late in life, that we were never going to find the words to tell each other how much we mattered to each other's survival, or how happy we were to have ended up in the same family roadshow. Robert was always the leader of that, of course, even if he was at times slightly uncertain as to where he was leading us or himself to.

Who was my father? Trying to answer that question is not altogether easy. If there was a thin or tortured man within him trying to escape, he certainly didn't make it. With Robert, what you saw was essentially what you got. Any analysis of him by me, or even by himself, was hindered first by our inbuilt reluctance to examine ourselves too deeply for emotional or inherited scars, and second by his unspoken but total belief in the maxim: 'Never complain, never explain'.

We, therefore, took it for granted that nature in her wisdom had put us together as a father and son team and that we'd better just play the roles as best we could without getting too far upstage of each other or interrupting the other's best speeches, no matter how repetitious they had become.

I suppose Robert's most demonstrative moment was when I told him I was divorcing my first wife, Margaret. He was very fond of Margaret, but though he rather laid any blame at my feet, he didn't really reveal his disappointment and anger. The worst I can say is that there was a distinct chill in our relationship for a time. I was slightly annoyed that he wasn't more on my side, but it wasn't his style to take sides. With his generation you tended to press on with a bad marriage, whereas mine was the first to say, wait a minute, this isn't working. There is a point when you don't accept continuing for the sake of appearances. Mind you, I still don't understand how anyone with children under 13 could get divorced. I think that must be agony.

Robert's own parents stayed together relentlessly even though his father went off a lot. I was 48 when I divorced, and there isn't much a parent can tell a son by then and he certainly didn't. Never once did he say, 'You mustn't do this, Sheridan.' All he asked me was if I felt I was doing the right thing.

Being very fond of Margaret, he kept in good contact with her after we'd split. She still lives in the village next door to my mother and sees her a great deal. Because my sister went to live in Australia more or less at the time I married Margaret, she became a surrogate daughter to my parents — the daughter they had lost abroad.

Robert grew very close to my children, which was lovely in a way, because by the time my children came along we were living very close to my parents' home in Berkshire. Again, all the words one uses now — input, caring, hands-on — he wasn't any of that, but we spent great times together eating, drinking, gossiping and swimming. Particularly swimming. He was almost the first person to have his own pool built in Berkshire.

We also travelled together on occasion. The *Evening Standard* sent us to Russia circa 1970 to write about tourism out there. We had a lot of laughs doing that trip. In 1975, when I was made arts editor of *Punch* by Alan Coren, Robert became my food critic and wrote a hilarious column every week about restaurants concentrating on the diners more than the food.

He turned more and more to writing during the 1960s and 1970s as he became more estranged from the plays of the day. They were no longer his sort of plays and he gave up doing them in the end. At the beginning he'd been in charge of each production. Writing about food and travel became more fun than appearing in plays he no longer terribly liked.

By the time he realised that he and plays no longer complemented each other he was 60. Therefore, he thought, 'That's it! I've done my best. I've done a lot of good work.' He really had and the films were still around as proof. He continued to do television and he especially loved chat shows.

When Robert began doing the chat shows in the very early 1960s there was but one chat show in America run by a man called Jack Paar. This was before the days of Carson or Letterman or any of the lesser people. Paar was the chat show host pioneer out there, and our British equivalent was, I suppose, Eamon Andrews. Now what they didn't do was invite someone who had something specific to sell. No chance of promoting a book, a film or a play. You were paid a lot of money to do about 40 minutes of genuine conversation and they would take a topic (sport or education) and Robert would go out there and earn his money. It was hard work. It was he and Ustinov and Muggeridge who really pioneered all that.

Robert would talk about politics for 40 minutes. It wasn't very accurate and wasn't very researched and I think if you were a politician it would have probably annoyed you, but it was a wonderfully wide-ranging view. You get the same with John Mortimer. He can do 40 minutes on socialism. It hasn't much to do with Blair or the narrow concept of the Labour Party, but it's a view of socialism that is kind of intriguing as it takes in the whole spectrum. You can see a lot of Robert in John, and a lot of Robert in Ustinov, too.

Pa's close friends were mainly actors and writers, needless to say. Peter Bull was his lifelong friend, very much the same shape as Robert, and who often played Nazis in films.

Rex Harrison and Pa went back many, many years to drama school in the 1930s. They had done their first plays together in rep and they had done their first film together, which was *Major Barbara* with Wendy Hilliar in 1937. After that, Rex had gone to America and become a very different kind of elegant, silk dressing-gowned actor.

The day after Pa had been on *This Is Your Life*, we were walking through the Burlington Arcade off Piccadilly when we bumped into Rex. Rex said, 'Robert, my God, I saw that programme last night. It brought back all the memories of our childhood. Mind you,' he went on, 'I wouldn't have dared do it myself. But for you, Robert, since we left drama school your life has been so different. One wife, one house, one family, and if I may say so, one performance.' It was amusing coming from Rex who hadn't changed an eyebrow in forty years of filming.

Robert would never allow himself to be angered by a remark like that, he always kept in control of himself and could laugh things off. It probably accounted for his longevity.

We live in a sort of psychiatric generation and people say, my God he must have been holding back all kinds of things. I don't think he was. I just think Robert was of the generation who didn't really think very deeply about their emotions. His anger was for immediate things, such as physical pain caused by stubbing his toe. I never saw him really sad. My wife, Ruth, who lived in America for years, says this is because we are so English, so stiff-upper-lipped. Of course, she's right. Only when Pa died did I see Ma cry. That made it all the more agonizing in a way. As I said before, she is 85 and if you asked how she was feeling she'd look at you in amazement and say, 'I'm fine, aren't I? What do you think I'm feeling?' The concept of are you happy, are you unhappy, are you worried, are you angry, never entered their lives, possibly, again, because of the generation they came from. We all just got on with it.

It's only when you meet someone younger that they say, 'But how could you have lived in a household where people didn't get very emotional?' Pa's emotions went on to the stage much of the time, and I believe he saved it precisely for that. We all loved each other and got along well. But my sister has now lived in Australia for 25 years, my brother lives in Florida, so physically we can't be described as close. I see my mother every weekend and we hug and share a kiss, but we're not a demonstrative lot.

I was originally discussing Robert and his writing, which not only did he enjoy immensely but which became very important to him as he grew away from the theatre. The first book was *Robert Morley, Responsible Gentleman* written with his dear friend Sewell Stokes in 1966. Throughout the 1970s and 1980s he continued to write books as well as articles, publishing eleven different titles in total.

I think whenever I remember Robert, it is his warmth that comes to mind. He was like a big cuddly koala bear and he was eminently easy. The more I hear actors' and indeed singers' and comedians' children talking about their parents and their childhood, I think, my God, we were so lucky in our family to have a man who, in a funny way — and it's not a word I like because it is misunderstood — in the best sense was amateur. By this I don't mean he didn't do his best every night, eight shows a week. He never missed a matinee except when there was a race meeting and then he would plan in advance. He never had a night off for illness. He was, to his fingertips, professional about the business. But his attitude to it was like that of a great gambler or traveller — he didn't really want to spend a lot of time talking to critics or playwrights or directors or designers about the art of theatre. He didn't really believe in the art of the business. He believed in the business. He believed he was there to make money for himself and to give the audience a good time. One of his great phrases was, 'spare them the agony'. He meant two things by this. Don't do plays that are very serious or depressing and sombre, and let's give the audience a two-hour break from the problems that beset their own lives.

It is best put in the man's own words: 'I am now 68 and, if have learnt anything in a long life on the boards, it is that there is not really a very great deal to acting, beyond a certain audacity. I do it mainly for the lolly, but I'm no longer capable of learning new tricks; so directors are stuck with this resolute, elderly comedian. I see it as my job to entertain whoever turns up at the theatre that night, to make sure that everyone is comfortably seated and kept laughing for a couple of hours. It's much like being a waiter, without having to serve the food or worry about the tips: just save the audience from as much agony as possible while they're with you, that's what it's all about.'

This attitude is now very unfashionable. No actor today thinks they are there to give the audience a good time. Giving them a good time, however, is what Robert was about. It is what distinguished him in his working life.

Robert didn't totally drift into his final years as a writer. Indeed, towards the end of his life, the work started to perk up again. There were a few scenes in *Little Dorrit*, Christine Edzard's classic Dickens film, and then a major role as the Dimblebyesque war correspondent in *War and Remembrance*. This was a sequel to Herman Wouk's *The Winds of War*, and gave Robert nearly a year on locations from Singapore to Hawaii, and a spectacular death scene in the desert.

For his 80th birthday we took over a restaurant near his home and gathered as many as we could of the family. Not long after that came work on what would be his last two books *The Pleasures of Age*, and a travel book, *Around the World in Eighty-One Years*. He was also involved in a possible television series about life in the office of a theatrical agent, not a million miles from his own existence.

He had slowed down quite considerably by now. My one big regret is that in these last and for the most part, I think, very happy years of his life, I rather lost touch with him. Once my marriage with Margaret had ended, I left Berkshire and moved to London.

We still sat around the pool during the summer months like a couple of old water buffalo, wondering if we'd be better employed doing something more active and deciding that on the whole we would probably not. And we still met at his home every Sunday for our ritual lunch. As Robert wrote himself: 'At my age now there is a fatal temptation to count one's days: sometimes, playing with someone else's pocket calculator, I find myself trying to work out the number of seconds during which I have survived ... I do seem to have spent approximately 40,000 Sundays on earth. For the first 1,000 or so I went to church, only to be told I was a miserable sinner, though I was usually only miserable at having to be there. For the last 39,000 or so Sunday for me has meant luncheon rather than church ... I have always believed in a choice of sweets, have indeed all my life been something of a pudding man, training my family from an early age in how to behave when the sweet trolley comes around, only glancing at one's plate with mock astonishment when the waiter has filled it with a selection of at least three different desserts. For me the two most awful words in the English language have always been "just coffee".'

He remained as uncertain about my choice of career as the day when I'd told him what I wanted to be. I think he wondered how anyone could possibly bear to go on reviewing plays, films, books and so on for a whole working lifetime. On occasion, I did try to point out that it was perhaps not that different from the life of an actor, although admittedly less creative.

Once we did an entire *Parkinson* together, which ended with Robert reciting the whole of Kipling's *If* from memory. Quite staggering. On another occasion, his last in front of a live audience, we turned up together for a platform performance on the Cottlesloe stage of the National Theatre to sell a couple of our books and generally relive the past years. That was near the end of September 1991, and backstage at the National I noticed, for the first time, how drawn and thin he was beginning to look, and how fragile it appeared to make him. He was concerned about his hearing-aid letting him down, so I promised him I'd repeat any missed questions. He seemed oddly unreassured, almost frightened of doing what he'd always done best. It then struck me that he didn't want to appear before an audience ever again.

Overall he was satisfied that none of his children had been that much trouble to him, other than the inevitable short-lived emotional or financial crises. After he had died, and much to my delight, I found a letter he had written from Australia to my mother some years earlier saying how much he had enjoyed and admired a hardback collection of my theatre reviews that I'd presented him with to help him sleep on the plane.

He became a celebrity guest at various functions and was never going to go quietly into that good night. On one of his last American book-signing tours he had almost had himself removed from the air after memorably destroying Bob Hope's defence of the Vietnam War while sitting beside the old comic and at home he continued to fight smaller campaigns, notably against the destruction of the local cinema, and in favour of a golf course being built next to his house by some old farmer friends.

'If life is a party,' Robert said during his last full year of life, 'I really should be leaving quite soon. After all, one doesn't want to outstay one's welcome; I'll just collect my shroud at the door and be off.'

In May 1992 we celebrated his 84th birthday and, for the first time in many a long year, were gathered around the table of a restaurant in Sonning my parents, my children and their mother, and Ruth Leon, with whom I had been sharing my life in London for the past four years. It was a joyous occasion, the first Sunday of summer on which it was possible to eat outdoors. Pa seemed genuinely delighted to have the clan gathered around him. This meant a great deal to me after an unhappy divorce, so much, in fact, that I think I was keen not to notice the signs that struck me later when my photographs taken on the day were developed, of Robert smiling, certainly, but also looking very grey, tired and drawn.

A few days later I was in New York. As the plane landed back in London, Ruth and Alexis were there to meet me at the airport. Even before they could speak, I knew at once why they'd come.

On that particular Sunday, my parents had been due to go to Margaret's for lunch. At around noon, Robert decided he felt just too tired and would take it easy at home, stay in bed and read the papers. During lunch, Joan and Hugo wondered that, if Robert were spending the day in bed, he may want to have the television upstairs with him. Hugo and Joan drove back to carry it up to the bedroom. When they arrived back, they found Robert slumped across the bed, having suffered a massive stroke. He died three days later having never regained consciousness.

I'm not into ghosts or that sort of thing, but something strange occurred shortly after Robert had died. I was doing a show of my own about Vivian Ellis who wrote *Bless the Bride*, and it was closing that night and it just so happened that I was the last person in the theatre. I was walking across the stage to go out the stage door and lock it when I heard Robert talking to the audience about himself. I've never had visions or extra-sensory experiences; I can't even tell you what exactly he was saying. But suddenly his voice was crystal clear and I knew it was Pa. It only happened that once — nothing remotely like it has happened since.

Ruth would say, and she has before now, that this is all so bloody English and clenched, and that I've spent most of my time talking about Robert and avoided the main issue. Ruth feels that everything I am, and everything I'm not, is due to Pa, and that neither of us ever really bothered to work out a relationship.

Why am I unable to deliver the filial goods when it is now so fashionable? Why, when I stare in the bathroom mirror every morning and see my father staring back, is he still not telling me anything of great psychological import about either him or me, let alone the two of us together?

Pa basically got bored of fatherhood. He was the only man I have known to catch the Trans–Siberian Railway as an escape from boredom rather than an invitation to ten days of it and there was deep inside him, I believe, a real terror of the family he so loved. Happy enough when leading us into restaurants or watching us splash around in his swimming pool, he would all at once remember that there was a world elsewhere and that fatherhood was never going to be quite as much fun as roulette.

Naturally, I was conditioned by him. For a start, he conditioned me to run away from any really emotional situation, to believe that loving a family was the same as looking after them, to know that my only real talent was for living on my wits, and that therefore I had to be careful to keep them about me, not allowing them to be interfered with by those who would wish to get too close. He taught me, by example rather than by conversation, that we were temperamentally observers as opposed to participants, and that in the end work was likely to be more fun than fun, provided we always found work we enjoyed and then made them pay for that.

I suppose if I never really found Robert on a psychological basis, I also never lost him except once, when I allowed my emotional life temporarily to paralyse me and he looked on in mild paternal astonishment at the lack of professionalism that had allowed me to put my life in front of my work when there were still children to educate and a family to feed. As always, it wasn't discussed as such, because we didn't discuss anything important that might lead to trouble or keep us from lunch.

Robert never scared me or bored me or tried to make me anything I hadn't already become by heredity or education or accident or desire. If

I disappointed him, he never told me. Yes, in our own clenched and curious way we loved each other very much.

Lynn Redgrave is 18 months younger than me and, like me, grew up backstage as the child and grandchild of actors. Unlike me, she had chosen to spend some 20 years in America, and is therefore accustomed now to a certain amount of soul-searching: indeed, there are moments when her autobiographical stage show hovers dangerously between theatre and therapy. But along the way, starting from the appalling and appalled discovery that Michael did not even note her birth in his detailed daily journal, she does at least begin to define the problem of being an actor's child, for Michael, of course, was one of us, too.

It's what they all were; just actors. Fatherhood was one of Robert's longer-lasting engagements, but he had to act that, too. I only hope he enjoyed the performance as much as I always did — for I was not only Pa's eldest child, but also his travelling audience, and it was a long and very happy tour with no more than a few bad houses along the way.

LORD OLIVIER
ACTOR, (1907–1989)

Laurence Olivier is generally regarded as the greatest actor of the twentieth century and was also a distinguished director. He was for many years associated with the Old Vic theatre and was director of the National Theatre company from 1962–73. The Olivier Theatre, part of the National Theatre complex on the South Bank, is named after him. He was knighted in 1947 and given a life peerage in 1970 'for services to the theatre' — the first time an actor had been ennobled.

His many classical stage roles included *Henry V, Hamlet, Richard III* and *Othello*. Other notable stage appearances included appearing with Noel Coward and Gertrude Lawrence in *Private Lives* and creating the role of Archie Rice in John Osborne's *The Entertainer*.

Olivier's film versions of *Henry V* and *Richard III*, in which he starred and also produced and directed, are regarded as the most consummate examples of Shakespeare on film. His other film appearances included *Wuthering Heights, Rebecca, Pride and Prejudice, Spartacus, Oh, What a Lovely War, Sleuth* and *Marathon Man*.

Laurence Olivier was awarded an honorary Academy Award in 1979 'for the full body of his work, for the unique achievements of his entire career and for his lifetime of contribution to the art of film.' His last role was as Harry Burrard in Granada TV's adaptation of J B Priestly's

Lost Empires in 1986.

Laurence Olivier was married three times: to Jill Esmond, Vivien Leigh and Joan Plowright.

The following contribution is from Richard Olivier, Laurence Olivier's son from his marriage to the actress Joan Plowright. He is a theatre director, author, teacher of acting and workshop leader. He founded Wild Dance Events to produce conferences and workshops on ritual, mythology and gender issues. His first book, *Shadow of the Stone Heart*, about his relationship with his father and his journey through the men's movement, was published by Pan Books in June 1995.

Richard has two younger sisters and one older half-brother from his father's first wife. He lives in London with his wife, Shelley, and two children, Alessandra and Troy.

Roger and Christian Moore.

Gary Morecambe with his parents.

p: Gary and Gail Morecambe with their parents and brother, Steven.

low: Eric and Gary Morecambe.

Robert and Sheridan Morley.

Lord Olivier and Richard.

Scott and Peter Stringfellow.

er and Michael Sellers and family.

Norman and Nick Wisdom.

RICHARD OLIVIER:

Generally, I wasn't aware that my upbringing should have been anything other than it was, but during the first seven years of my life my father was running the National Theatre full-time, and only stopped when he became ill with cancer.

The first time I saw *Wuthering Heights* was on television, one Christmas. Dad went out the room to drink port with uncles and aunts, coming back occasionally to peep around the door from time to time. At the end of the film, he came in with a 'Well, what did you think?' type expression, and I said, 'Daddy, you had black hair.' I think he was rather disappointed that this was the full weight of my reaction to his performance.

My basic feeling during much of my childhood was that there was this mysterious figure around the house, called Dad, who was at this magical place, called 'the theatre', which was situated in this far-away city, called London.

We were living in Brighton, my parents having made a conscious decision to move there so we wouldn't be so bothered by the Press, wouldn't be forever in the spotlight and around the theatrical scene. They were making a sacrifice, moving out of the area where they worked in order to protect us. From our point of view, they were away in London several nights a week playing and rehearsing while we stayed in this big house in Brighton looked after by nannies and housekeepers.

The first effect that Dad had on me, therefore, is more to do with his absence rather than his presence. Mum was around much more, but again she had her commitments, indeed her primary commitment was naturally to my father, to help him get the National Theatre off the ground. They both passionately believed in it, so they had a cause that they were both driven to serve, which took them out of the house and away from us. It was not until I was older that I developed a 'normal' relationship with them.

By the time I was born in 1961, my father had already covered a major part of his career. He had done so much that I could never be a part of or really know about — living in bigger houses, dining at home with Winston Churchill, two previous marriages, and many, many other things that would drop into conversation and that served only to make a great part of him a total stranger to me because of the age discrepancy. He was 54 when I was born.

He was basically ill-equipped to be a father. When his first son, Tarquin, was born he left his mother within a year. He always felt his first wife had become pregnant in order to try to keep the marriage together. He may have resented the responsibility of parenthood. He wasn't able to have children with Vivien Leigh, but there came a time later in his life when he did want a family.

At the age of 54, he was pretty set in his ways and at the peak of his profession, so it wouldn't have been easy for him to stop and enjoy us. He did what he could, though. I remember he'd come home at night and rub our backs to put us to sleep. I used to wait up for that.

But I'd missed out on his strength. By the time I was seven he had contracted cancer, so after that he could never really play any sports. Much of what I had to work through was related to his age, obsessive work habits and being Laurence Olivier, our most acclaimed actor.

Most holidays were at the houses of friends. We spent time at Franco Zefferelli's place in Positano and at William Walton's home in Ischia. Even on holiday, Dad would spend much of his time with his nose in a script. These times were strange for us kids, because you were in someone else's elegant home, not geared up for football in the living-room. We were genuinely well catered for and certainly never pushed out the way as if we were an intrusion. We could hardly have hung out at Butlin's with Dad — not without getting mobbed.

On one great holiday in Corfu, Dad had rented a motor boat and we pottered around the coast. It was brilliant; he and my mother were there the whole time with no distractions or excuses.

Other times together included the occasional football match. I remember a frightening moment when I was seven or eight, and we'd gone with Dickie Attenborough to see Chelsea play. We were in the directors' box, and Dad and Dickie marched out at the end not waiting for the ground to clear. Suddenly, part of the crowd surrounded them asking for autographs. Being small, I was soon pushed away from them. I found myself on the edge of this curb outside Stamford Bridge, trying to look over this sea of heads to spot my Dad.

My father wasn't a hobbies man, though he tended towards gardening at the end of his life. He'd built up an impressive garden at Notley Abbey when married to Vivien Leigh and he had this little country cottage in the middle of Sussex and suddenly started sculpting gardens round it. It ended up being lovely, but there were times when he got carried away. He tried to turn it into a mini-estate. It was something he could do on an irregular basis, but it was no substitute for the gap left by having little work during the autumn of his life. Interests, including the piano and painting, were taken up until work came along and then he'd drop them.

Many people are able to tell me things about Dad that I didn't know, but that's part of any son coming to terms with any father. After a parent has died, people who knew them tell you stories that give other angles to them. In the case of off-spring of well-knowns, people tend to remember the stories more and they're eager to share them. It is a claimed association of sorts.

My education was a fairly stable experience. As with the home in Brighton, my parents were keen to have a certain amount of security for us. I went to three schools before arriving at Bedales, aged ten, and I stayed there until I was eighteen. There was an earlier school that I didn't much care for, but I was sent there because I needed discipline. I have since worked out that the reason I required discipline was because I was reacting to my parent's absences.

It was an all-boys school run by an old colonel with a cupboard full of canes and I was terrified. Four years later, I emerged a nice polite boy. And slightly damaged. The disciplinarian attitude reinforced the sense that you should not say what you truly feel — keep the stiff upper lip.

I cannot claim that my arrival at Bedales was affected by who my father was. Boys of 10 tend not to be overly conscious of parents and I never felt additional pressure. I had a choice of being at home with a houseful of women paid to look after me, or being at school where I could make male friendships. The latter won out, only because the former was too frustrating.

If you are a working actor you're going to be away at night. You are going to disappear from four in the afternoon until around midnight. Sometimes we'd go to London, watch rehearsals, and hang out backstage, but not regularly; perhaps because Dad didn't want us to follow in his footsteps. He said the business was very much about talent, luck and being in the right place at the right time. Two of those things you have little control over, therefore it wasn't something he'd wish his children to do.

He usually left his character at the theatre, but I recall when he was doing *Long Day's Journey Into Night*, he would walk into the house and switch all the lights off. His character was obsessed about saving electricity, but generally he didn't bring his characters home. He was an 'outside-in' actor; a mask he would put on when he was in the rehearsal room or on stage, and then take off. I think his trouble was that he knew those masks better that he knew himself. That was his personal dilemma. He could manufacture characters who were totally believable to an audience, but he couldn't get to grips with the man beneath.

A great friend of my father's was Peter Hiley who he met in Australia back in the 1940s. I occasionally see Peter and we talk over the old days. Once Peter said to me that Dad was an ordinary man with an extraordinary talent and that part of his problem was he felt his ordinariness most of the time. When he was meeting other extraordinary talents who were also extraordinary people, he felt very much out of place. He would have been much happier having a pint at the pub with a mate than dining with Winston Churchill.

My mother tried to stay at home when we were very young, but she is a brilliant actress who needed that expression in her life and wanted to work as soon as she felt she could. Later on, when my father was very ill, she had to work to bring in the money. Once in the West End, she did a two-year run, which nearly killed her. I really appreciated her strength and dedication.

Now she is getting the film parts she would like and some that are just fun to do, and I feel totally at ease with who she is and what she wants to do.

It cannot have been easy for her with the discrepancy in popular fame between herself and her husband. I've always tried to defend her in conversations: 'Mother's one of the best actresses in Britain, too!', type of thing.

We have worked together twice. The first time I directed her in *Time and the Conways*, which was good but felt odd. The second time was this year, and it was just like working with a good friend. I didn't feel any maternal pressure.

I sometimes have dreams about directing my father. I never had the chance, but in my dreams I do. Quite often in the dream he is too old to do the part, and I'm in this awful position of having to go to people and tell them I think he cannot do it.

We were working on a couple of projects towards the end of his life because he did get depressed when he wasn't working, and later on he was too weak to be on a film set.

We would try to get him to tape things, about Shakespeare and so on, but it was a son prompting a father to reminisce than a director–actor relationship.

Professionally, I've shied away from Shakespeare, although now I've cleared away the shadows I could approach it without worrying what people think of a younger Olivier doing Shakespeare — something I couldn't have contemplated when I first started directing 10 or 15 years ago.

I used to worry about putting energy into his career rather than my own. After all, he'd had a pretty full one. But I'm glad I was around for the last two years of his life, because it healed a lot of early wounds and misunderstandings.

I regret never telling him the anger I felt about his being away and having all these plays that seemed to be more important than me. And how I felt the public was a rival I was fighting against.

Near the end, when I had the opportunity, it felt too mean, so I didn't. I did it in analysis afterwards and took it out on my therapist instead.

Dad's way had been to dedicate himself first to work, never really knowing how to dedicate himself to family. It was a pattern I was determined not to fall into. In consequence, I probably went too far the other way, over-compensating on the domestic front.

After my father died, I really did have to go through a long psychological process to get out of his shadow. One thing I found essential for me was to find other older men whom I could trust. First, to repair the gap left by a workaholic father, and second, to find mentors who could see who I was, and what my talents were, which is always difficult for the father to do.

Traditionally, one of the jobs of the mentor figure, is to be able to bless people, to give little gifts. He can just drop a jewel in an odd sentence that suddenly heals or builds a bridge over something that seemed like a chasm before. Michael Caine gave me one of those jewels. In 1977 I went with Dad to Hollywood. He was up for Best Actor, but pissed off because he was getting a lifetime achievement Oscar, too. He said, 'Oh, they're fobbing me off with this because they don't want to give me Best Actor.' But we went over together and were taken around all these Hollywood parties. I was in heaven. I was eating huge bowls of caviar and drinking far too much champagne. One huge party was given by Gregory Peck, and at the end of the evening Michael Caine came up to me. He said, 'You know, I've been watching you. Most people wouldn't, most people would be looking at your dad. But I'm not most people. I've been looking at you, and I just want you to know you're a good son.'

And that was amazing. Suddenly to hear that after two weeks spent following Dad around, aware that everyone was looking at him, while I felt an appendage. Just to have that feedback from someone who obviously had done what he'd said — been casually observing me — was terrific. I moved from feeling I was a useless hanger-on, to feeling like a good son, a blessing to have around.

Later on at Gregory Peck's party, Dad went up to Frank Sinatra and said, 'Oh, Frankie, it's lovely to see you. I love your music so much, but the kids won't let me put it on. By the way, have you met my son?' Sinatra just said to me through a steely gaze, 'I don't think I've set the old blues on you before.'

There was definitely a case of being able to use travels with my Dad as currency at school. You could acquire interest, yet you always knew they were interested in who you were talking about and not in you as an individual.

Older boys would bring girls over and say, 'Here, tell her about Steve McQueen.' It wasn't all good, but it was fun. But that time in LA was the first time I felt I had a really strong connection with my father while also being useful to him. That had its double-edge, because later I thought, 'Well, we only got on when I could be of use to you; that's not really what a father–son relationship is supposed to be.'

I am fascinated by what fame means in the modern world. I'm putting together a treatment programme for a book on the myth of fame — what fame is, who gets it, who dies from it, etc. ... When you skirt around the edges of fame there is a sense of excitement about being around these people who thousands, maybe millions, would want to be around, that gives you a buzz. Reflected glory becomes its own drug. I was aware early on of the danger of feeling important because I was with people others thought important.

I distrust people who are after fame for fame's sake. True talent, genius or vision, definitely deserves recognition, but I think it is also essential for these people to get out of the genius mode and do other things. If you become totally driven by fame, it will eat you up, one way or another.

The greatest lesson my family situation taught me is that fame and money don't make you happy. I want to try to get that message across to a younger generation who are inundated with media messages about fame. They should be careful about what they want; they might just get it.

The media attitude nowadays is, if you're famous, you're fair game. If you put yourself up there, we have the right to tear you down. Of course, it is just possible my father, and other famous people, actually didn't want a private life. It could be they wanted continuous adulation.

One destructive side of fame is the assumption that it gives you the right to behave badly. I don't think my father abused his fame in that way, which I'm proud of.

One of the things that I thought about while writing *Shadow of the Stone Heart*, was that my father had made a Mephistophelean deal. At some point in his life he had said, 'I will give up whatever you want me to give up if you'll make me the best actor in the world.' I think he wanted it so much that he was prepared not to develop other areas of himself and had no idea what result that would have.

My father left me enough money to buy a house without a mortgage, which is great. Occasionally little bits trickle in from the estate because we all share it. It's certainly not enough to live off, but it's great not to have to get a job at Safeway if I'm not working for a bit. My father could have earned a lot more money, but he decided to stay mainly with theatre rather than films. He did what was right for him, and I'm glad. He certainly didn't have money when he started out. After he'd left drama school, he didn't have a penny, so he worked on the Tube from about 11pm to 3am in the morning. He wouldn't get enough sleep and couldn't afford food so he'd end up at Lyons Corner Shops mixing ketchup and hot water to make free tomato soup.

I do get annoyed by what I call the 'vulture culture' — the people who pick over the bones and write books about supposed adventures or trysts that can't be proved. Everything else I can deal with. When I read about someone claiming my Dad had an affair with Danny Kaye or Sarah Miles, a part of me fantasises about revenge.

The Danny Kaye story shocked me. I heard quite a few rumours about my father down the years, but not that. We talked about my mother releasing a statement to the Press denying the rumour, although we feared it would only stir up more publicity.

In the middle of this, Ian McKellen, whom we know well, called and said, 'If you do make a statement, please make sure you're not saying anything against homosexuality.'

My mother came off the phone and said, 'I can't win!'

Derek Grainger, who worked with Dad at Chichester, is now doing an authorised biography. We are going to open all the archives in an attempt to get a balanced account.

What is important is to put Olivier in the context of the time he lived in and the whole theatrical history of which he was a part.

I have never read a single book about my father from cover to cover. I could never accept him as the subject of a book. Nowadays there is a tendency to dig for the dirt. It is a shift in society. Fifty years ago, people's private lives did not influence their ability to do a job. Now no aspiring politician who has been divorced could get nominated for Prime Minister.

Personally, Larry was extremely generous, but professionally he was jealous. When he was running the National Theatre, he didn't include his contemporaries and bring them in as equals. People have told me he deliberately excluded them through envy or fear that they might show him up. This was countered by his efforts to foster a young generation of great actors.

He never forgave the people who appointed Peter Hall to the National without consulting him. He told me once that he directed only seven plays and acted in seven plays there, but if he'd known Peter Hall was going to take over, he'd have directed and starred in them all!

We once got a letter from The Renaissance Company saying that Ken Branagh didn't know they were writing, but would Sir Laurence consider coming on the set of *Henry V* to wish everyone luck. Dad spent the rest of the day in a foul temper, because he didn't want anyone else to do something he'd put his stamp on. To this you can say, yes he made a great film, but surely every generation has the right to re-interpret. Just because a Shakespearean performance was done well in the 1950s shouldn't mean no one is allowed to do it again. He didn't want to share the glory. He loved that glory, the attention.

He was a Sir before I was born, and then he became the first Lord of the Theatre. He wouldn't accept his lordship for a year because he thought the Government was trying to get away without building the National Theatre. He thought it was a bribe. It wasn't until after everything had gone through that he accepted. I'm glad it is not hereditary though.

I think there are two basic ways that famous people operate. One is by giving from a full centre; the other gives from an empty centre and needs our approval to fill them up. They are giving talent and genius, but the deal is you give them attention that makes them feel OK about themselves. I would say my Dad fell more in the second category.

This is connected with not knowing who he really was. If you are uncertain if you're worth anything, then doing something becomes a fix, like an addiction.

Stage performance is very different from film performance. It is a different energy dynamic in that with stage you are out there. The star is still the centre of attention on a film set, however. There are always people around coming up to you, reassuring you. You are still receiving that kind of approval and appreciation. If you don't, you walk off the set. Then you definitely get it. Having said that, Dad was always the consummate professional. He prided himself on it and didn't get on with people who didn't.

There are times I do reflect upon with gratitude, particularly when I was at Bedales where he would arrive to watch football or cricket matches in the middle of a Wednesday or Saturday afternoon. It would take most of his day yet he wanted to be there and see me. But it was embarrassing for me. He was the only Dad on the touchline. He was putting in five hours of effort during which I would see him for five minutes at half time. I couldn't really be with him or talk about what was going on, so it didn't really work out. Now, as a memory, it means a great deal.

After my father died I went into a very numb place where I couldn't admit to any feelings. Then I tried to work it off, throwing myself into work in order not to have to feel anything. I did that for about a year, then realised that I was hiding something. There was something going on that I hadn't expressed. I hadn't ever cried for him, even though I did love him very deeply.

Still confused at this time by my stifled emotions, it proved a fortuitous accident that I was given a tape of an American poet called Robert Bly, who talked about a split that happens when part of you requires attention, but another part is just getting on with life as if nothing has happened. It struck a chord, and when he was in England some months later holding a Men's Workshop, I went along. He talked about the lack of initiation in modern society and the consequent pressure placed on fathers to be everything to their sons. His ideas made sense to me and I decided to pursue them. We meet every two weeks to talk on as deep a level as we can without the pressures of everyday life, and try to avoid the type of male conversations we would have at the pub.

It has helped me stop feeling sorry for myself, the son of a famous actor, always alone, no one understanding what it felt like. Not that I'd have wanted him to remain at home, unfulfilled. On the other hand there was emotional wounding, caused, in part, by his selfishness, egotism and fame, that I would rather had not happened.

Through these groups I began to feel I was a man among men, all of whom have different problems, all of whom have problems with fathers or parents. Those who didn't have an absent father often rued the fact that he was always there, pressuring them to succeed and putting them down if they didn't.

I begin to see this as a universal situation — the son's disappointment with the father. Now, I think, maybe it is part of the father's job to disappoint the son. If the father doesn't disappoint the son, maybe the son would never leave home.

I was able to get myself out of the victim position, 'Poor me, I need a father that I never had.' Five years later, I've figured out I probably got exactly what I needed. It's opened doors of understanding. Finally, I was able to let out the tears for Dad that I'd never been able to shed before.

My father's funeral and the subsequent memorial service at Westminster Abbey had been media events and I could not express personal grief. I carried that over into my life. I started to cut off a few emotions and ended up cutting them all out. I wasn't really able to be present with Shelley or the kids. There were large parts of me that were withheld. At that time, and without realising it, I was moving away from anything that exerted an emotional hold over me. I was on the run. And I made mistakes.

One such mistake was with a good friend of my father, the actor Dustin Hoffman. The family went to see Dustin as Shylock in *The Merchant of Venice*, as our first outing after the funeral. We relaxed backstage after the play, had a drink and reminisced about Dad. I felt moved to promise Dustin a memento of my father. The following day, I posted him the set of false teeth Dad had used as Shylock 20 years earlier. Larry and Dustin had worked together on *Marathon Man*, during which their most memorable scene together was about teeth. And these were a piece of National Theatre history! I was so pleased by my idea that I didn't pause to reflect on their possible effect. I still cringe when I envisage Dustin opening the box, expecting some treasured Olivier relic and finding ... gnashers! I never heard from him again. I'm not surprised.

I think a major pressure on the children of the famous is that they lose their right to fail. Part of growing up is trying things and failing, being outrageous, falling flat on your face and getting up again. When you fall flat on your face with a big name attached to you, it's rubbed into the dirt and it is more difficult to get up and try something else. If the parent were not famous no one would know about it not working. If Joe Bloggs directs a new play out of town and it doesn't transfer to the West End, no one knows. When I did that it was headline material for Nigel Dempster. I find that potentially destructive because it can end up putting pressure on you to make 'safe' choices.

Both my sisters went to drama school, which I think was very brave. I'm not sure they liked it very much, but I think there is a sense of expectation when you're following in parental footsteps. I went to UCLA in America, which was much easier. Whenever I tried acting I felt I was being constantly judged. Of course, that could have been my imagination, my third eye judging myself negatively.

There are very few obligations foisted upon me because of my position. I try to attend the Olivier Awards. When my Dad was first asked to put his name to the awards he discussed it with my mother. Mum said, 'Well, you have three children who, at this point, look like they are going into the profession. I'm still in the profession and it would probably be very difficult for any of us ever to be nominated for an 'Olivier' award. Also, this is the Society of West End Theatre awards, and you're the man of the National Theatre, not a West End, Shaftesbury Avenue actor, doing light comedies or musicals. So, do you think it's appropriate?'

Dad's reaction was, 'Oh no, you're absolutely right, Darling. I won't do it.'

Next year, they wrote to him again. He didn't confer with Mum this time, he just wrote back saying, 'Yes.' He wanted his name in the spotlight again. He wasn't being malicious, it was just, 'Bugger the rest of you.' We hadn't given him the answer he wanted, so second time around, he didn't ask us.

Many men find it hard to move away from their fathers. My

experience was doubly difficult being the son of Laurence Olivier, one of those rare men who are described as being 'the best in the world' at what they do. Perhaps the easy way out would have been for me to have rejected him, which, at times, I did. The harder task, which I eventually understood to be the right one for me, was to accept him as a human being who had lived his life as well as he could.

I remain proud of his achievements and of the inspiration he was to his profession. I continue to learn from his example. In terms of effort and discipline, I try to learn from what he did do. In terms of living a balanced life, I have to look elsewhere. A few years ago, I came across the words to an old African song, which sums up the way I feel now:

> *Do not seek too much fame, but do not seek obscurity.*
> *Be proud,*
> *But do not remind the world of your deeds.*
> *Excel when you must,*
> *But do not excel the world.*
> *Many heroes are not yet born, many have already died.*
> *To be alive to hear this song is a victory.*

Extract from *The Rag and Bone Shop of the Heart*, p 498

PETER SELLERS
ACTOR, (1925–1980)

Peter Sellers is best known for his role as Inspector Clouseau, in the 'Pink Panther' movies that spanned 14 years — from 1964 to 1978. Although having worked the variety halls through the 1940s and 1950s, it was through teaming up with Spike Milligan, Harry Secombe and Michael Bentine to form 'The Goons', that Sellers became a household name in the UK.

Through the 'Panther' feature films, he found international stardom, but he was first recognised as a rising screen comedy actor in the 1956 film, *The Ladykillers*, co-starring Alec Guinness, Cecil Parker, Herbert Lom, Danny Green and Katie Johnson.

His first feature film was *Penny Points to Paradise*, (1951), which co-starred Harry Secombe, Alfred Marks and Bill Kerr. His last film was *The Fiendish Plot of Dr Fu Manchu*, (1980), and co-starred Helen Mirren, David Tomlinson, Sid Caesar and Burt Kwouk.

In 1979, a long-awaited ambition was achieved with the release of the film *Being There*, a story that shows the amazing effect a man of pure innocence can wreak on a corrupt world. It co-starred Shirley MacLaine, Melvyn Douglas and Jack Warden.

The following contribution is from Peter Sellers' son, Michael, who is 41, and married to Alison, a maths teacher. She is his second wife. Michael is Peter's only son, although he has a sister, Sarah, from Peter's first wife, Anne Levy, and half-sister, Kate, from his stepfather, Ted, and a half-sister, Victoria, from Peter's second wife, Britt Ekland. Michael and Alison have two children, William, eight, and Hannah, five. They live in North London. Michael is a carpenter and builder by trade.

MICHAEL SELLERS:

I was aware from an early age just how curious people were about my father. To this day they're still curious. The question I'm most often asked is: 'What was it like?' Well, to me, who knew no different, it was just like having a father. That he was known the world over and was very wealthy with it, was quite normal to me.

I can remember my father showing moments of affection — a hug or a kiss or something — but he wasn't someone who gave of himself, he wasn't a demonstrative person. There were never any emotional moments, except when he lost his temper and then you'd quickly run for cover. My mother said I'd already learned to humour him by the time I was seven.

His attitude towards his friends and family was a whimsical one. An example would be a letter he sent me because he felt that we, the children, had been insufficiently grateful for Trust Fund money. It read as follows:

> *Dear Michael,*
> *This letter is to tell you how extremely upset I am by your behaviour toward me. You must, by now, have received the extra money from John Humphries, and your flat has been financed by the Trust I set up for you; yet you could not find the time to telephone or write a letter to thank me.*
> *I'm tired of being used as a source of finance, and contacted only when you need something. Whatever relationship we might have had is finished, the time has come for you to continue your own way. I no longer wish to be thought of as your father.*
> *Good luck with your career, if you ever choose one.*
>
> *Best wishes ...*

It was signed by a secretary and dictated by telephone from the south of France. A follow-up was sent the next day:

> *Dear Michael and Sarah,*
> *Further to your note, my final suggestion is that you have your name changed by deed poll to Levy.*

I was terrified of his temper. Once he was driving a new Bentley and a stone chipped the wing. I was about six, and the next morning I got up, got out the touch-up paint and fixed it for him. He went absolutely crazy. All my toys were cleared out of my bedroom, I was strapped with a belt and sent to bed.

In a way that fear lurked in the back of my mind until the day he died. My bedroom backed on to my parents, and I would wake up during the night listening to him screaming and shouting.

Looking back on the 15 years since his death, I realise I have a lot of reasons to dislike him. At the time, I loved him through everything as my father. He lost sight of that, I think. He probably thought I deserted him.

He was often away working for long periods, so our relationship was based on phone calls. In the holidays we'd be off to California or France or Italy — wherever he was filming at the time. People would be nice to us because they wanted to please him.

He enjoyed his fame. He liked to wield the power he had. A script girl turned up on the set once wearing a purple suit and he got her thrown off because he thought purple was unlucky. Like everyone else, we had to indulge him and do what he wanted to do. Never once did he do something purely for us, it had to benefit him as well, somehow.

Women were to play the biggest role in his life. The first notable occasion was when director Anthony Asquith asked my father to play an Indian doctor in a movie called *The Millionairess*. His interest grew when he learned that Sophia Loren was to take the title role.

Playing a leading role opposite a sex symbol like Loren was beyond his wildest dreams. Much to my mother's growing concern, he became obsessed with her. He brought Sophia to the house a couple of times. On her second visit, like the first, I went into hiding. I found her overbearing. She arrived wearing a yellow dress and yellow feathered hat. I told my mother I didn't like her. When she asked why, I said, ''Cos she looks like a chicken.' She was sweet and charming, but I still found myself reticent.

A part of my mother felt saddened for her husband in his emotional plight. Any man put under the gaze of those sizzling Italian eyes might have wilted in the same way he had done, but it got out of control. One night my father woke up and gripped my mother's arm as if their privacy had suddenly been invaded. 'Ssh, don't say anything,' he told her. 'I can feel her presence coming into the room. Yes, she is here with us ...'

'Who is?'

'It's Sophia ... Sophia,' he whispered back.

My mother, by then, had taken all she could of this. She moved into the guest room and said, 'I've left those two together!'

He began phoning Sophia at all hours of the day and in all parts of the world telling her in every conversation a dozen times over, 'I love you, darling.' He didn't seem bothered if the family were within earshot.

My mother's patience simply ran out. He'd just put the phone down after a half-hour talk to Sophia in Italy. 'What on earth is going on?' she shouted at him. 'Can't you see you're making an idiot of yourself? She is not going to leave Carlo Ponti for you.'

He was convinced she would leave Ponti for him, presuming always that she was as madly in love with him as he was with her. Sophia Loren gave no signs that implied she intended leaving Carlo Ponti or that she returned his feelings in any way.

He remained intent on leaving my mother for her; he was besotted, but every avenue he pursued brought him frustration. At home he became totally unbalanced — manic. If there was the smallest disruption to his day he refused to go to work. The studio appealed to my mother to exercise some influence over him, but that was impossible — everything he said or did was totally irrational and unpredictable.

Once he woke me up at 3am to ask if he should divorce my mother. 'That's the only thing we can do, Mike,' he went on. 'We must divorce. It won't make any difference to you. Sometimes you'll live with your mother and sometimes with me ... you understand, don't you?' I'm not sure I even understood what a divorce meant. I was only seven.

After further incidents and no respite, my mother moved in with friends. Sophia returned to Italy, and my father slipped into melancholy and drifted aimlessly about the house, which was strangely silent for once.

My sister, Sarah, was always pretty cheerful, happy-go-lucky, despite all the unrest at home. Certainly, she could be stubborn and unhelpful and also emotional at times, but nothing like as quick-tempered as our father. She has the greatest physical likeness to him.

Victoria's earliest memories are naturally of Brookfield, where my father lived with Britt. She remembers jumping up and down with us on the trampoline that our father erected in the grounds, and she recalls the geese and the chicken hut, the ducks and the fields beyond. Our father would call her 'Toria' when he was feeling affectionate, but he took little more interest in her than he did in us. She was 'Ekland's' problem, as Britt would be for ever known after their divorce, and if our stepmother was out for the day, then Inger the nanny would take over all responsibilities.

Victoria had barely started school when our father and Britt were already discussing divorce, and she grew up in the belief that divorce was a normal procedure. It wasn't until she was about nine, she discovered that we were only her half-brother and half-sister. In the coming years our hearts would cry out for Victoria, who was torn between Britt and my father. They didn't consider enough Victoria's own feelings. She was the innocent victim of her father's malice. She would start at one school only to find she'd been transferred to another. She ended up going to school in Sweden, America and England. She did a term at my old school, Ibstock. Our father visited her there and ordered her to get her hair cut. She did. Then Britt visited her and cut it even shorter. On seeing it he went mad.

'Don't listen to what your mother says,' he shouted, 'just listen to me.'

I never stayed at any school for very long — they were as turbulent and traumatic as any other aspect of life under my father's rule. His responsibility as a parent extended to our enrolment into private schools, kitting us out with the appropriate uniforms and paying the school fees. Helping with homework, attending speech days or concerts or even a general show of interest were not forthcoming. Fortunately, my mother and her husband, Ted, were not so remiss.

I was more rebellious than either Sarah or Victoria. My kindergarten days passed without too much incident and my school reports from The Hall School in Hampstead looked reasonably encouraging. After my parents divorced, I was moved to Ibstock, a preparatory school at Roehampton, seven miles south-west of London. I cried with anger and desperation the first day I arrived there, feeling my parents had abandoned me, which I suppose shows the unsettled nature of my upbringing.

Eighteen months later, my father decided it would be best for me to attend a more fashionable boarding-school. Frensham Heights wasn't very far from the family home at Elstead. My new friends were somewhat impressed to learn who my father was. On one occasion he came and collected me in his gold-coloured Ferrari and they got him to sign his autograph in their exercise books.

The general assumption among my peers was that, because my father was loaded, I, too, would have money to burn. They didn't really believe me when I told them that he gave me one pound a week pocket money and that this would be withheld if ever I upset him in any way.

I would dread any new introduction, just waiting for the moment when they realised I was Peter Sellers' son. On one occasion, aged eight, when being introduced to a new teacher, I decided it would be far simpler if I pre-empted the inevitable. 'I'm Michael, and my father is Peter Sellers.' I was told off afterwards for being big-headed. You couldn't win.

My crisis time at the school began when I started stealing. Not much at first — biscuits and goodies from the kitchens, that sort of thing. Later, though, I took a cigarette lighter for the gang I was mixing with, which smoked at break-times in a corner of the playing ground. For this indiscretion I escaped with a warning. When I swiped our gardener's wages from his home — well, that was entirely different.

My father had summoned the police to the house to track down the thief. All the staff were finger-printed. When he discovered it was me, he was horrified.

'Why in the hell did you do it?' he shouted. 'You've had every thing you've ever wanted, now you steal from me. Why? There must be an answer.'

I was unable to give him one, except I did point out he hadn't given me any pocket money for two weeks and the boys at school thought I was rich.

We resolved the situation — eventually. I offered to repay the gardener's wages in instalments from my pocket money.

I had a rough ride at Frensham Heights. Other kids would vandalise everything I had and smash up all my personal belongings. Their argument was, 'You can afford it. Your Dad's rich.' Even the teachers appeared to believe I'd been born with a silver spoon in my mouth.

The headmaster described me as wild and unsettled and called my parents to come in and discuss the situation. My mother met with Britt Ekland, whom she described as being concerned and sensible about my behaviour.

Things went on as they do at school, but because I lived so close to

Elstead, I took to slipping away secretly some nights and returning home on the bus. My father didn't question this, assuming, erroneously, that I'd had permission. Once my nocturnal jaunts were uncovered, that was it. I was expelled.

My father had warned me of the impending event, but told me not to worry about it. I asked what, exactly, this dreadful event was going to be. His reply was as typical as any of his classic Goon lines. 'That's what I am telling you, Michael,' he said, 'don't worry about it.'

The headmaster at Frensham recommended I had psychiatric treatment and put this in writing on my final report, which wasn't very helpful when it was time for my mother to try to place me in another school.

My father had put my name down to maybe half a dozen schools before I was born. As well as Eton, Harrow and Westminster, he had fortunately chosen a less prestigious establishment called King Alfred's. This was at Golders Green and Sarah would join me there in later years in the co-ed system.

I went from a doctor to a child psychologist as part of the agreement in accepting me to the school. He told my mother in one report, 'Michael is an insecure child lacking the attention of his father.' It went on that I was going through an identity crisis and that my disruptive practices in the class were made in order to get attention.

The psychologist was getting near the truth. I no longer wanted to be Peter Sellers' son. I craved my own identity. Whenever I'd tried talking to him about school, he was always too busy to listen. His own activities left him no time to spare for anyone else, not even his children.

After a time my psychologist was becoming more harassed than the headmaster had been. I'd already been grilled by the headmaster in front of my parents for smoking marijuana. My father hadn't looked too comfortable about that, knowing he would be a hypocrite to criticise me. A few months later, he gave a lecture at the London School of Economics and came out on the side of the pro-marijuana movement!

I wore a long overcoat at the time and had long, curly, shoulder-length hair. My mother couldn't understand why I wanted to look like a tramp. 'When people see me,' I told her, 'they say, "There's that boy with the long hair" rather than, "There's Peter Sellers' son".'

It wasn't difficult to get hold of pot at school. In my case even easier as my father was into it as well, and he kept the grass in empty film canisters in the house. There was so much grass about the place I knew he wasn't going to miss a bit. It was the same with pills — he had thousands of them — and I'd help myself to amphetamines or Mandrax sleeping pills. He called his bathroom 'Boots'.

When my mother found out about the pot, she suspected we were getting the stuff from pushers outside venues where the day's big bands played at weekends. Some of it did come that way, but she didn't realise I was also poaching the stuff from my father's hidden supplies.

At King Alfred's, I wasn't alone in having famous parents. Jazz musician Humphrey Lyttleton's kids were there, so, too, was Kathy Kubrick, daughter of Stanley who had directed two of my father's films.

My father wanted me to be a film director, but I'm afraid I didn't live up to expectations on that one. When I eventually became a carpenter, he simply asked me when I was going to get a real job. A real job, by his definition, meant a glamorous life-style with rich and famous friends.

Like me, my sister, Sarah, had slowly learned how to humour our father, by weighing all her words very carefully before saying them. She once started praising Ted and the new house with a swimming pool and billiards room that we had just moved into, and she found he was jealous of our family life, and the fact that Ted could now give us a home as luxurious as he could. He seethed with anger and played his familiar line, saying Sarah didn't love him and didn't she realise Ted was only her stepfather?

My father could be an unexpectedly generous man, although he was fickle and had most of the traits he's accused of having. Once, I was trampolining with Stan, the stable boy, and Stan broke his Timex. My father turned up next day with a new Rolex for him.

I ended up by the age of 12 finding myself telling my own father to be sensible about his purchases. He would pay for anything. Once, in St Tropez, he paid two bagpipe players there to march on to Peter Ustinov's boat with his compliments.

It shouldn't be forgotten that my father had a humorous side and things could go wrong in a very funny way. There was the time when we had a firework party at home. The house caught fire, and as the television exploded, he pushed me and my sister into the car only to find the car's battery was on charge. As he tried to disentangle the wires, he ended up getting trapped under the bonnet. He was still struggling with it as the fire engines turned up. He was about to sell this house to Alfred

Marks. He rang him up and said, 'Do you want to choose your own decorations? We've burnt the lounge down!'

While recovering at home from a heart-attack one summer, my father received a visit from aviator Tommy Sopwith, who turned up at Brookfield in his own helicopter. We all put white sheets out as markers in the field.

Tommy invited us aboard for a ride and suggested paying a surprise visit to some friends only three or four miles away. My father made a minor navigational error and we landed in an elderly couples' garden during the middle of their afternoon tea. They were fairly flummoxed to see Peter Sellers climbing out of a helicopter on their lawn asking for directions.

My father's health was an ongoing problem. He had his first heart-attack at the age of 38, not long after marrying Britt. He'd been using the stimulant amyl nitrate, which is supposed to intensify your sex drive. In later years, he threw his heart tablets away, sure that he'd been cured by some psychic doctors he'd met in the Philippines.

We first heard about Britt Ekland when he was staying at the Dorchester Hotel, in London, while shooting *Shot in the Dark*, for United Artists. Ironically, it would be at the Dorchester that he would eventually have his final heart-attack many years later. He was given superstar treatment there, occupying the plush Oliver Messel suite. It even had a garden terrace reached through French doors.

Sarah and I would visit him at the hotel most weekends. On our third visit, he sat us down on a sofa and told us he had some very special photos to show us. He produced a set of pictures of this exceedingly glamorous-looking girl. 'Who do you think that is?' he asked.

We didn't know, of course. 'Is she a film star like you, Dad?' I asked.

'Yes, she is,' he beamed, 'her name is Britt Ekland and she comes from Sweden. Isn't she beautiful? How would you like Daddy to marry her?'

By this time, he'd already proposed to Britt. He had spotted her only days earlier in the foyer of the Dorchester choosing magazines at the bookstand.

He discovered she was filming at Pinewood. Only two months earlier Maurice Woodruff, a clairvoyant he regularly consulted, had told him he would shortly become involved with a person whose initials were 'B E'. Now he had found her.

His love, as always, had to be conveyed through extravagant gifts. He bought Britt a triple-banded Victorian engagement ring of emeralds, diamonds and rubies. He also bestowed on her a black mink coat, a diamond-studded gold brooch, a sports car, and a Dachshund dog she called Pepe. He also hired the Queen's couturier, Norman Hartnell, to design her wedding dress for their marriage at Guildford registry office on 19 February 1964.

A week after the marriage, my father had to go to the States to start work on a new comedy movie for director, Billy Wilder. As Britt had to stay on and finish her film at Pinewood, he decided I would accompany him. This wasn't a good move as far as I was concerned. I'd just changed schools and made new friends. I was ten years old, and felt man enough to tell Dad that I just didn't want to go with him.

An argument inevitably unfolded. 'Right,' he finally stormed. 'I want to ask you one question. Who do you love most — me or your mother?'

Knowing it would irritate him, I said, 'I love Mummy best.'

He went berserk. He dashed next door and fetched Sarah and applied the same question. 'I love you both the same,' she answered tactfully.

Sarah was excused, I was told to pack my things. 'You're going back to your mother's and I never want to see you again.' In any emotional conflict, tears would stream down his face, and now we were both crying our eyes out.

He left for America alone. Eventually he talked Britt into quitting her film and joining him in California. Britt's three weeks' work on the movie had to be scrapped and my father paid $62,000 in compensation to the film company.

It was Easter and my birthday was approaching. He felt it was time for us to make up. He rang our mother to invite Sarah and me over to see Disneyland.

I was feeling apprehensive when we arrived. The last time I'd seen him I'd been told he never wanted to see me again.

The house was wonderful. It stood astride Beverly Hills among a colony of Hollywood stars. We were to see quite a bit of our neighbours, Cary Grant, Steve McQueen and Shirley Maclaine.

We visited Disneyland, but not by road. My father hired a helicopter. Britt came with us, and it was her first ride in one, too.

We had no inkling that stalking this moment of happiness was a series of heart-attacks that were to take him to the brink of death.

He dreaded the thought of another attack. Any small pain, be it indigestion or otherwise, was the beginning of an attack in his own mind. Spike Milligan said, 'Your father was always searching for a bloody heart-attack as if it were a letter that he knew had been posted and hadn't arrived.'

His marriage to Britt began deteriorating in the same fashion as his first had done. Britt, normally bubbling with spirit, became low and vacant.

Their marriage lasted four years. She was granted a divorce, on the grounds of mental cruelty, in London on 18 December 1968. She was also given care and control of Victoria, with joint custody. My father didn't accept the fact he was divorced, just as he didn't when he was divorced from my mother.

Britt was staying at the Dorchester just prior to her departure to Sweden where she was returning for Christmas. He offered her his flat in Clarges Street to use. As she had Victoria, it was convenient in the circumstances, so she accepted the offer.

That evening, she even went out to dinner with him in a party that included Warren Beatty, Julie Christie, Roman Polanski and Sharon Tate.

By the end of the evening he was apparently feeling morose and began questioning how their divorce could have come about. As Victoria went off to bed, he took down a double-barrelled shotgun that he used on royal pheasant shoots and pointed it at Britt, his finger on the trigger, threatening to kill her.

With great presence of mind, she pacified him by pointing out such things like spending the rest of his life in prison and so forth, and eventually took the gun from his trembling hands. But we didn't see Britt for a long, long time after that.

He continued to want to take his revenge on Britt for all their past troubles. She was referred to in conversation as, 'a lousy actress', 'a gold digger', 'a professional girlfriend who was an amateur at everything else'. All of which was very distressing for Victoria.

My father's friendship with Princess Margaret had seemingly increased. They'd known each other for some years by now. She, at that time, was going through marital problems of her own with Tony Snowdon.

The Princess entertained my father at Kensington Palace one evening.

He said she was dressed in a low-cut gown and after dinner all the servants had disappeared. They were sitting all alone when he suddenly noticed how attractive she was. 'My God,' he thought, 'if I don't behave myself I'm going to end up in the Tower.' One assumes he did — and therefore didn't!

There then followed Miranda Quarry and, of course, Lynne Frederick, and there were plenty in between. He was beginning to establish a pattern — good-looking, blonde, impressionable 21-year-olds. I really don't think he could have handled a relationship with a more mature woman.

Miranda was of a classical English mould, one of the debutante breed whose place in society was enhanced by the fact that her stepfather was Lord Mancroft, the former Conservative cabinet minister.

The following summer after the start of their romance, we sailed to Cap Ferrat to visit David Niven and his wife, Hjordis. We then tied up in Monte Carlo. We were moored next to the boat of Hollywood mogul, Sam Spiegel. My father had met Miranda through him. Miranda didn't like going on the boat. She was scared of the water and would have preferred to stay in waterfront hotels.

One day my father called on the ship's radio and sent a message for me to go to Cap Ferrat to pick him up. I took his Riva speedboat, *Bluebottle II*. I arrived at the spot and waited off-shore for 90 minutes, but there was no sign of him. I got through on the ship-to-ship radio to discover he'd changed his mind but hadn't bothered to let me know. He'd gone to lunch with Miranda, joining a party with Leslie Bricusse, Tony Newley, David Niven and Roger Moore.

Friendship wasn't in fact my father's strongest point. Spike, Graham Stark and Bryan Forbes, had all suffered his unpredictability. I suppose they must have known they would be insulted and abused at some point. Anyone who could stand up after that sort of treatment and remain loyal to him was indeed a true friend.

Orson Welles found him quite mystifying. Working on *Casino Royale* together, my father didn't want to work in the shadow of this metaphoric and literal giant. His friendship with Elliott Gould, on the other hand, just drifted into obscurity. There wasn't any particular reason, except that my father just couldn't be bothered to keep in contact. Most friendships with other artistes went the same way.

As ever uncertain about marriage, my father kept his relationship with Miranda in limbo for about two years, but it survived the usual bout of tantrums, suspicions and general qualms.

Once they were out in his Rolls-Royce and she said something that so incensed him he deliberately crashed the car. The police were called, he was arrested and taken to Gerald Row police station in Belgravia. He didn't talk to Miranda for some weeks after the incident.

Perhaps through loneliness, I'm not sure, he decided to marry Miranda. It's what she wanted, and he claimed that she'd called all the shots forcing him into the situation. In fact, just hours before the ceremony took place, he actually telephoned both my mother and Britt to lay the blame for his marriage to Miranda squarely at their feet. Miranda must have found the celebrity world fascinating, but as a marriage it was doomed before it had even taken place.

My father promised me a car for my seventeenth birthday. I was with a pop group by then playing odd gigs and thought it would be better to have a van to ship us and all the equipment around. He agreed, and a van was duly ordered. When I went to the garage, they told me the order had been cancelled. I asked my father for an explanation and he just pleaded poverty. As an excuse I could just about have gone along with it had he not so recently bought a saloon car as a present for one of Miranda's sisters. He'd already recently bought another of her sisters a Pentax camera with all the accessories. The family were coming very low on his list of priorities — certainly second to Miranda and her family.

Despite showing a total lack of enthusiasm for the things she wanted to do, Miranda didn't let him interfere with her social calendar. It was his bad luck that he was bored with the nobility set she mixed with. 'Why did I marry her?' he asked me at this time.

Without any evidence, he cornered her one day and accused her of having an affair. She pleaded her innocence, but he wouldn't believe her.

'I want proof of your innocence,' he shouted.

A legal separation between them soon followed and, once she'd gained her freedom, she married Lord Nuttall. 'That's what she always wanted,' said my father, 'a title.'

In 1973 he announced his intended marriage to Liza Minnelli. She was as dazzling and brilliant as her mother before her, Judy Garland.

No one could recall two stars falling in love so instantaneously. It was an open affair and they would share kisses and hold hands in public.

The media, of course, loved it. My mother laughed when he told her about their relationship, but, on meeting Liza, said, 'I think she's great. I do hope you'll be happy this time.'

'Yes,' replied my father wistfully; 'well, I did love her mother's old films.'

During their third blissful week of romance, I began to detect that something was amiss. My father began complaining he never saw her on her own, that she was always surrounded by an entourage.

'How do we get rid of these people when we marry?' he asked her.

'Get rid of them?' said a shocked Liza. 'These are my friends, Peter. They're always gonna be my friends.'

This, apparently, was the beginning of the end. For Liza, it came when she consulted the London clairvoyant Fredrick Davies who predicted on a radio broadcast that she'd not marry Peter Sellers.

My father was furious with her for seeing a clairvoyant. 'Why didn't you tell me?' he demanded.

But it was too late. The whole affair was to be no more than that and now it was finished.

My father's type of women didn't appeal that much to me. Britt was the exception. I formed a closer relationship with her than I did with the others. I could have passed as her boyfriend when I was 15 and six feet tall and escorting her to discos and on the ski runs in St Moritz. As I grew older, I realised his lifestyle was beyond me and that included his women. I was young, but had no riches or social standing. And I wasn't famous. I was happier with girls within my own reach.

There was the time when we thought he was going to marry Mia Farrow. One afternoon, I'd gone with him on an excursion to his tailor. Once outside, he said, 'Come on. We're going to Frank Sinatra's flat in Grosvenor Square.'

Fair enough. We rang the bell and the door was answered by a nervy, fair-haired waif. This was Mia Farrow, and she began talking films with my father.

But Mia's warmth was easier to detect on her visit to Brookfield. She found the house compelling, and Sarah and I walked her around the grounds. It seemed she was one of few female friends who was just a friend with no strings attached. The Press began speculating on a romance, but when she returned to America, her name wasn't mentioned again.

I guess Lynne Frederick saw my father as a megastar. She was going out with David Frost at the time. The shame of all that is that my father was so stupid about it. I don't know why he allowed himself to believe we were all against him and that he should feel the need to write us out of his will, which is exactly what he did.

Lynne was just a few months younger than me, and we got on all right before they were married, even for a while after they were married. She was nicer to me than to the girls. Unfortunately, due to difficulties with the girls' relationship with Lynne, my father, Sarah and Victoria had not spoken to each other for three months before his death, but the same problems with Lynne didn't drive a wedge between me and him.

My father's last Easter found him at the Dorchester Hotel with Lynne. I could see he was doing his best to save what was left of his marriage to her. He'd bought her a new fur coat in Paris, and acquired a specially equipped Range Rover that they could share in Switzerland.

He saw the holiday as an opportunity for a family reunion, perhaps reconciliation, and Victoria flew in specially from Los Angeles. She was very excited about seeing her father, but naturally jet-lagged. She crashed out when she arrived, laying across a sofa in the suite, headphones on listening to some tape.

The presence of Victoria and Sarah must have irritated Lynne enormously. First she criticised Victoria. 'Well, darling,' she said to my father, 'if Victoria's going to listen to cassettes throughout the holiday, at least you won't have to talk to her. That's your problem solved.'

Shrugging off her remark, he put on a video clip from *Being There*, his penultimate movie and one he was most proud of. He'd hoped it would bring him an Oscar, but it didn't.

He asked Victoria if she'd liked the film. Victoria, removing her headphones, nodded. 'I thought it was great, Dad,' she said innocently, then added, 'You looked like a little, fat, old man in the part.'

Lynne was shocked. 'Did you hear that, darling? Victoria thought you were a little fat old man.'

His face turned to thunder and he spun around and threw his drink all over Victoria. She didn't cry, she was too bewildered. Sarah towelled her down and Lynne acted as though the whole thing was a big joke. Dad scowled and went into his bedroom and remained there until dinner.

No one except Lynne had noticed that at dinner Victoria was dressed from head to foot in the dreaded purple. Even her shoes.

Abruptly, my father got up from the table saying he was going to bed and turning to Victoria, he said, 'Never let me see you wearing purple again. Never, do you hear?'

The next morning Victoria requested some cash to buy clothes.

'I'm afraid your father's not going to do it,' said Lynne emerging from the bedroom. 'Your mother must give you plenty of money for your clothes.' Lynne, who was of our generation and indeed several months younger than me, sometimes talked to us as though we were kids.

Victoria stuck around until her dad appeared. His face was white with rage. 'As far as I'm concerned you can get the next plane and go home. I never want to see you again! Your behaviour's disgusting. I give your mother enough money for clothes. What does she do with it? You've no right to ask me for any more. You're going back on the next plane.' Knowing he gave Britt no clothes money for Victoria, and having heard enough of this, Sarah stepped in. 'Look Dad, it's nothing to do with Victoria what goes on between you and Britt. You're making her the scapegoat and that's not fair.'

They stared at each other a moment, then Sarah and Victoria marched off to a bedroom in tears.

A little while later, Lynne came into their room and patted Victoria's head. 'There, there,' she cooed, 'you know what your Dad's like!'

Contrary to all this, he could be very caring. When he discovered my first marriage to Kathy had broken up — a situation that had both perplexed and devastated me all in one blow — he was very understanding about it. The marriage had lasted only six weeks. She met someone else and that was that. She'd had problems understanding my father, and it wasn't helped by his phone calls, which could come through at any time, sometimes at 3 or 4am.

I didn't tell him at first, as he had enough problems of his own at that time. Also, I was worried he might send over 'one of the boys' to 'fix' Kathy's new boyfriend. He was always talking about sending over 'the boys' in these types of situations. The only evidence I ever found of their existence was when he sent a film 'heavy' to give someone a little encouragement to settle an overdue bill.

I spent some time with him at his house in Gstaad, and we began to get on with each other on an adult level. At last, the future began to hold some real possibilities as regards our personal relationship. But then he came back to London, had a heart-attack and died.

Blake Edwards, who directed the Panther movies, was once reported to have said about my father, 'The man was insane.' But that's not true at all. He was someone who'd been given a free rein. With that opportunity any one of us could look crazy. If you were given a couple of million pounds and told you could do what you like, you'd develop strange habits and certain idiosyncrasies. The truth of the matter is he was a comic genius with a childish nature that was spoilt by stardom. Hangers-on said, 'Come on, you're a star,' and he would go along with it to sustain the image. Finally, he died exhausted from this role.

Just before he died everyone was throwing money at him. He told me, 'They're offering a new "Panther" film and will pay me one million dollars to agree, another million to shoot it, a third million to finish and a percentage of the profits. And Pamela Stephenson is up to star.' It was as if they were all out to squeeze the last bit of magic from him.

I think that just before his final heart-attack in 1980, aged 54, he had changed a bit. It was as though he'd looked back and said, 'Who the hell is this person? I don't like him at all.' He had used up his life and had no fight in him when the big attack came. I believe he accepted it as a release from purgatory.

At one time, my father was in his house in Switzerland, while Lynne was in Paris. They spoke to each other every day, but one night she went missing. He rang every one he knew in Paris to try to track her down. He also rang through to various restaurants where he thought she might have gone.

In the end, he told the manager of her hotel to go up and unlock the door to her room, convinced she'd fallen ill or taken sleeping pills. The manager, recognising the caller's voice, did as requested. She wasn't there and the bed had not been slept in. He was stunned. When Lynne surfaced, it was only to discover she'd been out with Sue Evans, my father's PA. A furious row ensued between him and Lynne.

After the Paris incident, they talked in some detail to each other — a conversation he recorded. He played the tape to me. They talked a lot about his health. 'I got a bit low because things weren't functioning sexually between us,' he said on the tape. 'I got so desperate about this. I want to lead a normal married life again. There's got to be a reason for it.' It went on with him expounding the practices of an American doctor who claimed cures for the problem of impotence by utilising video slides. 'I can tell you one thing,' he told her at the end of the one hour tape, 'I've been completely and totally faithful to you.'

'Oh, that's good,' said Lynne.

When it finished, I found he was gently weeping. 'I still love her,' he said.

In the course of time, Lynne suggested my father should see a psychiatrist, but he wasn't disposed to. He talked his troubles through with me. 'What's the point of going to a shrink, Mike?' he said.

He was deeply divided about how he felt towards Lynne at this time. He became suspicious again and told me he was going to hire a private detective, but then he was overwhelmed with guilt and pulled him off the case.

Being There opened in America to rave reviews. He had convinced himself he would at last achieve his life's dream — a Hollywood Oscar. Then he remembered all the derogatory comments he'd made about Hollywood over the years and guessed he didn't have a hope in hell. He was right.

Some time back he'd tossed his CBE medal in the dustbin. The actual scroll, which is signed by the Queen, he had framed and put up in the toilet. It was because he hadn't received a Knighthood like Sir John Mills or Sir Richard Attenborough that he dismissed the CBE as too insignificant to keep.

'I guess I blew it because I became a tax exile,' he told me. 'John and Dickie played it by the letter. Trust them to do the right thing. Do you think I live out of England by choice?'

One of my father's biggest regrets in life was not having taken the opportunity of heart surgery from his friend Dr Christiaan Barnard, the world-famous heart specialist. He had gone over to South Africa to see open-heart surgery being performed by Barnard, the idea being to reassure him before having the same treatment himself. He watched and photographed the operation. Afterwards he said, 'There's no way you're doing that to me,' and caught the next plane home. Had he had a by-pass then, he could have been strong enough to survive and maybe live into his seventies which he always believed he would do. He was already carrying a pacemaker that cut two ways — it gave him a new lease on life, but disguised the genuine condition of his heart.

The last days I spent with him, just the two of us in Switzerland, he pondered over a forthcoming heart operation in Los Angeles that he knew he had to have. 'I'm worried about it, Mike,' he said. 'It's a big operation. If only I'd gone through with it when I had the chance with Christiaan Barnard. I'm not as fit now ...'

'Don't think like that,' I told him, knowing how morose he could make himself. 'Once you've had the operation you won't have to take the hundreds of pills you do now.'

After some further chat and reassurances, he reached for a sleeping pill and his glass of water, which were always at his bedside. I squeezed his hand and said goodnight, not knowing I was saying goodnight for the very last time.

A few days after my father died, the lawyers told me of the provisions he'd made for us — basically nothing, really. As it was, this woman not only had all my father's money, but all my grandparents' personal effects, all the items my parents had when they were first married — our entire past, really.

In the first few years after his death, I would have bad dreams about it, and part of me still cries out in frustration. When tax demands drift in, you think about it again in a wistful way.

I've got to the verge of being sued by my bank manager several times. The legacy of my father is that I just don't know how to deal with money.

Had I realised what was in store, I might have done things differently. I could have been successful as a musician, but I didn't want fame. I would have done better to have taken the Sellers name and used it as I saw fit.

My life is now on an even keel, and I'm happy. That has to be more important than what might have been.

Usually, at the end of any conversation with my father, he'd say, 'Is there anything you want?'

I'd say no, because he always bought loyalty and I didn't want my love to be for sale to him. Just before he died, he had a Porsche and asked me if I wanted one. I said, 'No, I'll get my own when I can.'

I've cursed that day many times.

PETER STRINGFELLOW
Night-Club Owner, (1940–)

Peter Stringfellow is even more famous than his nightclub in London's West End. He has spent much of his life working in and owning clubs, from Sheffield to Leeds to Manchester to London. In the 1980's he owned clubs in America as well as Britain.

He has been married and divorced twice, and in recent years has had a succession of girlfriends. His sense of fun and flamboyant nature have sustained his popularity with the public and popular press alike.

Scott Stringfellow was born in 1966, and is Peter's son from his second marriage to Coral. Scott, who is a racing driver and instructor, has an elder half sister, Karen, from his father's first marriage to Norma. The family all originate from Sheffield.

SCOTT STRINGFELLOW:

The early days were really good. Before my father got to the position he is in now with the big nightclub scene, he had already started out with church halls and, subsequently, small clubs. When I came along he had his first proper nightclub.

Mojo's was the main one in his life because we literally lived right above it. I don't remember much of Sheffield. What I do remember is when we moved from Mojo's to a small house. Dad would come home in his suit and dickie bow from doing D.J. work at the club, and then promptly fall asleep on the sofa. I've got a photograph of this somewhere as proof. He used to totally spark out.

Snippets I remember from being a kid are things like watching *Doctor Who* with my mother, and my father being at the club a lot of the time. A stronger memory is being in Wakefield for a year while Dad was building the Cinderella Rockerfellas in Leeds. From there we moved on to Leeds itself. That's when things started to happen for us, because he went from being small-time nightclub owner to fairly big-time nightclub owner.

He was becoming very well-known for putting on turns — particularly comics such as Morecambe and Wise, Cannon and Ball and Freddie Starr. Dad was an innovator in that he brought soul music over from America. Artistes like Stevie Wonder and Wilson Pickett appeared at the Mojo club, as well as rock bands like The Small Faces and The Who.

We had a big house in Leeds with a huge garden. Some would probably say I was spoilt, but I've never regarded my upbringing as being an indulgent one. My sister, Karen, and myself had motorbikes in the back garden which made for a nice upbringing, but then you tend to go through life thinking, 'Well, hasn't everyone got a motorbike in their garden!' But we were a normal family, never encouraged to act in an aloof way. He was really good at bringing us up even though he wasn't always there.

Throughout my schooling I can never remember having breakfast with him. He was always asleep at breakfast recovering from the night before. We had a nanny called Nancy. She was always looking after us, but Dad was available at certain times during the day, particularly in the early evening when he was getting ready for the night.

He would either watch the news or *Star Trek*. I'd watch *Star Trek* with him, and that time together was wonderful. Typical of a father, he would tear apart all the programmes on television; but he did like *Star Trek* so that became a regular event. Watching the re-runs now still makes me feel good because of the memories of those earlier times.

Come the evening, he would be off to work again, so it was an unusual upbringing as opposed to a strict one. Myself and Karen were well cared for but not over-parented.

He was very keen to have us do well in school. I think, academically, I was bad at everything. One of the few things I actually liked at school was acting. I went to stage school much later on.

I never took it on board that he was a well-known person. I remember being stopped by some kids in the local farmer's field where we used to go and play. 'You're Stringfellow's son, aren't you?' they said. 'Yes,' I replied cautiously. 'Has your Dad got a thousand pounds?' they asked. A lot of money back then. 'I think so,' I replied. I'd always answer people honestly. I wasn't very good at being deceitful.

Once I went into town with a few friends and we decided to nick something from the sweet shop. They took their Twix bars and whatever, and I took a single black-jack. Later on, I returned to the shop and put it back. I felt really bad about nicking this single sweet. In a way, It's down to parent-fearing. I never want to upset my Mum or Dad, and so I can't do anything that would make them look down upon me. I've always wanted to make them happy and proud of what I'm doing with my life.

I didn't get bullied at school. I was very lucky. I seemed to get on with everybody. When I look at my Dad, it's been much the same thing with him: he more or less gets on with everybody. I either inherited it or learned it from him. There was always that little bit of one-upmanship at school, though. I think there always is. But again, I don't think I really looked down on people: we just got on with living life. This was home, that was school, and never the twain shall meet, sort of thing. I never got into showing off at all. If anything, it was instilled in us by our parents to be like everyone else.

I always dreaded the school reports coming in. You always know that there's something in them you don't want your parents to see. I look back now and see that he wasn't ever disappointed in me but just wanted me to do better all the time. But he wasn't overbearing about it.

It wasn't until many years later when I saw his school books that I found out why he wasn't too overbearing. He had the same shortcoming as me on the academic front. And he did far more doodles than he ever did work in his school books! But he was good at maths, unlike me.

Karen and I just saw school as something to be got through for the few years you're there. We would tell Dad that we were going to do nightclubbing when we'd finished the education thing, so it's always been there.

I became very keen on motor racing in my earlier years, but I never thought I would do any racing. I just saw it more as a hobby. It was conditioned in the brain that my real work would be in the clubs.

I wasn't a well child. At 18 months, it was discovered I had asthmatic bronchitis. I spent the first couple of years in and out of hospital visiting an oxygen tent. I seemed to be ill all the time with something or other. Strangely, I grew to like hospital. It meant my Mum and Dad would turn up with presents. The down side was the medicine.

One time when I was in hospital in Sheffield, Dad brought me a small red racing car that I could sit in. Now I've ended up in motor racing he probably blames himself for conditioning me with things like that toy car. But really I do think it was more me than anyone else. I don't think I was specifically pushed in the direction of motor sport.

Even when I was very young, Dad and I would go to the club together every now and then. We'd go to the Rockerfella side, which was a calmer atmosphere with middle of the road music, whereas Cinderella's was very noisy and had a strip bit at the side as well. I remember getting dressed up in a suit to go and see a comedy turn. I was only about seven or eight, so it all began making a great impression on me. It got to the stage where once I grabbed the microphone and told a load of jokes on the Cinderella side of the club. All these jokes were ingrained in my head. Dad hadn't pushed me, but he could see it was possibly useful in terms of learning the business for the future. And I went down okay. It was a kind of baptism to dealing with people, and the ability to deal with people has stayed with me right into my motor sport career.

When I got into my teens, I felt marginally less comfortable with people my own age than people older than myself. That has proved quite useful in motor sport when you have to instruct people older than yourself.

Back to Leeds. That was a really good time because, as I mentioned, we seemed to have everything. Dad started to get into fast cars like the Jaguar E Type and the Jensen Interceptor, then came a Rolls Royce. Then in 1977, we moved to Manchester. My school was directly behind the house. Not much chance of skiving. And the motorbikes didn't come with us. There wasn't enough room. Actually, the bikes were stolen a couple of days before we moved. I guess the house was being watched while we packed up, and they nipped in quick in between a big load being transferred.

The transition was a difficult one, but I found some new friends there, and

Dad was doing a lot of innovative things which was helping his business. He would put on fashion shows and other special items which went down well.

We had a big house in Manchester, if not much land around it, and this was a period when Dad bought cars thick and fast. The Rolls went and next was a Corvette Stingray. A lovely car. The first car I ever drove. I was a very short kid, so Dad sat me on two cushions and took me to a disused airfield. Other kids were there with remote control aeroplanes, but I was much happier driving the car. It was automatic, which made it easier. I saw a friend from school driving there in a Mini clubman. 'He can only drive automatics,' he told everyone at school next day. 'Well, how many Corvette Stingrays have you driven?' was my reaction.

In one of Dad's cars, he'd let me sit on his lap on the motorway and drive. He would hold his arms up to make it look like he was driving.

Throughout the years in Manchester, I was keeping an interest in the clubs and in cars. And life just went on. We seemed to have a lot of dinner parties, I recall. It's been reported that his parties were a bit wild. Karen and I would sit at the top of the stairs listening to the various conversations. I remember hearing remarks like, 'Peter's outside playing tennis naked!' Karen and I looked out the window. He was naked and so was the woman the other side of the clothes line which was the tennis net. Nearby was a block of flats so a few people must have been entertained.

In your teens, you want to try all kinds of things, such as get your hair coloured or wear an ear-ring. And your parents say, 'Oh, you're not going to do that are you?' With my Dad, it was the other way round. My Mum, Dad and sister all had perms done, and I wouldn't do it. I tell you, it was like living with the Jacksons. 'Come on, you've got to do it,' Dad would nag, and I'd refuse because I knew I'd come out looking like a girl. Then he'd say, 'Well why not have an ear-ring? Look, I've got one.'

I relented when we moved to Islington in London in 1981. I said I'd have the perm once we were out of the area and away from my school where I'd have been ribbed to hell.

I had this perm done and needless to say it looked terrible. I couldn't wait for it to grow out. But it served its purpose: it pleased him that I'd gone along with it, but he saw, as anyone could, that it didn't look good. Mind you, he pushed me into peroxide blonde hair later on, so it wasn't a complete close to the subject of my hair. I think he basically wanted me to become showy.

I was enjoying acting a bit, and before we moved to London my mother asked me if I wanted to do Manchester Youth Theatre. I did that for a

Summer Season in 1980. So I had the taste for acting by the time we moved to London. My mother and I went to see the producer Bill Kenwright. He was a friend of the family, and my mother asked if he'd take me on for a week and train me up and get me into the Arts Educational School, which was then in the Barbican in London.

I did the audition for stage school, and my Mum and Dad were pleasantly surprised at this new interest in life, especially Dad as it's a natural link with the entertainment industry.

I did three years there and it was wonderful. Half the day was taken up with normal school work, and the rest of it was drama or jazz dancing. In the third year, although I was in drama, you had to do ballet, tap and jazz. I did six months and hated every minute of it, especially the ballet. I was not a ballet dancer; I was a northerner who thought ballet was for poofters! I did develop a great respect for those who could master it, however. It's physically incredibly demanding.

The whole experience changed me from being somewhat withdrawn. It took me out of my shell. I left feeling very confident of myself, and went straight to join my Dad who was by now building the Hippodrome.

That was a real change after being on a high from the acting school. Suddenly I was involved in a massive refit of the building which is now the Hippodrome. I was sent on a door survey. Dad assigned me to a crew and said I'd do lots of various things and that it would be a worthwhile experience.

I went into it hook, line and sinker. Doing a door survey meant tape measure, pencil, pad and hard hat, and walking around the bowels of the place measuring up for doors. I can assure you this was a monotonous job. After that, I was put on to fixing rivets in the lighting systems. When the whole place was up and running, I was doing the lighting in the follow spots, working up in the gods on bands such as Hot Gossip.

We did a satellite link-up for the Grammy awards with the band Culture Club. The band came in during the day with their song piped, so there was just a drum and Boy George walking around singing the number. We did the follow spots. We did several run-throughs, then it came to the satellite link-up live with America. 'From England, Culture Club'. Big cheers came through my cans. The number ran and at the end they were meant to wave to America. But at the end of the song I thought that was it, and blanked them out. Dad went spare with me. 'What the bloody hell do you think you're doing?' He went up the wall. I thought it was the end of the world.

At the end of the same day, I saw Dad with his new girlfriend, Frizzbi, canoodling together. She saw me and went, 'Oh, oh!' He had gone crazy with me, and now I'd seen him with her for the first time, and all in all it made for an almighty tricky day.

At the club there was a very open plan seating area with a Royal box affair to one side. It was all leather and over-the-top in typical Hippodrome style. Dad led me over there to talk, and I was saying, 'I don't know if I want to talk about it.' This was my father with somebody else, and it just blew me way. 'Ask any question you want,' he said. 'Why?' I replied. 'She's so fucking ugly — my Mum's brilliant. Why?' Now don't get me wrong, because Frizzbi is actually a really nice person, but at the time this was my father with another woman, so she was the worst person in the world.

He went on about him and Mum, and I really didn't want to know any of this. I couldn't go telling my mother: it wasn't anything to do with me on that level. I could see he was going to trip himself up at some stage and all would be found out, though a part of me thinks that perhaps she already knew something was going on.

I analyzed it as well as you can when you're in your teens, but it was really strange for the next few days. I just didn't know what to do or say. In the end, I tried to blot it out of my mind, and every time I saw him it was a bit strained. But we got through it, and eventually it all came out, and I've never been so relieved in my life because it dealt with all the secretiveness and the awkwardness between us. It was a natural loyalty to my mother that I guess had made me react in the way I did.

I've always been a faithful person, and I believed the same of my Mum and Dad. I went to schools where other kids had got divorced parents and had assumed that mine were really happy together and weren't like these others at all. As soon as it happened to me I felt, no, this can't happen: my Mum and Dad have been happily together for nearly twenty years. What's going on here!

It suddenly dawned on me why my sister, being from my Dad's previous marriage, had never got on that well with me when I was a kid. It was, of course, because I represented the same thing as Frizzbi had done to me. I was her father's wife's son from another woman, as opposed to being her brother. But the interesting thing is that when my parents divorced, my sister and I got closer than we'd ever been. We developed an affinity.

They split up and I hated it for a long time, but years down the line I see it was a lot better that they were apart. They were always arguing violently by the later stages: we went down on crockery quite quickly! For noise value, if nothing else, it was a lot more peaceful.

Dad moved out at a time when we were starting to grow closer, as you do when the relationship becomes one between two adults as opposed to a father and his son. At the end of the day, he still loves me and my sister for what we are, and we still love him for what he is.

There have been subsequent girlfriends, but that doesn't bother me now — so long as he's happy, that's fine by me. It just took me a long time to understand this other side of life compared to the life I had known through my upbringing.

Moving to London and setting up home with his family and taking on the challenge of Stringfellows was a huge upheaval for him. Until he wrote a book, I never realised he built three clubs on virtually no money. I'd never even thought of money as being a big problem in our family at all. It was just there, or so I had always thought. I never even thought of money as a commodity except when we went down to the market together and he'd whip out a great wad of cash. I'd be thinking, 'Jesus, we're going to get mugged any second.'

At the time we were in London and my parents were splitting up, I'd started racing. I got involved with it through a charity night called 'Race Night'. There was an auction and one of the items was a race package containing tickets to Le Mans, the British Grand Prix at Brands Hatch, a day's tuition at Brands Hatch Racing School, and various other bits and pieces. Dad made a bid for it and got it, and that was the start. I found myself in a Formula Ford for a day.

In 1984 I did about twenty races here and there. In 1985, we had 'Hippodrome' on the car when Dad decided to do a bit of a sponsoring. It was good of him — it helped get it all going. I learned a lot that year though in racing terms it wasn't a good year, because my team manager at the time was a total arsehole who shall remain nameless. He nearly ruined my career before it had even started. Fortunately, a friend and fellow-driver, Richard Dean, put me in the right direction to Jim Lee racing, and at the same time Dad remained very supportive just putting it down to a bad year, and still came up with the money the next year.

During 1985, I felt slightly embarrassed with the 'Hippodrome' motif emblazoned on the car, and Stringfellow across my suit. I think it was because I wasn't doing very well, and I had my Dad's business plastered all over the place. I didn't want my crashes and various failures to taint him in any way.

1986 was, fortunately, a brilliant year. We won two championships and it gave me the opportunity to give something back to him. He came to a couple of races and one I remember distinctly because I'd spent the whole race in second place just behind the race leader. In the second to last lap, I thought it was time to make my move. I went down the inside at a hairpin and braked too late. I rejoined the race in sixth place. I was so upset as I was going to win this race because my Dad was there. Afterwards he told me it was the best race he'd seen me do and that it didn't matter that I came in sixth, and that he knew I could have won it. It was great to know he was supportive, because he was wary of my racing — naturally, he just didn't want me to have a crash.

He sponsored me for a further three years in Formula Three, so he knows how embroiled I've become with racing.

I went to try and find my own sponsorship and shot myself in the foot a little bit in the fact that when a sponsor sees what you've had on your car they will assume, as in my case, that my Dad could afford it, and that they weren't really needed.

Both my parents have remained supportive, neither dissuading or persuading me to continue. They just learnt to accept that it is what I want to do.

Every year Dad still says, 'So when are you going to come and work for me?' I think he would be very happy for me to come in to the club and start to D.J. like he did. Maybe eventually take over, even. But I'm never going to give up on the racing, so somehow we're going to have to meet in the middle.

I do like the clubs a lot. I enjoy visiting them, and I worked briefly at Stringfellows in Beverly Hills doing D.J. lighting, but it's not really my working environment.

There's one thing about the Stringfellow clubs: he's the club and the club is him. If I was to take it over, I would find it very difficult. I would be in the shadow of the man who has built up the name. It's always difficult for a son to top his father; or just be on the same level as his father. Even if he wants you to be on the same level, no one else wants you to be. If my dad suddenly retired and I announced I was taking over, I'm sure the club would lose a lot of clientèle very quickly, because people are used to coming in and seeing him there.

There's a lot involved with running a club; it doesn't just start and finish at night, this thing goes on day after day after day. And he's never off the TV — he's constantly being interviewed for something or other, and while that's good publicity, it's also time consuming.

I got involved in instructing and I think Dad felt concerned that I had found something to keep me involved in motor racing. I'm working for a magazine now, called *V10*, which I like. I do a bit of writing and test driving. And they're supposed to be helping find sponsors for the motor racing thing which I'm trying to kick start again.

Dad's been with me to circuits so that I can instruct him. In 1987 he drove a Ford Escort XR3 in a pro-celebrity race where you share the race with the racing driver, swopping over half-way through the race.

I spent the day with him at Brands Hatch. It's a fairly hilly circuit with some difficult bends. I was in the car with him saying, 'Brake! Brake! Brake!' He was going, 'Why?' I was saying, 'Because there's a fucking corner coming up!' 'But there's so much room,' he's replying. We had a lot of banter that day, but I've taught him how to get around the circuit without falling off, without going too slow, and without going as quick as he'd like to go.

The test drive was done in nice dry conditions. Come race day, it rained. I watched him coming down the back part of the circuit, and I could see his eyes were wide open, and he was gritting his teeth, and his knuckles were white on the wheel. He was frightened to death. But he went from seventh to third position because half of them fell off. Then they got going again and passed him. Paul Warwick took over for him and got them back to fifth, so they did quite well.

I instructed him at Snetterton down the back long straight to the esses bends, and I had my foot hard down going 110 mph. I told him how fast we were taking it. 'I know, I know, you mad bastard,' he said.

I've also got a tape of him in the car, something we did for TV for the Midlands. That is hilarious. Something to treasure forever. Teaching him to race was horrendous, but the last ten minutes he'd got it. It was scary and it was fun.

It's definitely during the last ten years our relationship has grown even closer. As well as my being older now, which I've already mentioned, I think it's also that I'm relaxed about his other relationships. Especially the really young ones, who I can't take seriously at all. They're all out there hoping he'll marry them, but he'll never get married again: he's out there to have fun. He's happy at what he's doing, and as long as he doesn't think about marrying anybody, he'll be fine. I say that because I don't think he could ever be faithful to one woman. A girl will come along who will stick for a while, but it never lasts because I doubt he's ever really faithful to them, either. And what with the midweek appearances of the Cabaret of Angels at Stringfellows, his girlie club, that's like he's got the sweet shop.

I was once asked in a clothes shop if I was related to Peter Stringfellow. 'Yes,' I said. 'He's my Dad.' A look of doubt crossed this lady's face. 'Not happy with him,' she said. Here we go, I thought, and explained that they mustn't believe what the press say, and that some people like him, some don't, but really he's a nice guy. It can be tricky being his son in those circumstances.

My Dad's enjoying life to the hilt at the moment. I'm naturally very glad. Some sons or daughters of such a person involved in all his club stuff may cringe and go, 'Oh my God!' But this is the way he is and the work he does. And it's a strange thing with my Dad that everyone has accepted that this is the way he is. It took my sister and myself possibly longer than others to accept it, but we're both of the same mind now.

The girlfriend thing is really funny. Personally, I've never been one for younger girls; they're generally older than me. That's not, by the way, a deliberate plan to get back at my Dad by saying, 'Look, I'm going out with someone more mature,' and so forth. I just know that, and no disrespect to younger girls here, I have to be able to talk to them on a similar level. Dad's deaf in one ear. You can always tell when the girlfriend is on the way out, because he turns the deaf one towards her.

Recently there was a girl he was with, and she was on the deaf ear side. I asked him how it was going, and he said he didn't think it would last. I told him I'd seen it was coming. 'What do you mean?' he said. 'She was sat on your left the last time,' I told him. He still didn't twig. It must be an unconscious thing he does, because he fell about laughing when I explained, saying he'd never noticed himself doing it.

Dad is happy the way he is, he wants to mess about all the time, but he's not going to get anything deep and meaningful from his relationships, I wouldn't have thought. The way I perceive it is there are too many women out there for him, and he's going to enjoy himself — he's not finished yet.

I still think the perfect woman for him was my Mum, because she understood him and took the time to understand him. She gave him a good deal of freedom as well, but at the end of the day it was more the club than anything else which separated them.

Although he's a lot more relaxed these days than when he had the four clubs going, I think he'll tire of just having the one and there will come the time when he'll expand again.

There was so much travel involved when he had the clubs in America. At one stage, he contemplated buying a jet, because he was spending more time in planes than in cars.

Some of the girls I've met think I'm loaded and that I spend all my time in the club. Neither is true. If I go to the club, it is usually with a potential sponsor or with good friends. I never go in looking for relationships or because it's the place where I'm supposed to be.

Instructing does earn a little money — nothing incredible — but I'm definitely not loaded. Like many others, I'm doing as much work as possible while at the same time doing what I want to do in life.

My life is very rewarding in so many ways, because everything I'm involved in I actually want to be involved in. No disrespect to my Dad, but that's more than the club can offer me. And I have a girlfriend who doesn't mind that I don't work every single day, and we share the same interests including the racing.

I have a different outlook to life from my father, yet we're both single-minded people. His single-mindedness is the nightclub, of course. Mine is motor racing. I think he understands that that is the way it is, that if anything it is a great similarity we share.

Dad is someone who always has people around him, so when we get together — usually at his place — he cooks us a meal, and I insist he takes the phone off the hook and we really enjoy some quality time in each other's company.

It's a bit of a turn around as in modern families it's the parents looking for quality time with their kids. When I do see him, which I have to say is fairly rare nowadays — he's been to my house once in the six years I've lived here — I like to make the most of it.

It's difficult for him to do regular things like go to the cinema and eat out, because he's recognised wherever he goes, and I do understand that. He's too much of a showman to go out in disguise. If he's going out then it's, 'Hey, how are yer doing?' to everyone.

He had a black BMW for a while which had blacked out windows. It was to avoid getting recognised at traffic lights and so forth, and this does happen. I've taken him in my car and dropped him outside the station for him to go and visit his father down in Brighton. But you can't drive through a city or town with him without people knocking on the windows. Often it's a messenger bike. 'Hey man, how are ya? I love your place. . .' etc. . .

Interruptions to do autographs while you're eating in a restaurant is the worse. You sit there hoping you're not going to get disturbed, but there's always one who'll come across. But you can never really turn anybody down, and he's always nice to them.

I had dinner with him at the club once when it was meant to be just me and him. We had a press photographer come and plonk himself right next to Dad and start talking away. I'm slowly seething, and Dad's looking at me knowing what I'm thinking. This photographer then gets himself a menu at our table and orders himself some food. 'You ignorant bastard,' I thought. Dad gave him the raised eyebrows and the this-is-how-it-is dialogue, and he went. Afterwards, I said to Dad I thought it was the rudest thing I've ever seen. 'I know,' said Dad, 'but the press guys have no manners, and you just have to deal with it.'

That's another reason why I couldn't do the nightclub thing. The majority of people who come into the club are okay. But there's the odd idiot who comes up and I can't deal with the idiots, I really can't. I can wind them up, which is more fun, but I can't deal sensibly with them.

Sat at a table at the club, I've had a bloke come up and ask me if I knew where he could get some good coke. 'We've got Pepsi,' I told him. I think he got the message.

The other thing with club life which will keep me away from it, is that you don't get to have a social life. Everyone thinks it must be brilliant, all the bright lights and the girls and stuff, but it isn't, it's a business. My father has managed to turn it into an art form. His life and social life is him in the club at night. Remarkable. I think he very rarely sees daylight.

Nightclubs have a dodgy reputation, and that's one thing I'm proud about with my Dad: he's never done any drugs. Some people thing he must use them because he's a night person, but after twenty or thirty years of keeping these hours, his body has become accustomed to it.

He goes to the gym occasionally and keeps reasonably fit and in shape. When I worked at the club doing the light for him, I wasn't accustomed to the hours and lost too much weight and got very ill. For Dad, it's not a problem.

But with the business, Dad knows that I'll probably be around to help in running it in some form eventually, but I want to get myself set up in other things, such as maybe running my own race team in Formula Three. That's a good ambition to have going.

No doubt Dad'll continue to ask me from time to time if I'm going to join the business, and I'll reply, no, but I'll keep coming in for a visit!

NORMAN WISDOM
COMEDIAN, (1918–)

Norman Wisdom is a British icon. Born in London in 1918, his childhood was disturbed by the separation of his parents when he was nine years old. He was subsequently brought up by a guardian. He joined the army at 15 as a band boy in the 10th Hussars and became adept at playing a succession of varied instruments, from the xylophone to the clarinet. He was also an accomplished boxer and was the flyweight champion of the Hussars at 18.

Demobbed in 1946, Wisdom toured music halls perfecting his comedy. His first TV appearance came quickly in 1948 and after his first appearance in a Royal Variety performance in 1952, he was given his own TV series. That same year followed his extremely popular film comedy, *Trouble in Store*. That film saw him sing what was to become his theme song: *Don't Laugh at Me 'Cause I'm a Fool*.

One of the most accomplished British exponents of slapstick comedy on film, Wisdom's undemanding comedies scored well at the box-office for over a decade. His more famous comedies include *One Good Turn* (1954), *The Bulldog Breed* (1961), *On the Beat* (1962), and *The Early Bird* (1965).

His subsequent film appearances have been sporadic, although he has continued to appear constantly on TV and in the theatre. Wisdom has varied his work so assiduously that audiences can accept him equally as his evergreen fool with the ill-fitting suit and the cap with the upturned peak, or playing a dying cancer patient in a serious drama.

Wisdom, who is as popular as ever, is one of the last variety stars still working continuously and has achieved a longevity unequalled by most of his peers.

Nick Wisdom is Norman's only son. He has a younger sister, Jackie, who lives in Surrey. Nick is a former county cricket player, who now runs a sports retailing business. He is 43 years of age, and lives in West Sussex with his wife, Kim, and their two young sons, Laurence and Greg.

NICK WISDOM:

I started life in Barnet, but since the age of four I've lived in West Sussex. I have a sister called Jackie, who lives in Surrey. We get along fine, although I don't see her that often. She works in an art gallery.

I began schooling proper at Arundale School in Pulborough, then moved to prep school at Aldro near Guildford. My final schooldays were spent at Charterhouse. I really enjoyed my school years, especially my prep school years. If you're reasonably good at sports, schooling can be quite fun. Fortunately, I have always been reasonably good at sports. My father was always good at sports, too. It's where the two of us are on the same wavelength — we're both sports mad and we've been to quite a few sporting events together. Our biggest joint sporting interest was Brighton and Hove Albion F C where he was a director for a number of years. I went to loads of matches with Dad and occasionally on the team bus for the away games. I was lucky that I could get quite involved through my father's own involvement. You could go into the players dressing-room, sit in the Directors' Box — all the sorts of things that a young sports-crazy child could dream of. My father always felt the need to perform on these occasions — to give something to the club by being the Norman Wisdom they expected to see. The crowd would always be waiting for him to take his seat, and it became a thing that they would wait for him to guess what the score was going to be. He would hold out his fingers and signal something like two-one, which they used to hold him to if he got it wrong.

It became very difficult for my father to be endlessly committed to Brighton, because you spend your life as a comedian touring, then suddenly you're at the club attending board meetings. He involved himself for the enjoyment of it, but I think a directorship at a football club these days is a little more serious than it perhaps was back in those days. He would come back after meetings and I'd ask him what they had discussed. He would say, 'Oh, we discussed things like a complaint about the quality of the tomato sauce on the hot dogs, and why there was no toilet paper in the West Stand. Then, at the end of the meeting, the Chairman asked if there was any other business, and apparently so-and-so had asked for a transfer.' I think things are a little bit different now with consortiums and take-over bids and what have you.

I don't think there came a moment that sticks out in memory as the moment when I realised my father was unusual because of his success and fame.

During my schooldays, I never found it a problem to have a famous father. I was given a little bit of a hard time by one of our school matrons at Aldro, who for some extraordinary reason thought that having a famous father made me the chosen one, and that life should therefore be made difficult for me. Other than that, I can honestly say I was treated fairly and normally throughout my education, which is precisely how it should have been.

There were never any jibes made about my Dad being a comic. It's possible they may have privately thought it and I merely remained blissfully ignorant of their thoughts. It's such a long time ago, but I must have had comments made that never struck home in a way that I can recall them now.

I can certainly recall that, after events like sports days, the lads at school would come up and say, 'Your Dad was on good form today,' or words similar to those, but that happens even now. It is something that has for ever been a part of my life. The only difference is that now I'm an adult running a sports shop, but people still come into my shop and say how much pleasure my father's given them over the years. I find that very pleasant, and invariably I'll talk to them about him for a while because you can sense they are genuine in their affection. It's usually the films that people like to remember fondly.

My father would visit me at school to take me out on exeat, but he also came to play in the Fathers' matches. It was never uncomfortable for me, because both my schools took to him very well. Naturally, it was always quite a big occasion when he turned up as he was in his heyday at the time.

On one sports day, he was asked to do his party piece, which he always obliged them with, although deep down I sensed he would have preferred to have just come and watched the events; that deep down he thought, 'God, I wish I could be just like everyone else and sit down and watch this instead of having to perform.' If they wanted him to entertain the parents for a few minutes, he would. Once they had him giving the Headmaster a donkey-ride. There was always something going on around him, but it was all good fun. He's basically never been good at saying no. The only time he refuses to give an autograph is when he's eating. The public can't grasp that. They can't accept that he's at a restaurant eating a main course and is being expected to put his knife and fork down to sign their bit of paper. They look offended when he's sent them away. Apart from when he's eating, he always tries to please.

I was sitting with him at the Palladium watching a pantomime. Sid James was on stage and very tactfully said, 'My mate Norman Wisdom's in the audience.' He got my father to stand up, and this was about ten minutes before the end of the show. It took an hour from the moment we made to leave to get out of the auditorium because of the line of people wanting to talk to him and ask for autographs, but he always kept cheerful about it.

I would say, generally speaking, people respect his privacy. When we went to restaurants together, you would inevitably have the chef come out of the kitchen to say hello and so on, but he wouldn't play up to those situations, he would remain very calm and pleasant and not suddenly burst into a comedy performance.

As he's got older, he's started to play up more. I think he feels he's on the stage all the time. In fact, he's possibly more eccentric than he ever was. I quite enjoy it, as do my two sons. He's great fun to be with. Our relationship has always been one of good pals as opposed to father and son. Much of this was due to his inability to instil us with fatherly discipline. He simply wasn't a disciplinarian. We could get away with murder. It was my mother who was the disciplinarian. That became one of the main problems between them.

My upbringing with my mother, plus having boarded at schools which knock you into some kind of positive shape, stood me in good stead. I felt I was always reasonably well behaved as a child, but it was my father who drove my mother crazy at times. We would be sitting down at tea, and she would be saying, 'Less talking, more eating,' then he'd lift up the dog and put it on the table, which would totally undermine her. The dog would look at my father, and he'd give it a wink, then the dog would look at my mother, and get the face of thunder. It wasn't done deliberately to undermine her, it was just his way.

I knew I could get away with so much before my mother would step in and say enough was enough, but you could feel the iciness between the pair of them. One was trying to bring you up into the real world with proper discipline, and the other wasn't so fussed.

I moved to Charterhouse when I was 14, which was a different experience from junior school but, again, a very pleasant one for the most part. I feel very privileged to have gone there. It's a bit out of my financial bracket, so I doubt I'll be sending my own children.

The biggest upset for me during my time there was that my parents' disagreements developed into a painful divorce. The Headmaster called me in and asked if everything was OK, and I replied that it was, and in terms of the divorce affecting my schooling, that was an end to the matter.

In terms of the divorce itself, it was a much harder emotional upheaval. I didn't see my mother for five years after it happened, which was a wrench. I would have to confess that this was my own choice. I was only 15 at the time. If I had been older, I would have handled it differently, more maturely. It was too long a time to be without each other — bad for her and bad for me. We slowly drifted back to each other, and by then it was all water under the bridge. My mother lived with another man but never remarried and my father never remarried, either.

We had a housekeeper at our home in West Chiltington, so it was possible to spend time with my father during the school holidays. She was there to look after us as and when needed, such as when my father was in America working. He was very busy during this period so we didn't see a great deal of him.

He was doing summer seasons in places like Yarmouth and Margate. Jackie and I would go along with the housekeeper and stay with him for our two-week summer holiday. I enjoyed these times because we would do things together as a family during the day, then pop along to the theatre at night and watch the proceedings backstage.

I always loved standing backstage when I was a child. You could really get the feel of the theatre and be a part of it. Backstage at the Palladium watching Aladdin is one of my greatest memories. My father has a wonderful oil painting by Russell Flint's son, which is of people standing in the wings looking on and you can see the orchestra and part of the audience. A fabulous picture. It's exactly as I can remember it: standing at the side of the stage and watching spellbound.

The privileged spectator aspect always appealed to me, but I have never wanted to go down the entertainment line, and I'm sure much of this decision is based upon these early memories of witnessing my father feeling obliged to entertain. I would say my sister, Jackie, took it a step further than me by taking up singing. As a serious career option, it fizzled out after a time.

I think it would have been a little more acceptable for her to move into the business. There's more of a direct comparison between father and son. If it's the daughter involved, it is more difficult to make an obvious comparison.

Often were the times I was asked by people if I was going to take that route, but it never really crossed my mind as a serious option. Some things have rubbed off on me from my father. I like to think I have some of his style of humour, but I would never have tried to emulate him — I'm sure that that would have been a recipe for disaster. If I'd had the calling and been good enough, possibly a straight actor is the direction I would have chosen, but that has never developed as a serious possibility.

There was one occasion around the mid-1950s that, if anything, cemented my decision to avoid the entertainment industry. For a bit of fun, my father arranged for me and Jackie to make a brief appearance in a film called *Follow the Star*, which was being shot at Pinewood Studios. My role was to be seen as a young lad having a piano lesson. Hattie Jacques was in it, but the actress playing my teacher was June Laverick. I remember it well because I was very nervous and I think that comes across in the film. All the keys were on the piano but no noise emanated from them because the music was dubbed on afterwards. I did manage to find one key that still worked, and I repeatedly hit it, much to the irritation of June Laverick.

Her final line to me was something like, 'And I'll see you next Wednesday, Nicholas.' I got out of that chair and bolted for the door in my keenness to get off the set, so I come across in the film as a very reluctant piano student. It was quite overpowering for a little lad to be on a film set lost among cameras and crew. When the director shouts 'Action', you tend to freeze at that age.

That era was the pinnacle for my father — things were really happening. He was *the* star of that time. It can't have been that easy for him. He couldn't even walk down the street without being recognised. Yet, he was always so good about the attention aspect of his success. Like most performers, a certain part of him thrived on it.

He is certainly a workaholic. He'll think nothing of working through the night getting something like a dance routine perfected. During the

1950s his compulsion to work caused him to collapse and he had to spend several days recuperating in hospital.

We didn't have that many family holidays, other than the ones that combined his working seasons. Unlike many other entertainers, he has no villa in Spain. It never really appealed to him to own property abroad. He always had a passion for Spanish-designed property so he built a Spanish-style house at the end of his garden which, in my opinion, didn't quite work. I think you need the right climate to go with that sort of house.

Once, we visited Majorca together. We cruised on the *Andes* and on the *Queen Mary* for six days, but going to Majorca was probably our first real family holiday.

My father relaxed a bit more out in Majorca. He would still do all the visual comedy with the waiters, not really caring whether they recognised him or not. My father's classic party-piece was stepping over the imaginary rope when it was getting dark outside. He would pretend to be hoisting his legs over this non-existent rope, and anyone coming up behind would start looking for the thing.

He wasn't someone who could sit on a beach for very long. We would go to Bournemouth to visit my granny who lived there. Once, he sent me off to buy a couple of ice-creams. I came back with one ice-cream in a cornet, and just a cornet, because the other ice-cream had fallen on the promenade. I said, 'Sorry Dad, yours dropped out,' and I remember him laughing loudly about that.

He once owned a yacht, but that became more of a headache and disaster than a form of relaxation. He had it built on the coast near home, but he was away in America while construction was going on. It cost him a hell of a lot more than he'd anticipated. It became a noose round his neck and he chartered it out as a business, although I know he was glad when he finally got rid of it. One of the chief problems was that he couldn't use it for his own pleasure. The tax man deemed it unsuitable for him to use it for more than about a fortnight a year.

During my time at Charterhouse, I can recall a small incident that has always stuck in my memory. An American film producer sent my father a prototype clockwork razor blade. When you wound it up, this thing shuddered in your hand and wouldn't stop until it had wound right down. Dad was happily shaving away with it one day when suddenly it got hold of his throat. It was like having metal teeth attached to his skin.

Being clockwork, it was feeding itself deeper and deeper into him. He managed to wrench it free leaving a hole in his throat with blood pouring from him.

He came downstairs saying, 'That's the last time I use that bloody razor.' We all thought it was quite amusing, although it could have been quite serious.

He put it away in its case and, before returning back to school, I whipped it. I began showing all the lads at school. Being 15 or 16, we'd all started to shave by now. We all gave it a go.

My father went to his bathroom cabinet and saw that it had gone. He rang up the housemaster at school and put the whole place on full alert about this unpredictable razor. Fortunately, none us suffered the same painful results that he had suffered.

I've told him he should use the anecdote on a chat show, because you can visualize him acting out the scene where it judders on his neck.

I went to the States with my father in 1966 when he was on Broadway doing a show called *Walking Happy*. He was still with my mother then, and we went out there for Christmas. As an event, it sticks in my memory because it was a unique thing to have done.

After Charterhouse, I returned to West Chiltington. I hadn't done very well in academic terms and drifted into Chichester College, which I didn't stick for too long.

My next move was into cricket. I felt I had a bit to offer there and that I could give it a real go. I was signed up by Sussex, so much of my time and thoughts were channelled towards cricket for the following three years that I was playing for them. The standard was very high and, for me, it just wasn't to be. That sort of level is very competitive, and mentally I didn't feel I was quite strong enough for professional cricket.

My father was a good supporter during this period. He would come along and watch whenever he could.

I chose to stay in the sports industry. It was an easy decision, as sport has always been the main motivation in my life. I had worked in a sports shop over the winter breaks, so my next step was to open my own sports shop. Although shop work can be a bit laborious, you meet interesting people. It's my own set-up and so I enjoy it. I've been running the business for about 20 years.

I met my wife, Kim, during the time that I've had the shop. I went to two parties. Kim wasn't at the first one. I was talking with a group rather than an individual so it became difficult afterwards to recall who was who. At another party soon after the first, I met Kim and did speak to her quite a bit, although I noticed she'd arrived with a guy. So that was that, or so I thought.

A while later, I received a phone call in my shop. It was Kim saying that she was the girl I'd met at the party. For some reason, I'd completely forgotten about Kim, and my mind was switched on to a blonde I'd seen at the previous party. So when Kim asked me if I'd like to come for supper, thinking it to be the other girl, I said yes.

I turned to a rep who was in the shop and said how strange it was as I'd hardly spoken to this girl and here she was asking me to her place for supper.

I made a complete mess of finding the house, confusing the name of the house with the name of the road. Eventually, I found the house and Kim opened the door. All I could see was her silhouette so I thought it was the blonde girl with a new haircut. Then I stepped inside and realised it wasn't the person I'd expected to see. My jaw could have dropped, but to my credit I retained control.

My father visits the shop occasionally and usually causes a bit of mayhem. He'll see a customer pondering over a cricket bat and tell them they shouldn't buy it because it's no good. The customers are never quite sure whether to take him seriously or not.

I've had the Press on to me at the shop, and I have to admit that I don't really care for it. If something controversial is happening in town, such as business rates on shops, they might phone me up to see how I feel about it. I make some innocent and unchallenging comment, and next day open the paper and read, 'Nick Wisdom, son of Norman Wisdom, says it's disgraceful that. ... blah, blah, blah.' If it had been anyone else, it wouldn't have even made the paper, and I really don't like that. Consequently, I'm perhaps not as obliging as I could be.

My father's lived in the Isle of Man for nearly 15 years. Up to a point, he's based himself there for tax reasons, but it was from doing a summer season in the Isle of Man that convinced him it was a place where he would like to live.

His house is at the Scottish tip at the end of the island, so it's a bit remote. It's a very nice place to visit for a week. As a family, we've only visited once, but I've stayed there several times down the years. Christmas would be a good time to visit him, but more often than not he's away on a winter cruise giving talks.

He has what, in principle, is a huge house, but unbelievably has only three bedrooms. Someone usually has to sleep on the landing. All the space is confined to the ground floor, which is absolutely vast.

It's interesting that he's so popular in places like Russia, Turkey, Iran and Albania. I think in Albania, Norman Wisdom films are about all they're allowed to watch. It's quite likely that they can relate to his downtrodden character — a little like the Chaplin character — but most of all its safe material, and I think, particularly in Albania, they're not allowed anything remotely suggestive. You can't get it much cleaner than my father, so I guess it's Norman Wisdom or nothing.

He reciprocates their interest by making visits to the countries in question. He visited Chernobyl during the last year and, of course, Albania where he's treated like a visiting dignitary. His visits have even made the news over here. On his last visit, they had overthrown some dictator and given his car to my father to drive around in, which I found both amusing and unbelievable.

The sheer numbers that greeted him was a bit frightening. If he was put up for President, I don't think he'd have any trouble getting elected. I'd love to have gone with him for the experience. The chance may come, for he's sure to go back.

He remains a strangely naïve man in some ways. He was doing a film in Southport called *What's Good for the Goose*. A group called The Pretty Things were also in the film. It was the producer's birthday so the whole film set took over a hotel, which was due to be knocked down shortly afterwards. The Pretty Things said they'd throw a party that would tear the roof off the place. They played live music, and my God, they nearly did tear the roof off. They took a break after a while, and the lead singer came up to my father and asked if he was coming out for a smoke. My father smiled and said, 'Yes, fine.' So he goes outside, where the lead singer produces a joint that he takes a drag of before offering it to my Dad. 'No, it's all right,' said my Dad, 'I've got my own,' and promptly brought out a Senior Service. He totally missed the point — he was on a completely different wavelength.

As a granddad, he's fantastic, absolutely unbelievable. The boys just love him. Kim reckons he's a bit of a misogynist, so having two grandsons probably makes it even better for him.

I took Laurence to see his granddad receiving the OBE at

Buckingham Palace. Somehow, Laurence ended up with his picture in all the papers. I was happy for him to do this, as it was a very rare occasion but Laurence looked a bit nervous — a bit like me in that film. It was something that just happened and there was nothing pre-arranged about it. Even so, I was very conscious that I didn't want him to be made a fool of.

My father's greatest hobby is spending his free time looking around car showrooms. I always say to him, 'If you're thinking of changing your car then let's get looking, but if not, let's get back in our car and get going.'

He plays quite a bit of golf. He has his own tournament, the Norman Wisdom Golf Classic. I don't think he plays that seriously, he just hacks around the course. With the cap and all the gear, he looks like Gary Player.

I played golf with him on the summer seasons. He was playing really badly and started tossing golf balls at me that I tried to hit into the sea with the end of the golf club.

Freddie Starr used to close the first half of my father's show in summer season, and he wanted to get in on the golfing act. Without having taken a single golfing lesson, he went out and bought a fabulous set of clubs. Once he was on the tee trying to hit the ball, he realised too late that there was a bit more to it than he'd thought. He ended up throwing all the golf clubs as far as he could into the sea. A quite extraordinary man.

He had the habit of interfering with the other acts on the show when they were performing. He'd think nothing of suddenly driving a motorbike across the stage, but he never interrupted my father, so great was his respect for him.

In a sense, my father's success has come full circle. It's on a different plateau now, mainly talk show stuff, but he's back in the public eye, and people seem to remember his work with great fondness. Much of this is because he's one of the survivors.

I held a surprise 80th birthday party for him a couple of years ago at my house. I decided it would be lovely to get some of those from his own era to come along, and actors from his films whom none of us in the family had seen for years. I couldn't find any. Sadly, they've all gone. My father is the last. It does emphasise how much of a survivor he is. It's very sad for him to be existing with a totally different generation from his own and this isn't a recent occurrence. Many of them have been dead for nearly 25 years, but because he is such a survivor, he just goes on and on in a relentless way, and I hope he will do for many more years to come.

EPILOGUE

When Michael and I first started work on *Hard Act to Follow*, the one fear we had was that there would develop a sameness in what our contributors had to say. We were somewhat surprised, therefore, to discover as we went along how diverse the backgrounds of our contributors have been and that, while there are definite similar strands that can be pulled together, they are far fewer than originally anticipated.

My own upbringing with a great comedian compared with Michael's upbringing with a great comedian, is an opening example of this diversity. Eric Morecambe and Peter Sellers were very different people. Eric, with his solid, almost Victorian attitude to life, married only once, a firm believer in family values, a comic genius who seemed to shrug off this fact through his total disinterest in the intellectualising of comedy. And Peter, a human chameleon, changeable and whimsical, married three times, rarely living in any settled state, occasionally happy, more often lonely, particularly near the end of his life, a man disappointed with how life had treated him and how he had treated life; a comic genius who felt pressured into living up to his own huge reputation.

For Michael and I, our upbringing couldn't have been more dissimilar, yet we both knew the good and bad sides of living in the shadow of a great comedian. Both of us agree that we went through our youth with a certain expectancy hanging over our heads. People wanted us to be our fathers, to look like our fathers and be as funny as them. You sensed an air of disappointment when it sank in that you were, in fact, yourself and no one else. We, in turn, began deliberately going out of our way to disassociate ourselves from what our fathers represented rather than basking in all the glory, and I know my sister, Gail, felt exactly the same. For the most part, we all came to dread the connection between ourselves and our parent being made.

What I also find particularly interesting about Michael's and my upbringing is, that although very different in so many ways, we both felt overshadowed by our fathers and didn't really develop as people until after our fathers had died.

This theme runs through Richard Olivier's contribution, where Richard went in search of finding what manhood was all about once the huge shadow of his father had been lifted by his death. He even wrote a book on the subject called *Shadow of the Stone Heart*.

Conversely, this clearly wasn't the case for Sheridan Morley. Sheridan is not unlike his own father, Robert, although perhaps more in the physical than emotional sense. But there is a very deep-rooted similarity between the two men. Meeting Sheridan, one cannot help but feel that one is meeting Robert by proxy. Both men seemed to cast their shadows concurrently, never noticeably encroaching upon the other's space or reputation. Both were often seen together — big, affable men enjoying and being seen to enjoy shared interests. They always appeared to me, and my opinion hasn't altered during the writing of this book, to be more like brothers than father and son. There doesn't appear to have been any conflict of interest between the two men, which presumably gave rise to a more relaxed relationship. And, of course, Robert comes across as having been excessively unfussy and easy-going, which may have given Sheridan a greater sense of freedom and space within which to enjoy his youth.

There is a sense of ongoing struggle in the offspring who chose to follow along similar lines to their illustrious parent. The benefits of having a film director as a father when you wish to pursue an acting career have been less than I would have imagined for Jennifer Edwards, who clearly has not had an easy ride. I sense that Hayley Mills laughs off what must have been a difficult moment in her life when her own buoyant film career was momentarily showing signs of eclipsing her father's.

Kate and Eunice Gayson have volatile contretemps which has probably made life uneasy for both of them at different times. I sense and hope that, in terms of their relationship, a happy outcome lies ahead. Indeed, Kate says that contributing to this book has inspired her to re-open dialogue with her mother.

Martina Jones toyed with the idea of going into music, but it was clearly becoming detrimental to her well-being to be seen moving in an area that her talented father came and saw and conquered. She has begun to find and establish her own identity by removing herself completely from his high-profile world.

The ones that seemed to have had a smoother ride are Ian McCorquodale, Felix Francis, Nick Wisdom and Scott Stringfellow. It cannot be coincidence that these four gentlemen have not competed with their famous parents. As mature men, Felix Francis has moved into the family business as advisor and accountant and, likewise, Ian McCorquodale works for his mother, Barbara Cartland. In their youth they chose radically different paths from their parents. Had both men chosen to be novelists — particularly while still in their early twenties — leaves me wondering just how cheerful their recollections of their youth might now read.

Nick Wisdom is perhaps the best example of establishing and retaining a free spirit. Until now, he has not even given an interview about his father, Norman, let alone tried to emulate his father's career in any way. Both men are keen on sports, and Nick decided to make his career out of that interest, keeping well away from the entertainment industry. It's also interesting that he describes his relationship with his father as that of being pals as opposed to father and son.

I can empathise with Nick. My father took me to football matches and became a director of Luton. Like Norman, he somehow felt obliged to entertain the team, the staff and the crowd. On holidays, he would play the fool in restaurants and grow bored if he was away from work for too long.

The feeling of being a kindred spirit with a parent is a very strong theme to this book. I've just mentioned Nick and Norman Wisdom, but there's also Christian and Roger Moore who keep in daily contact, and share a relationship that again is described as being pals rather than father and son. And I can personally vouch that they share the same wonderful sense of humour.

It would seem that Michael Sellers and Christian Moore had the worst time of schooling in terms of suffering for their parent's fame. All the other contributors seemed to pass through their educational era without too many problems.

Jenny and Blake Edwards seem to have grown very, very close, and Hayley and John Mills have apparently been close since she first cut her teeth.

This isn't to say that the others were not close to their parent, because closeness can be expressed in different ways. I would say I was close to my father, but I would also say he and my sister, Gail, understood each other better than he and I probably did.

Richard Olivier had moments of closeness with his father, but perhaps suffered from the age gap. As Richard says, his father had lived a full and separate life before Richard was even born.

A book of this nature can produce no real conclusions. To do that, we would need to interview at least a thousand sons and daughters of famous parents. But strands can be pulled together, similarities spotted, and differences, too.

One thing is clearly evident — every one who has contributed to this book has in some way or another, either in a negative or a positive way, or even both, been strongly affected by having a famous parent.

The most important thing to my mind is that we all appear to have survived the journey.